Political Economy of Reforms in India

Political Economy of Reforms in India

(Essays in Honour of Prof. K.S. Chalam)

Edited by

Prof. D. Pulla Rao

SERIALS PUBLICATIONS

NEW DELHI (INDIA)

First Published - 2011

ISBN: 978-81-8387-427-4

Published by
SERIALS PUBLICATIONS
4830/24, Prahlad Street, Ansari Road
Darya Ganj, New Delhi-110002 (India)
Phone : 23245225 Fax : 91-11-23272135
E-mail: serials@satyam.net.in

Contents

Foreward

I am very happy to write a few words about the book edited by Prof. D. Pulla Rao in honour of his teacher who was a great teacher, scholar and administrator.

The last six decades have witnessed probably the most sweeping changes in the landscape of the political economy of India in modern times. Several policy initiatives undertaken by central and state governments have led to drastic changes in the socio-economic power structure, some intended and some unintended. These changes have not been uniform all over India in character or extent. Hence any study of these changes needs to be broken up region wise for arriving at valid conclusions even though some patterns do emerge nationally. In many ways, a study of the changes in the political economy of Andhra Pradesh promises to be extremely interesting as it not only is one of the largest states but also straddles the divide between the Deccan Peninsula and the Northern Plains.

The Andhra region that was part of the Madras Presidency under British rule and the Telangana region that was part of Hyderabad state under Nizam had different histories of tenancy structure evolution and socio-economic transformation. The policies adopted by the British rulers to meet the requirements of World War II led to the emergence of non-Brahmin upper caste landowners as the most powerful and influential political and economic force in Andhra whereas the old feudal structure remained undisturbed in the Hyderabad state until its integration into the Indian Republic and subsequent merger with the state of Andhra Pradesh.

The churning in the agrarian economy of Andhra started with the commercialization of agriculture for providing raw materials for Britain's manufacturing industries at the turn of last century and consequent emergence of non-Brahmin upper castes as a major economic force. The new farming elite used the cash surplus generated from commercial farming for further strengthening their economic prowess by acquiring more land and engaging in money-lending activities and for investing in processing industries. At the same time, the introduction of diarchy by the colonial rulers enabled them to acquire political power and tighten their grip on rural economy. The steps taken by the governments in independent India for termination of Zamindari system in its various forms and the green revolution established this class as the dominant socio-economic and political force in Andhra. What happened in Andhra in this respect was different from the scenario in most other parts of India where the industrial sector has come to be dominated by the traditional trading community and professionals and farming by non-Brahmin upper castes and middle castes. Nevertheless, the common feature of the scenario of rural economy in the whole country is the marginalization of the lower castes, agricultural labourers and other poor sections of society. Lion's share of the benefits of industrialization and green revolution was cornered by upper and middle castes and trading communities all over India while the poor have continued to suffer. This has led to the alarming phenomenon of violent struggles and the creation of what is commonly described as Red Corridor.

Fortunately, however, there is now a growing awareness of the serious threat posed to the social fabric and unity of the country by this alienation of a very large segment of society. The new emphasis on inclusive economic development is the result of this realization. A deep understanding of the factors responsible for the violent disturbances rapidly spreading through vast swathes of India is needed in order to come up with appropriate and effective programmes for correcting this serious social imbalance.

This volume on *'Political Economy of Reforms in India'* is a collection of papers presented at the intellectual festival organized to mark the 60th birthday of Prof. K. S. Chalam, presently a Member of the Union Public Service Commission. Prof. Chalam is a leading light in the study of the political economy of modern India and his contributions in this field have received international acclaim. His book *'Readings in Political Economy'* is a pioneering work that has been accepted as standard text in Indian universities. As an educationist, author and a perceptive observer of the evolution of social architecture in independent India, Prof. Chalam has acquired a unique intellectual stature. At a time when many of those fighting for empowerment of the lower strata of Indian society still remain wedded to old slogans and recipes, Prof. Chalam presents a refreshingly different approach of transforming this section of people into a confident, dynamic and forward looking force rather than a bunch of weaklings addicted to walking on crutches.

The papers included in this Volume deal with an interesting mix of subjects ranging from analysis of the socio-economic changes in Andhra and elsewhere in the last century to the impact of the changing global economic scenario on India's agriculture and rural society. The intellectual rigour that is the common characteristic of these papers is a befitting tribute to Prof. Chalam and an index of the high esteem in which he is held by his students, colleagues and admirers in the academic world.

I commend this Volume to the policy makers and all those who are interested in understanding the dynamic forces at work in Indian society.

I congratulate Prof. D. Pulla Rao for bringing out a useful and purposeful volume.

K. Roy Paul

Former Member of Union Public Service Commission & Former Secretary to Government of India

Acknowledgements

This book is an outcome of the Seminar on "Human Development and Social Exclusion" conducted in the Department of Economics, Andhra University, Visakhapatnam on the occasion of Shastiabdi Poorti Celebrations of my Guru and Director of my Ph. D work Prof. K.S. Chalam, Member, UPSC, New Delhi. About 350 delegates participated and more than 250 delegates presented papers and participated in the discussion and deliberations. I am highly thankful to the paper contributors for helping me in bringing out this book which will be of some help to the researchers and also policy makers in India. I am very much beholden to the Prof. K. Rama Krishna Rao, Chairman, Indian Council of Philosophical Research, New Delhi, for his financial assistance. My special thanks are due to our honourable Vice-Chancellor Prof. Beela Satyanarayana and Prof. V. Satyanarayana, Honorary Director, Indian Council of Social Science Research, Southern Regional Centre, Hyderabad for their financial assistance.

My sincere thanks to Prof. L.K. Mohana Rao, Principal, College of Arts & Commerce, Andhra University for inaugurate the seminar session. I express my grateful thanks to Prof. Beela Satyanarayana, Vice-Chancellor, Andhra University, for his inaugural address of the seminar. My sincere thanks are due to Prof. K. Rama Krishna Rao, Chairman, Indian Council of Philosophical Research, New Delhi for sparing his valuable time for preparing and delivering the keynote address. My special thanks to Sri D. Raja, M.P (Rajya Sabha) for attending as a guest of honour and released the Souvenir. My sincere thanks to Prof. Y. Satyanarayana, Vice-Chancellor, Andhra Pradesh University of Law for attending as a guest of honour and delivered valuable message.

I am very grateful to K. Roy Paul, Former Member of Union Public Service Commission & Former Secretary to Government of India for having kindly written the foreword to this book sparing his precious time. I express my thanks to Sri S. Reghupathy, Hon. Minister for Environment and Forests, Govt. of India for attending as the Chief Guest for Shastiabdi Poorti Celebrations of Prof. K.S. Chalam and valedictory function of the seminar session and released the book 'Dravida Udyamam Katha' written by Prof. K.S. Chalam.

I express my gratitude to Ms. Parveen Talha, Member, UPSC for attending the Shastiabdi Poorti Celebrations of Prof. K.S. Chalam and released the book 'Political Economy of Underdevelopment of Kalingandhra' written by Prof. K.S. Chalam.

My heartful thanks to Sri. P. Janardhana Rao, Mayor, Greater Visakhapatnam Municipal Corporation who presided over the function of the Shastiabdi Poorti Celebrations of Prof. K.S. Chalam.

I also thank to Prof. R. Sudarsana Rao, Head, Dept. of Economics and Prof. G. Ramachandrudu, Chairman, P.G. Board of Studies for their continuous support for the successful completion of the seminar.

Finally, my special thanks to the teaching and non-teaching staff, research scholars and students of the Dept. of Economics, Andhra University for their support for the successful completion of the seminar and Shastiabdi Poorti Celebrations of Prof. K.S. Chalam and also in bringing the book to the present shape. I place on record the excellent work done by publishers in bringing the book on time.

Prof. D. Pulla Rao

Introduction

Political economy as a study of policies of the government is distinguished from the Marxian political economy that interrogated the dynamics of economic and political power. The subject, political economy is interdisciplinary in nature and therefore encompasses several disciplines; history, political science, economics, sociology, education etc. The economic reforms were introduced in India in the year 1991. Though the reforms have directly affected industry, agriculture and other important sectors of the economy, its impact on society and development was extensive. There are several studies that have brought out the meaning, scope and content of political economy of reforms. Prof. K.S. Chalam in whose honour, the book of papers are dedicated is a known political economist. His book on "Readings in Political Economy" by Orient Longman is a pioneering work that has provided a standard text book from the Indian prospective. This is being used in several universities as Text Book.

The present book is basically looked at the structure of the economy in relation to land, caste and other Indian parameters that have undergone a sea change during a period of time. The reforms that were initiated in the country two decades ago have influenced several areas including food security, weaker sections, sustainable development and even the strategies of planning. Therefore, the papers are arranged in such a way that they focus on reforms in general and its impact on the economy, society and development planning in particular.

The present book consisting of 28 papers were presented at a national seminar on "Human Development and Social

Exclusion" at the Department of Economics, Andhra University during 6-7 October, 2008. The seminar was organized in honour of Prof. K.S. Chalam on his 60th birthday on 7th October, 2008.

In this book,

1. **Adapa Satyanarayana** in his paper on "*Land, Caste and Kulak Pettandars in Andhra Pradesh*" observed that the caste based feudal domination was increasingly challenged by the emerging rural rich class, the Kulak-Pettandars in Andhra and Telangana regions. However, it should be pointed out that although political power has shifted from the land lords to the rich peasants, it has not gone into the hands of the backward sections of Andhra Society, as concluded by the author.
2. **G. Surya Prakasa Rao and K. Ramachandra Rao** in their paper on "*Implementation of Land Reforms in India*" observed that in the parts of India, which were under indirect -impact of the British and were part of various kingdom, various forms of feudal tenures prevailed. The authors concluded that the implementation of land reforms should be faster and more inclusive, i.e. all sections of farmers like small, marginal, medium farmers and tenants of the rural area. For effective implementation of land reforms in our country the policy makers would utilize institutions like rythu mitra sangalu and self-help groups, which are well established in rural Andhra Pradesh.
3. **K. Kishore Babu, A. Balakrishna and K. Mahendra Kumar** in their paper on "*Agrarian Economy of Andhra Pradesh*" observed that most citizens of Andhra Pradesh have thus already achieved the level of socio-economic status that the majority of Indian citizens are unlikely to experience in their life time. This seems to have been made possible by using the agrarian economy of the state. It was concluded that considerable scope exists for further land redistribution particularly when waste and cultivable

lands are taken into account. In order to develop the lands, complementary inputs for cultivation–initial land development, input mini kits, credit etc should be provided to all assignees. The future assignments of land should be in the name of women.

4. **P.P. Satyanarayana Rao** in his paper on *"Modernisation– Mobilisation: A Means of Development"* observes that the current indicators of development include both economic and non-economic factors. Development cannot be achieved without involving the people since, the prime benefactor of development outcomes are for the people. He concludes that modernization of man thus becomes at once the means to development and the goal of development because the modern man not only facilitates development but also ensures sustained development.
5. **D. Pulla Rao** in his paper on *"Dry Land Farming in India: constraints and opportunities"* observes that a large tack of cultivable land is dependent on rain fall without assured irrigation facilities. And such lands are kept out of the so called green revolution. It needs a separate strategy to bring in the dry land farming under high yielding variety technology. He concludes that farmers should utilize well in time what ever improved technology varieties suitable for dry farming are available. They should be extra careful about the utilization of available rain water, selection of crops and protection of crops from different harmful physiological or biological agencies.
6. **P. Kothandarami Reddy** in his paper on *"Challenge of Food Security in India"* observes that even though self sufficiency of food production has been achieved, the population still lacks access to balanced food. In his concluding statement he remarks that the government at different levels should try to strengthen the existing programmes like food for work programme, public distribution system etc. and also immediate steps are to be taken to provide food security to the target

groups by introducing new programmes in the country.

7. **M. Venkata Ramanaiah, B. Parameswara Reddy and G. Ranganath** in their paper on *"Land Reforms and Agrarian conditions in Andhra Pradesh during Post Independent Era"* observed that land reforms of agriculture as well as in spite of all the limitations in implementation, did play an important role in changing the agrarian structure in Andhra Pradesh. They concluded that the spirit of land reforms not yet nationalized in all the way. The political will have to translate then into government policy and on the ground-level implementation.
8. **D. Pulla Rao** in his paper on *"Area, Production and Productivity of agriculture with special reference to Rice in Andhra Pradesh"* observed that in spite of the fact that nearly 70 per cent of our working population was engaged in cultivation, the country was not self-sufficient in food grains. Most of the cultivated land in Andhra Pradesh is still under dry farming because they do not have irrigated facilities. Construction of minor-irrigation projects, scientific and optimum use of available water resources in these areas, development of new methods of water utilization etc. are some of the steps required to extend green revolution to dry areas as well.
9. **A. Vamsi Krushna, S. Marulu Reddy and K. Kiran** in their paper on *"Progress Of Food Grains Production In Andhra Pradesh: An Analysis Of Post Reform Period"* observed that nearly 60 per cent of an average Indian's food expenditure gets spent on food grains. The demand for food grains in India, as in most developing countries is increasing rapidly because of population growth and raising income. It was concluded that to attain food self-sufficiency and to arrest the health obstacles such as malnutrition among children the governments both at the centre and state level must draw attention towards increasing food

grain production by giving incentives to farmers who are cultivating food grains.

10. **V. Divya Thejomoorthy and I. Narendra Kumar** in their paper on *"Impact of Five Year Plans on Rural Industries"* observed that the essential processes are functions of the Indian economy are: production, consumption and growth. It was concluded that socialist society will naturally bad to the removal of poverty and misery and rise in the standard of living of the people in India.
11. **G. Gangadhar Hugar** in his paper on *"Land Reforms and Agrarian Relations"* observed that the debt crises of the early 1950s and the subsequent multilateral lending programmes provided a decisive opening for the international financial institutions to impose a neo-liberal agenda of fiscal restraint, open trade and capital accounts and privatization on indebted developing countries. It was concluded that despite women's increasing participation in paid work labour markets continue to reproduce gender-based segmentations and inequalities in wages/income, work-related social benefits, and social security.
12. **K. Janardana Rao** in his paper on *"Eleventh Five Year Plan- A Vision for Faster and Inclusive Growth"* observed that India has entered the Eleventh Plan Period with an impressive record of economic growth. Besides, there was acceleration even within the Tenth Plan Period and the growth rate in the last four years of the plan has averaged 8.6 per cent making India one of the fastest growing economies in the world. It was concluded that although, the government has provided more resources for the development of education sector, health sector and for the welfare of the socially disadvantaged groups of SCs and STs in the first two years budget, that determination be required to carry on in the est of the three years to realize the vision of faster and inclusive growth.
13. **Jesurathnam Devarapalli** in his paper on *"Economic Hardships and Social Denigration of Dalits of Ayodhya*

Lanka: A Case History" observed that in the efforts to understand social and economic conditions of lower castes, it is inevitable to make an inventory in to the very nature of caste system. It was concluded that the mere ownership of land could not solve the problem as the quality and quantum of land and availability of technology and investment are also equally important to raise the economic levels.

14. **S.V. Lakshmana Rao** in his paper on "*Sustainable Development through Innovative Strategies of Political Economy"* observed that all governments in the industrialized as well as developing world have undergone pressures to reform their public administration system to adequately respond to the needs and requirements of increasing democratization, globalisation, liberalization and market economy. It was concluded that thrust between the administration and citizens can only emerge from the process of building authentic relationships interweaving the two wills in the larger whole.
15. **M. Ramesh and B. Addai** in their paper on "*Agrarian Crisis and Agrarian Struggles–A Global Scenario"* observed that peasants and farmers have strongly opposed the WTO, growing penetration of giant agribusiness firms and attempts to corporatize agriculture. It was concluded that land reforms could significantly relieve pressure on marginal and ecologically fragile lands, because in many developing countries land distribution is highly skewed with most agricultural land being concentrated in small percentage of holdings.
16. **CSN Raju and B. Sudheer** in their paper on "*Cooperative Societies and Weaker Sections"* observed that thrift and savings constitute fulcrum of the working of cooperative banks. Cooperative lending is the means to promote the thrift and savings and service, and the profit is not the motto. It was concluded that

society should provide certain facilities to the artisans also belonging to the weaker sections, besides providing literacy programmes to the illiterates, so that they could require awareness of the society and its utility. Cooperation constitutes credible continuation to compensate the weaker sections to achieve socio-economic development.

17. **T. Geetha Madhuri and P. Shoba Rani** in their paper on *"New Generation Financial Institutions and Poverty Alleviations in India"* observed that the eradication of poverty has been an integral component of the strategy for economic development in India. It was concluded that the impact of microfinance on poverty alleviation is a keenly debated issue, however, when implemented and managed carefully and when services are designed to meet the needs of the clients, microfinance has had positive impacts, not just on clients, but on their families and on the wider community.
18. **B. Lakshmi Bhavani, S. Appala Naidu and N. Bhaskara Reddy** in their paper on *"Indira Prabha: An Evaluation Study of Land Distribution Scheme: A Case Study of Visakhapatam District"* observed that failure or land reforms in the country indicate the living conditions of rural poor particularly agricultural labourers. It was concluded that the political parties should aim at poverty alleviation programmes for social upliftment in rural areas in a stabilized manner. Keeping in view of their financial and revenue sources otherwise the very objective of the programme may fail.
19. **M. Rukmani, M. Raghava Reddy and S. Rathna Kumari** in their paper on *"Impact of DWCRA on income and Employment Generation (A Study in Chittoor District)"* observed that the excess burden of poverty has been borne by women because of the responsibility of the survival of the household rests on the shoulders of women. It was concluded that inter-developmental

coordination is an essential pre-requisite for the effective and successful implementation of DWCRA programme as potent instrument for the economic empowerment of rural women.

20. **Santhosh Singh Bais** in his paper on "*HRD Practices in Small-Scale Industry (A Study with special reference to Gulbarga District in Karnataka)*" observed that it was rightly remarked that HRD is the process of increasing knowledge, skills, capabilities and positive work attitudes and values of all people working at all levels in a business undertaking. It was concluded that every organization required ensuring sound human resources planning, acceptable policies regarding recruitment and suitable performance appraisal, sound motivation policies, sincere effort towards selection, proper training and development, adequate education, fair promotion policies.
21. **D. Francis, D. Pulla Rao** in their paper on "*Impact of Green Revolution on Agricultural Development in India*" observed that the significance of agriculture in India arises from the fact that the development in agriculture is an essential condition for the development of the national economy. It was concluded that the green revolution was mainly due to hybrid seeds, which raised agricultural yields. In addition to the High Yielding Variety Programme (HYVP) the government has taken several steps to increase agricultural production. The other aspects are short duration crops, multiple cropping, farm mechansiation, extension of irrigation, price support, processing, storage and marketing facilities, improved credit facilities, institutional changes, production of supplementary food products etc.
22. **A. Vamsi Krushna** in his paper on "*Influence Of Inter Sectoral Linkages On Nature And Volatility Of Growth Of Major States In India*" observed that while framing development strategy the linkages between various sectors, especially the inter linkages between

agriculture and other sectors must be taken into account. The contribution of agriculture to growth of the non-agricultural sector, and vice versa is determined by the strength of their linkages. These linkages were defined in terms of forward linkages, backward linkages, demand linkages, and employment linkages etc.

23. **D. Pulla Rao, D. Francis** in their paper on "*Progress of Agricultural Production during Plan Period in India*" observed that population has been increasing at a rapid rate, leading to increase in demand for food and other consumer good, many of which have an agricultural base. It was concluded that the adoption of chemical fertilizer is the main factor, which determines the productivity of agriculture in the Indian economy. However, it has to be supported by other important agricultural inputs like irrigation, HYV, rainfall etc.
24. **V. Krishna Murthy and R.V.L.N. Rathnakara Rao** in their paper on "*Political Economy through Education*" observed that political economy should include Education For All (EFA), so that the political action as well as its economic intention result in national development. It was concluded that education provides employment, economic freedom and thereby empowerment along with fulfilling the national objectives and goals.
25. **R.V.L.N. Ratnakara Rao and V. Krishna Murthy** in their paper on "*Political Economy – Workers' Education Programme*" observed that usually workers education is outside the scope of an organisation's functions. Hence workers education is organized by the Central Board For Workers' Education (CBWE) set up in 1958. It was concluded that workers education is an opportunity to provide update knowledge, skills and attitudes necessary for workers to improve their socio-economic status, productive skills and political economy so that the overall organizational position and status can be improved.

26. In her paper on *"Impact Of Social Capital On Poverty In India"* **Kavita Venkatachari** concentrating on the role of social capital in development and examining whether there are economic payoffs to enhancing social capital. It can be seen that within the developing country context, the former has been the exclusive vehicle for analysis; allowing detailed study of the effects for broadly conceived social capital. However these approaches suffer from a limitation, in that they provide no means for aggregating up and looking at social capital from the macro level. In the developing country context, this kind of data is scarce making analysis more problematic. It can be seen clearly from the analysis that those states which were initially well endowed with social capital were also more successful at reducing poverty.
27. **Kavita Venkatachari** in her paper on *"Learning New Computer Skills In The Workplace: A Stress Or Pleasure?"* observed the adoption of ICTs and its far-reaching effects have attracted considerable interest. The majority of earlier literature centers around the effects on productivity and job quality. Specifically, having to learn new computer skills is more likely to cause stress for middle age employees in the age group 35-44. Because of the recession and job cut, people who are having higher level of education they are greatly affected by stress. There is also an issue of equity - all workers are affected in different ways in different sectors. Their indeed exist substantial variations in these effects over demographic and job specific characteristics.
28. **G. Durga Prasad** in his paper on *"Intellectual Property Rights in India – a Case for Their Protection"* made an attempt to study how IPRs are protected in the country. Patenting of inventive ideas is the need of the hour in the light of the fast picking up globalization trends in the country particularly in view of the globalization of higher education. Though the

government had provided several fiscal incentives for encouraging innovative ideas by the industries, academic institutions, the R&D expenditure is at a lower level. Therefore, encouraging research activity by an intensive funding mechanism on the part of the Universities, IITs, IISc, research institutions is urgently called for. They must be encouraged to go for patents.

Prof. D. Pulla Rao

Profile of Prof. K.S. Chalam

Prof. K.S. Chalam in whose honour the present book is edited is an Alma Mater of Andhra University. He is a well known Educationist, Political Economist and an innovator of Staff Development Programme in India. He has entered the U P S C in 2005 after a brief stint as Vice Chancellor at Dravidian University, A P.

He served the Department of Economics, Andhra University as a Lecturer, Reader and Professor for more than three decades with dedication and distinction. He was trained as an Economic Planner at Central School of Planning and Statistics, Warsaw, Poland during 1981-1982. He has obtained first rank in the international diploma programme of the school. As a student of Prof. B. Sarveswara Rao, he has strengthened the teaching of Economics of Education and Human Development. He has delivered endowment lectures on Public Sector and on issues relating to educational development at several universities and institutes in the country. He has published so far 20 books in English and 6 in Telugu and about 90 research papers covering areas of Economics of Education, Political Economy, Public Economics, Dravidian Studies etc,. Some of his articles published in Economic and Political Weekly are still cited in several reference works. In his forthcoming book on "Economic Reforms and Social Exclusion" he has made an attempt to bring interdisciplinary approach to study the impact of reforms on the socially excluded groups in India. His book on "Caste-based Reservations and Human Development in India" published by Sage Publications in 2007 was reviewed in around 20 leading newspapers and journals including the Hindu, the Tribune, etc appreciating the author for the innovative approach used to understand and solve the contentious issue of our times. The reviewers in Pakistan and DFID commended the book as "immense topical relevance, this book will be of interest to students and scholars of development studies....useful to policy makers and practitioners working in this area". The book is being translated into Tamil and Telugu. An honours diploma thesis was submitted by Natasha Azad to California University on this book.

Prof. K.S. Chalam is an internationally recognized scholar, teacher in Staff Development and Economics of Education. He is known in the country as the father of the famous Academic Staff Colleges Scheme as he was the one who initiated the concept in 1985. At a time when the professors of the university system were not given any structured training to improve the quality of higher education, Prof. Chalam initiated a training course with UGC support in 1985. The UGC has recognized his contribution and asked him to conduct the first national workshop to design the proposed Academic Staff Colleges in India. He himself founded the college in 1987 and organized the first orientation course. It became an important part of the system of higher education to improve the Quality of Higher Education. The UNESCO has appreciated the scheme as one of the largest schemes of Staff Development in the world. He was responsible in strengthening the scheme with his 3 important publications on staff development. The latest (2006) book on 'Modern Techniques of Teaching and Staff Development' is a reference volume for all teachers in higher education. He has delivered lectures on Staff Development and participated in deliberations of the Prof. Rastogi Committee. It has helped to consolidate the scheme in the interest of Quality of University Education.

Chalam K.S. was the first student trained formally in a university system in Economics of Education in 1972 at Andhra University under Prof. B. Sarveswara Rao. Late J.P. Naik inaugurated the specialization. He has worked for his Ph. D on 'Finances, costs and productivity of higher education'. The study published as a book was reviewed both in India and abroad. Late Dr. Malcolm Adiseshiah acclaimed it as 'an excellent analysis of the economics of education in Andhra Pradesh as such is an important addition to the limited literature in India'. Another reviewer Dijon Jean-Claude Eicher commended it as a "courageous and useful book". He was Professor of Economics in Andhra University and taught the specialization both in the Departments of Economics and Education for a generation of students. He has pioneered interdisciplinary research and published 'Education and Weaker Sections' in 1988. Prof. P.R. Panchamukhi in his review of the book mentioned that 'the interdisciplinary approach to the study of educational problems is a useful framework'. Some of his books are offered as Text books for P.G students. He is one of the very rare research guides who has trained a dozen research students on a variety of issues starting from Human Development in A.P (before HD Report, 1990), Child Labour, Primary Education, Dalit Poverty, Impact of Technology on Agriculture, Liberalization to name a few. He is a prolific writer in Telugu. Apart from 6 Books in Telugu, scores of edit page articles were published in all leading dailies. He has supervised 12 scholars successfully to obtain their Ph. Ds in Economics, conducted research studies funded by UGC, Govt. of A.P, UNICEF, etc.

The contributions of Prof. Chalam are cited by scholars and activists across the globe. He has kept a legacy of teaching at Andhra University. One of the citations of an award rightly remarked that he is a 'scholar with social consciousnesses'. A Volume of papers were contributed in his honour in the name of 'Development of Weaker Sections' in 1998. As the third Vice-Chancellor of Dravidian University for a brief period, he has produced a programme of action for the university. He is also known as the first Director of Swamy

Ramanand Teertha Rural Institute, the first institute of NCRI, Govt. of India. His experiments with rural higher education for one year at Pochampally published later in a book are useful as a reference work. He is the founder Editor of 'South India Journal of Social Sciences'.

Prof. K.S. Chalam commands respect among the academicians and activists due to his committed service in public affairs over a period of three decades. He is not an armchair scholar. He has been actively involved in public affairs relating to education and social development. All his studies in economics are interdisciplinary in nature and contain social issues with economic analysis of development. Therefore one of his biographers Avinash Misra called him as Simon Kuznets of India.

He has single handedly projected the underdevelopment of North Andhra with his publications and lectures for the last three decades making the Govt. of Andhra Pradesh to appoint a separate development board for the region in 2007. He is not an idealist but a practical person who got himself married outside his caste and implemented the same principle for the entire family. He has performed more than hundred social marriages in A.P.

Prof. Chalam is not only a serious scholar and teacher, but also a social activist. He served as the National Secretary, Amnesty International during 1984-85, Secretary and Vice-President of Professional bodies like A.P. Economic Association, Indian Political Economy Association etc. He has participated in international debates on caste and race at Durban, Cairo etc. He has presented papers on Education, Poverty, Political Economy at Cambridge, Wisconsin, Manchester, Colombo, Bangkok and at other international fora. He has been on several expert committees at center and State levels and has served on the World Bank teams. He is a builder of institutions. The Academic Staff College that he has nurtured at Andhra University became a model for the entire country. He has started Mahendra Degree College in his native place, Pathapatnam a decade ago to provide higher educational facilities in a remote tribal region.

He got his Economics honours from S K C G College, Parlakhemundi, Orissa. He studied in the college as a day scholar walking the distance from his native place in Andhra crossing the border everyday for 4 years. He was the first Telugu person to receive honours degree from Utkal (Berhampur) University in 1968 at an age of 19. He became a Lecturer at a very young age that helped him to develop passion for teaching and research. The passion for teaching made him to continue his advice to the UGC as Hon. Chairman of a 'High Power Committee on Academic Staff Colleges' even after joining the UPSC. He is on several committees including NCRI, ICPR on an advisory capacity. He has an impeccable character and sound knowledge in social sciences that helped him to become Member, UPSC. It is said that his presence in the UPSC made people from lower socio-economic background to get inspired to enter into civil services to serve the country and people. This is reflected in the results of recent Civil Services Examination.

List of Contributors

1. Prof. A. Satyanarayana, Department of History, Osmania University, Hyderabad.
2. Dr. G. Surya Prakasa Rao, Associate Professor, Department of Economics, G.V.P. College for P.G. Courses, Visakhapatnam-45.
3. K. Rama Chandra Rao, Assistant Professor, Department of Economics, G.V.P. College for P.G. Courses, Visakhapatnam-45.
4. K. Kishore Babu, Research Scholar, Department of Economics and Applied Economics, Acharya Nagarjuna University, Guntur, (A.P.)
5. A. Bala Krishna, Research Scholar, Department of Economics and Applied Economics, Acharya Nagarjuna University, Guntur, (A.P.)
6. K. Mahendra Kumar, Research Scholar, Department of Economics andApplied Economics, Acharya Nagarjuna University, Guntur, (A.P.)
7. Dr. P. P. Satyanarayana Rao, Associate Professor, Department of Education, Andhra University, Visakhapatnam -03.
8. Prof. D. Pulla Rao, Department of Economics, Andhra University, Visakhapatnam-03.
9. Dr. P. Kothandarami Reddy, Associate Professor, UGC - Academic Staff College, Sri Venkateswara University, Tirupati, (A.P.)
10. M. Venkata Ramanaiah, Lecturer in Commerce, Department of Commerce and Management, Dravidian University, Kuppam-517 425 (A.P.)

11. B. Parameswara Reddy, Research Scholar, Department of Commerce, Sri Venkateswara University, Tirupati-517502, (A.P.)
12. G. Ranganath, Lecturer in Commerce, Department of Commerce and Management, Dravidian University, Kuppam-517 425, (A.P.)
13. A. Vamsi Krushna, Research Scholar, Department of Economics, Andhra University, Visakhapatnam - 03.
14. S. Marulu Reddy, Research Scholar, Department of Economics, Andhra University, Visakhapatnam - 03.
15. Dr. K. Kiran, Teaching Associate, Dept. of Economics, Dr. B.R. Ambedkar University, Etcherla, Srikakulam, (A.P.)
16. Dr. V. Divya Thejomoorthy, Assistant Professor, Department of Rural Development, Acharya Nagarjuna University, Nagarjuna Nagar - 522 510, Guntur , Andhra Pradesh.
17. Dr. I. Narendra Kumar, Academic Consultant, Department of Econometrics, Sri Venkateswara University, Tirupati - 517 502, (A.P.)
18. Prof. G. Gangadhar Hugar, Faculty Member, IBS – Mumbai, Opp: L.H. Hiranandani Hospital, Off: Technology Street, Hiranandani Gardens, Powai, Mumbai.
19. Dr. K. Janardana Rao, Economic Officer, Planning Commission, Room No. 332, Yojana Bhavan, Sansad Marg, New Delhi-110 001.
20. Dr. Jesurathnam Devarapalli, Lecturer, Department of Anthropology, Pondicherry University, Puducherry – 605 014.
21. S.V. Lakshmana Rao, Research Scholar, Department of Education, Andhra University, Visakhapatnam - 03.
22. Dr. M. Ramesh, Post – Doctoral Fellow, Department of Rural Development, Dr. B.R. Ambedkar University, Etcherla, Srikakulam. (A.P.)
23. Dr. B. Addai, Associate Professor, Department of Economics, Dr. B.R. Ambedkar University, Etcherla, Srikakulam,. (A.P.)

24. Prof. C.S.N. Raju, Dean, Faculty of Social Sciences, Department of Economics and Applied Economics, Acharya Nagarjuna University, Guntur, (A.P.)
25. B. Sudheer, Research Scholar, Department of Economics and Applied Economics, Acharya Nagarjuna University, Guntur, (A.P.)
26. T. Geetha Madhuri, Assistant Professor, GITAM Institute of Management, GITAM University, Vishakapatnam-45.
27. P. Shoba Rani, Assistant Professor, GITAM Institute of Management, GITAM University, Vishakapatnam-45.
28. B. Lakshmi Bhavani, Research Scholar, Department of Economics, Andhra University, Visakhapatnam - 03.
29. S. Appala Naidu, Research Scholar, Department of Economics, Andhra University, Visakhapatnam - 03.
30. Prof. N. Bhaskara Reddy, Department of Economics, Andhra University, Visakhapatnam - 03.
31. Dr. M. Rukmani, Academic Consultant, Department of Economics, Sri Venkateswara University, Tirupati - 517502, (A.P.)
32. M. Raghava Reddy, Research Scholar, Department of Economics, Sri Venkateswara University, Tirupati - 517502, (A.P.)
33. Prof. S. Rathna Kumari, Department of Economics, Sri Venkateswara University, Tirupati - 517502, (A.P.)
34. Dr. Santosh Singh Bias, Lecturer, Department of Studies and Research in Management, Gulbarga University, Gulbarga - 585106. Karnataka.
35. Dr. D. Francis, Teaching Associate, Dr. B.R. Ambedkar University, Etcherla, Srikakulam, (A.P.)
36. Prof. V. Krishna Murthy, Flat No. 201, Vijaya Apartments, APSEB Colony, Seethammadhara, Visakhapatnam - 13.
37. Dr. R.V.L.N. Ratnakar Rao, Department of Physical Education, Andhra University, Visakhapatnam - 03.

38. Kavitha Venkatachari, C-7, 201 Vedant Residential Complex, Vartak Nagar, THANE (W) - 400606.
39. Dr. G. Durga Prasad, Associate Professor in Economics and Deputy Director, PG Courses & Research Centre, DNRCollege, Bhimavaram – 534202 (AP)

1

Land, Caste and Kulak-Pettandars in Andhra Pradesh

A. Satyanarayana

The objective of this paper is to analyse the inter-relationship between caste/class, land and dominance in rural Andhra Pradesh. Central to this is an examination of the role of caste in relation to land control and changing forms of agrarian relations. Expansion of commodity production and agrarian market since the late 19th century, resulted in the formation of a new social class, namely "The nascent peasant bourgeoisie". The emergence and cyrstellization of this class signified the redefining and reshaping of agrarian relations and class structure. It also meant a very complex mixture of caste and class. The caste based feudal domination was increasingly challenged by the emerging rural rich class, the kulak-pettandars in Andhra and Telangana regions.

A word about kulak-pettandars: The dynamic, market oriented rich peasantry as kulaks, (a Russian concept used by Marxists) substantially possessed the characteristic features of a capitalist peasant bourgeois class. To put it in the words of Carol Boyack Upadhyay, they are "Farmer-Capitalists". They also possessed the characteristics of dominant caste landed gentry, hence they are pettandars. Apart from economic power, they also exercised considerable socio-cultural and political authority over the vast mass of the peasantry belonging to lower and middle castes. In caste terms, the kulak-pettandars invariably belong to the sudra upper castes such as kapu, reddy, velama and kamma. The term kulak connotes economic and class relationship, while pettandars signifies caste and social power of the dominant peasantry. Cambridge historians like Baker and Washbrook have described them as "rural magnets", "rural elite", "village boss" etc.

This paper is divided into four sections: The first section briefly describe evolution of agrarian social structure under colonial conditions, with emphasis on caste and land relationship. Commercialisation of agriculture and its impact the peasantry is discussed in the second section. The third section examines the nature of agriculture entrepreneurship in colonial Andhra. An overview of the relationship between caste and power in post-colonial period is presented in the fourth section.

Land and Caste in Colonial Andhra

During the colonial period, the agrarian social structure in Andhra closely corresponded to the structure of landownership, power and authority. Although the British abolished the existing caste-defined position over land and other resources and imposed juridico-legal relationships of landownership (property right, private property in land, etc.), the caste hierarchies continued to exist and often overlapped with the hierarchies of economy and power.

The socio-economic transformation during the colonial period (1802-1947) resulted in the formation of new classes, formally separated from the traditional caste system. Yet the categories of caste and class were, to a large extent, converged and continued to be interlinked. Broadly speaking, the fusion and convergence of caste and class in the colonial context contributed to the emergence of two distinct groups of classes, namely, landlords (zamindars) and peasants/tenants.

The evolution of the land tenure system under colonialism strengthened the position of zamindars as well as the big ryotwari landlords in terms of their control over land. It may be pointed out that for years the zamindars had been able to command and exercise immense power and authority in the countryside mainly because of their grip over land. The zamindari agrarian structure enabled the landlord class as a whole to appropriate a larger share of agrarian surplus by means of extraction of exorbitant rents. The landlords' authority was, in fact, maintained on the basis of rack-renting. The zamindars in Andhra held vast estates and obtained unfettered access to communal, waste, forest lands and other resources. It may be noted that they exercised rule and control over not only land and forests but also over ponds, sources of irrigation, etc. Thus, the zamindars' power was further reinforced since they acquired enormous wealth and affluence based on rack-renting and illegal cesses. Acquisition of wealth and control over resources enabled the landlords to maintain their higher status. It also sustained their hold and hegemony over rural society, economy and polity. Thus, the landlord class in the Andhra consisted predominantly of the non-Brahmin upper class, viz., Kshatriya, Velama, Kamma and Reddy. Most of the big zamindars like the Rajas of Bobbili, Venkatagiri, Pithapuram, Mirzapuram, Chellapalli, and Vuyyuru were also moneylenders. By leasing-out lands and advancing money they were able to tighten their grip over the dependent tenantry. As creditors, the landlords always commanded authority over debtors. By virtue of 'proprietorship' over land, the zamindars could lease-out lands to whomsoever they wanted and displace the tenants-at-will at their will and pleasure. The threat of eviction coerced the tenantry into submission. The colonial land legislation, although it granted certain rights of occupancy to tenants, on the whole failed to protect the tenants. The growth of population and land hunger further strengthened the hold of landlords over rural population. In caste terms the vast mass of the tenantry, both in the zamindari and ryotwai areas, consisted of the peasant and artisan castes. Particularly the lower castes among the backward communities such as Goundlas, Yadavas, and Telagas used to lease-in lands from landlords. They were the most exploited lot as they were subjected to frequent rack-renting and illegal exactions.

Control over land and acquisition of wealth and affluence helped the landlords to exercise power and authority. The growth of non-Brahmin movement and establishment of the Justice Party led to the rise of landlord power in Andhra. The opportunities provided by the colonial state in terms of local self-government and 'diarchy' were utilized by zamindars to their full advantage. Their ability to extend patronage and exercise control and domination over their dependents contributed to the monopoly of power by them. As a matter of fact, the working of diarchy (in the 1920's) witnessed the emergence of landlords as 'political bosses' in the Madras Presidency. Due to the colonial patronage, between 1921-36, out of four chief ministers three belonged to the zamindars class. The legislative council and the local board elections provided opportunities for the landlords to emerge as the dominant political elite. An examination of the electoral data (of the mid-1920's) reveals the fact that landlords successfully competed with the professional elites (lawyers), in occupying positions in the Madras Legislative Council. The strength of the landlords in the council increased from twenty-eight in 1920 to thirty-eight in 1926; whereas the representation of lawyers declined from forty-eight to thirty-six during the same period. Some of the zamindars in Andhra like the Rajas of Bobbili, Pithapuram, Venkatagiri, Mirzapuram were active and took leading part in the Justice Party as well as in local and provincial politics. They held positions (Chairmanships) in the district and taluk boards. A perceptive scholar remarked: "Landlords with local influence discovered that as presidents and members of local boards, they could wield a large amount of influence in their locality, and exercise greater power over their neighbours" Being powerful men in the countryside they could and did command the votes of their creditors and dependants. Therefore, between 1920-40, many local boards were controlled by landlords belonging to zamindari and ryotwai areas. The landlords' control over provincial politics remained unchallenged till the late 1930's.

Commercialisation and the Rich Peasantry

The integration of Andhra's economy into the world market commenced since the late 19th century. It facilitated and accelerated commercialization of agriculture in terms of the export of raw material like cotton, oilseeds, tobacco, jute etc., and the import of manufactured goods from England such as cotton textiles, gunny bags and oil. Thus till about the depression years in the 1930s, Andhra economy tended to primarily cater to the needs of export-oriented foreign trade. The growth of trade and commerce in agricultural commodities necessitated the establishment of agro-processing small-scale industries such as rice mills, cotton gins, jute presses, and groundnut decorticating factories. The total number of such industries, which came under the Factories Act increased from 11 in 1899 to 242 in 1920.

The works of Baker and Washbrook, though debatable, contain an interesting analysis of the impact of commercialization on agrarian society in modern Andhra under colonialism. They have argued that in the 'dry' regions of the ceded districts, because of unfavourable ecological conditions like low rainfall, infertile lands, lack of irrigation, etc., and the widespread prevalence of small holdings, the vast majority of the peasantry had to depend on credit supplied by a 'rural elite' to carry on agricultural production; while in the 'wet' districts of coastal Andhra, the 'middle peasantry' with secured irrigation and fertile lands carried on agricultural production without the absolute domination of the merchant-moneylenders. To quote Baker:

"The dominant men of the village formed a very distinct elite in the rural areas... The members of the village elite loomed large in the rural economy. To begin with, most of the other members of the village in some fashion depended upon them for their livelihood. The village leaders were the chief patrons of many different artisans and of the other services castes... Many of them in the village did not own enough to support their families and thus supplemented their holdings by renting land from the village elite... many of the villagers had at some time to come to the village bosses for a loan".

Washbrook maintained that the expansion of commercial agriculture and the establishment of an integrated market economy in the countryside since the late nineteenth century led to the concentration of rural wealth and power in the hands of minority of rich peasants. He characterized the agrarian society in terms of 'rural magnates' and 'agrarian dependents' to explain the process of peasant stratification in the countryside. He also suggested that the 'rural magnates' were able to control the dependent peasantry, by virtue of their control and monopoly over credit, land and commodity markets. According to him, the process of commercialization of agriculture, in a crucial sense, strengthened the domination of the 'rural elite' over the 'agrarian dependents'. On the basis of available evidence it can be argued that the penetration of market relations into a stratified peasant society led to the widening of the gap between different sections of the peasantry. It can also be suggested that the impact of the commercialization of agriculture was not uniform and equitable; the upper stratum of the peasantry with substantial landholdings responded favourably to market and price incentives and benefited immensely from commercial agriculture. The expansion of commercialization was beneficial to them because they were not under the domination of the merchant-money-lenders; whereas the majority of the medium and small peasants were compelled to grow cash crops in order to meet subsistence and debt obligation.

The chief characteristic feature of coastal agriculture at the turn of the 20th century was the predominance of food grain cultivation. During the first half of the twentieth century, nearly four-fifths of the cultivated area was devoted to the cultivation of paddy, jowar, bajra and other cereals and pulses. However, among the foodgrains, paddy occupied a significant place. It accounted for more than 50 per cent of the gross cultivated area in the Ganjam, Godavari and Kistna districts; and in the non-delta districts of Vizagapatam, Nellore and Guntur it occupied more than 25 per cent of the total cropped area. Although paddy remained as the dominant crop in coastal Andhra, the cropping pattern since the turn of the century was characterized by the cultivation of a diversity of commercial crops. The relative importance of different cash crops in the cropping pattern had undergone significant change over time. The importance of some cash crops like indigo and opium declined; others like cotton, sugarcane, oilseeds and tobacco gained prominence in the twentieth century. In particular, the cultivation of cotton, oilseeds, tobacco and sugarcane expanded as a result of growing demand both in the external and internal markets. The phenomenal growth of two important crops in coastal Andhra, viz., tobacco and sugarcane, during the first half of the twentieth century was a clear indication of the expansion of commercial agriculture. The expansion of the area under tobacco was possible because of the growth of external (foreign) demand, whereas sugarcane catered to the domestic market.

In the Rayalaseem districts, cultivation of jowar, bajra and other cereals and pulses became popular, while paddy was 'scantily cultivated'. Given the lack of adequate irrigation facilities and infertile soils, the Rayalaseema area was mostly suited to the cultivation of millet and other rain-fed crops such as cotton and oilseeds. Although the area under foodgrains was more than 70 per cent of the total cultivated area at the beginning of the twentieth century, it began to decline thereafter. The cultivation of cotton and oilseeds, the most important cash crops, gradually eroded the traditional crop structure of the Ceded Districts. The area under commercial crops registered a remarkable increase during the first half of the present century. In addition to crop statistics, available data from the Settlement Reports and other sources also clearly indicate that there was a shift in the cropping pattern of the Ceded Districts over time. Most of the settlement officers and other revenue officials noted that 'the most striking feature' of the cropping pattern in the region was 'the large increase of area under industrial crop'. Therefore, it is clear that in colonial Andhra there was a rapid reduction in the area under cereals and pulses, while the area under commercial crops significantly increased. The crop pattern in the Rayalaseema region, in particular, underwent a clear-cut reorientation with cash crops progressively swallowing up the area under subsistence crops.

The process of commercialization in modern Andhra can also be explained in terms of the price responsiveness of the peasantry. Higher prices for agricultural commodities certainly induced the cultivators to grow valuable cash crops. According to Dharm Narain's study of the cotton crop in the Madras Presidency: 'The price factor alone would seem to account for most of the change in the area... price bears an unusually large degree on the variation of cotton area'. Similarly in the case of groundnut, he pointed out, 'the directional affinity between the movement of price and area is positive and persistent'. In coastal Andhra, rising prices from the early decades of the twentieth century encouraged the cultivation of more remunerative crops such as tobacco and sugarcane.

The growth of commercialization of agriculture was also possible in Andhra districts mainly because of the rapid expansion of trade (both internal and external) in agricultural commodities from the late nineteenth century onwards. A perusal of data on agrarian trade indicates that, while coastal Andhra districts exported rice and paddy to places within the Madras Presidency, to neighbouring states and outside the country (Ceylon, Mauritius, etc.), the Deccan districts exported cotton and oilseeds to international markets. Internal trade statistics indicate that the surplus foodgrains of the deltas, Nellore and Vizagapatam districts, were exported in large quantities to the southern Tamil districts and the West Coastal. Besides foodgrains, the coastal districts also regularly exported jaggery (unrefined sugar), provision, spices and condiments to the neighbouring states like Bombay, Hyderabad and Mysore. The pattern of internal trade suggests that while the coastal districts exported primarily rice and provision, the Ceded Districts exported jowar and bajra. Imports from the neighbouring provinces and states into Andhra districts consisted mainly of sugar, grains and pulses.

The growth of sustained internal trade in Andhra districts was possible due to the expansion of the rail-road transport network. In addition to exporting rice to places within the province and outside by rail, the delta districts also exported rice to foreign countries from the late nineteenth century. An examination of the composition of the export trade of Andhra districts indicates that food grains, rice and oilseeds occupied an important part. The fact that the area under oilseeds rapidly increased was confirmed by exports to foreign markets. Groundnuts grown in the Ceded Districts enjoyed an excellent reputation with European customers. The benefits commodity production and market incentives were not equally shared by all sections of the peasantry. Given the inequality of landownership and resources in the countryside, the upper stratum of the peasantry could and did have free access to various markets, viz., commodity, land and credit, and benefited from commercial agriculture; the small and middle peasantry, on the other hand, were forced to depend on the merchants and moneylenders for credit, because they possessed inadequate 'working capital' and were burdened with subsistence costs. The dependence on the trader-usurers deprived them of the benefits of expanding commodity production. In particular, indebtedness was wide-spread among the poor peasantry and it caused land alienation. Increasing transfers of land from the indebted poor peasantry significantly contributed to the process of pauperization and differentiation among the peasantry.

Therefore, the main characteristic feature of the rich peasantry in modern Andhra had been its price responsiveness and market-oriented production. The dominant caste peasantry directly participated in the commodity market and benefited by the rising prices of the early 20th century. Accumulated surplus of the rich peasantry was invested in land purchase, money lending, trade and agro-industries. Recent studies on the emergence a new class of businessmen out of the class of capitalist farmers in coastal Andhra Pradesh and some of its social and economic characteristics have explained the convergence of several historical processes: the development of a productive and commercialised agrarian economy in the later nineteenth century and the emergence of rich peasant class, the integration of town and countryside, an early interest in education on the part of the rural elite, the politicisation of caste identity and, later the green revolution and land reform. Thus the rich peasantry emerged as a dynamic commercial and industrial entrepreneur class. Recent literature on the emergence of regional capitalism and entrepreneur class also indicates that big landholders and substantial peasants actively participated in the development of agro-based industrialisation. Accumulated profits of the rich peasantry were increasingly ploughed back into agriculture in the form of money lending, trade and land. Available evidence clearly indicates that in Coastal Andhra rich peasants who belonged to the dominant peasant castes like Khamma, Raju and Reddi replaced the traditional bania-caste in the rural credit market. Various government reports and village surveys conducted by Slater, Ranga etc., make it abundantly clear that the wealthy peasants and big landholders of Coastal Andhra districts were able to diversify their surplus into various activities. In the delta region, in particular, they took to agrarian trade during the early decades of the 20th century. Besides trade, the rich peasantry also invested in agro-processing industries such as rice mills, oil mills, cotton gins and presses and groundnut decorticating factories.

The above discussion makes it clear that expansion of commodity production, agrarian market and trade resulted in the emergence of a class of prosperous rich peasantry. In terms of caste, they predominantly belonged to Kamma, Raju, and Reddy. Upto the end of 1920s agrarian surplus of the rich peasantry was primarily invested in money lending, trade and small-scale agro-industries. However, the onset of the world economic depression in the 1930s led to a "shift of capital, entrepreneurship ... from country to town". Economic compulsions during the depression period forced the rural rich money-lenders and speculators to transfer their profits from agriculture to industry. The rapid decline of agricultural prices and collapse of rural credit market prompted the rich peasantry to search for new avenues for investment.. Baker's studies have shown that there was a substantial increase in joint-stock companies in the Madras Presidency during the post-depression year. Big landholders in coastal Andhra had invested their surplus in the agro-industries such as Sugar and Cotton mills and in other joint-stock companies. The co-operative sugar factories emerged as an important sector within the sugar industry of the Coastal Andhra in 1930s. In the establishment of sugar mills, particularly in the cooperative sector, landlords played a vital role. The Etikoppaka and Thummapala cooperative sugar factories were established by Rao Bahadur C.V.S. Narasimha Raju, an ex-president of the Madras Legislative Council. He was also a Zamindar in Vizagapatnam district, who paid Rs.1200 peshcush to the Government. He was member of the Madras Legislative for more than a decade. For some time he was the president of District Board and a Governor of Imperial Bank. In the case of the Bobbili factory, the Raja took an active part in its formation. His family members along with the Raja of Venkatagiri who are related to the Bobbili family, invested an amount of Rs.4 lakhs as share capital. Unlike the majority of the Andhra Zamindars the Raja of the Bobbili and Venkatagiri, who belonged to the dominant Velama Caste, played an important role in entrepreneurial activities. In the establishment of the Vuyyur factory the local Zamindar(of Kamma caste) Adusumalli Gopala Krishnaiah, who owed 1200 acres of wet land in the Krishna delta including 300 acres in the Vuyyur seemed to have played an active role. In co-operative factories the shareholders consisted of the rural rich who belonged to the non-Brahmin upper caste. It is also reasonable to argue that the growth of sugar industry in Andhra was a clear example of the emergence of industrial entrepreneurship based on agrarian capital.

It is possible to suggest that since landlords enjoyed state patronage and political power they could take keen interest in the development of sugar industry, during the period of Diarchy (1920-37) for instance, four out of five Chief Ministers of Madras were Zamindars: one of them was the Raja of the Bobbili, the leading landed aristocrat of Andhra. The Government of Madras also nominated big Zamindars like Raja of Venkatagiri, Pithapuram, Paralakimidi, Nuzividu, Kallikota etc., as members of Board of Industries, Honorary members of the Advisory Council for Agriculture, Cooperative and Veterinary department and Honorary Visitors to Agricultural College and Research Station at Coimbatore. As a privileged socio-political group they took advantage of available financial resources of the colonial state. For example as members of Board of industries, it was easy for them to obtain Government loans and other concessions, while access to the political power enabled them to influence the policy formulation of departments like agriculture, industry and cooperation. In other words the acquisition of political power has allowed them to secure control over such agencies, which influenced the execution of state policy at the local levels. While the big landlords took lead in establishing sugar industries, rich peasants with substantial holdings were enriched by the extension of cane cultivation.

Caste and Entrepreneurship

The multidimensionality of the formation of industrial capital and the evolution of modern capitalist class can be better understood on the basis of detailed micro -level studies. Regional studies will clarify some of the issues regarding the process of evolution of indigenous capitalism and capitalist class in the colonial context. Hence, in this paper an attempt will be made to highlight some aspects the changing nature of caste system and the disjunction between traditional occupation and modern entrepreneurial activities. On the basis of empirical evidence at the regional level, the validity of certain assumptions of Max Weber that the Hindu caste system and the irrational doctrines of Hinduism are not conductive for the economic/technological transformation of India can be tessed and contested. He also asserted that the caste system, which reduces occupational mobility and prevents innovation, was not favourable for the emergence of dynamic industrial capitalist class.

However, recent studies by some sociologist, economists, historians etc., have suggested that the dynamics of Indian social structure did allow certain adaptive strategies towards occupational mobility and modernization. Nafziger remarked: "despite the powerful socio-religious sanctions given the caste system, there are several dynamic factors making fluidity and flexibility in occupational and caste structures possible". Moreover, "modifications of the caste system and the modernization of traditional occupational cultures have gone farther than Weber seems to have believed possible".

In this paper certain aspects of convergence and divergence between caste system and class formation, viz., caste/class origins of entrepreneurs in modern Andhra will be explained. The inter-war period (1919-39) did witness industrialization in terms of the development of import-substitution consumer industries in India. The Telugu speaking districts of Madras Presidency had also witnessed the rise and growth of several domestic-market oriented medium and large-scale industries. Among them the agro-based industries like rice mills, oil mills, cotton mills, tobacco and sugar factories played a significant role. As the Andhra region was endowed with considerable natural and agro-economic resources, it offered excellent scope for the growth of such industries. For instance, the growth of modern rice mills was possible because of the better irrigation and canal system of the delta districts like Krishna, Guntur, and East Godavari. Landlords, rich peasants and local Komati merchants took active part in their growth. It has been found that by the end of 1940s rice mills, in numerical terms, accounted for more than half of the total industries in the coastal Andhra districts of Krishna, Guntur, East and West Godavari and Nellore.

The growth of major agro-industries in Andhra districts during the 1930s and 1940s marked an important turning point with regard to capital investment in industry. The depression years, which changed the terms of trade between agriculture and industry in favour of the latter, brought about a significant shift of capital from agriculture and money lending to industry. The boom in investment in local industries was also encouraged by the changes in the industries policy of the Madras government, viz., tariff protection to sugar and cotton textile industries and the post-war development plans with regard to oil mills and cement factories. Certain other factors like the availability of abundant raw materials also accelerated the growth of the agro-based industries. The growth of sugar industry in Andhra was sustained by increases in sugarcane area over time, particularly in localities where sugar mills sprung up where there was a prospect of their establishment.

Thus we find the predominance of merchants and landlords in the establishment of large-scale industries in colonial Andhra. It is generally admitted that merchants, being men in possession of capital and entrepreneur skills entered into the industrial sector, i.e., conversion of merchant capital into industrial capital. So in Andhra, merchants constituted the largest single occupational group, which invested in industry. Studies on entrepreneurship in other parts of India had revealed a negligible number of entrepreneurs drawn from agricultural background. In most cases merchants first, then artisans and finally professionals have been the principal groups from which capitalists have emerged. But the findings of this study show that the agrarian classes were as prominent as the traditional merchants and professionals in industrial development in Andhra during the period under study. An examination of the available data on the socio-economic background of the Board of Directors of various industrial and commercial concerns reveals that two groups, viz., that merchants and landlords dominated the manufacturing sector. Industrial enterprises in colonial Andhra, during the period under study were dominated by the entrepreneurs drawn mainly, if not solely from, the twice-born castes (Brahmins, Kshatriya, Rajus andArya Vaishya Komatis) and the non-brahmin upper castes (Reddi, Kammas, Naidus, Velamas, Lingayats etc). The participation of Brahmins in industrial activity was also significant, as they acquired skills and knowledge in technical and professional education they ventured into industry. Whereas the Komatis were involved in trade and commerce for long and when occasion favoured they diversified their investment. The entrepreneurs belonging to peasant castes like the Kamma, Velama and Raju castes in coastal Andhra and Reddis, Naidus and Mudaliars in the ceded districts were conspicuous by their overwhelming presence on the Board of Directors of many companies. The predominance of entrepreneurs drawn from the dominant land holding castes and communities like the Reddi, Kamma, Naidu and Mudaliar was quite pronounced in certain industries, viz., cotton mills, oil mills, and sugar mills. For instance, the Chittoor Sugar Cane Growers Association, which proposed to establish a sugar factory consisted of ten Reddis and two Naidu landlords. The Bank of Chittoor Ltd., was dominated by landlords of Kamma-Naidu, Reddi and Mudaliar castes. The Kammas, a sizeable and prosperous cultivating caste primarily in the coastal districts were together with the Reddis and Rajus among the economically dominant castes in Andhra.

The rich Kammas of coastal Andhra were very active in the establishment of many rice mills, sugar factories at Vuyyuru and Tanuku and trade at Guntur. Although the export trade of tobacco was dominated by the ILTD Company, rich and enterprising Kammas increasingly participated in it. Some of them also became big exports of tobacco to foreign countries. The Kamma entrepreneurs also took keen interest in establishing other medium scale industries such as tiles and brick factories, fruit canning and ceramics. Interestingly, lower castes (i.e. backward and untouchables) were conspicuous by their absence in industrial entrepreneurship. Hence there seems to be a positive correlation between the caste ranking and representation in entrepreneurial activity. There was also a significant positive relationship between caste ranking on the one hand, and education, income and occupational status on the other. Available evidence indicates that The twice-born castes together with the non-Brahmin upper castes had educational advantages over lower backward castes. The literary rates of different communities/ castes in Andhra confirm this.

The emergence of industrial entrepreneurship in colonial Andhra was certainly conditioned by social as well economic factors. Accumulation and access to capital, possession of business experience and the opportunity to acquire technical and managerial skills were far more important. Moreover, it should be noted that the prevailing social structure and caste system in colonial Andhra had profound influence in determining who acquired capital and obtained business and technical knowledge. It may also be noted that no single caste or community solely dominated the industry, rather industrial entrepreneurs belonged to several castes-excluding the lower castes. A perusal of the lists of Board of Directors of several companies in Andhra indicates that Komati merchants, Brahmins, Kammas, Naidus, Reddis etc., were the main share holders. Most of them had either landed property and/or previous experience in commercial enterprises. It appears that initial capital accumulation by the entrepreneurs was obtained through profits in commercial agriculture. Many of the Directors of industrial concerns were "men with considerable influence and good financial resources". Local merchants assumed an increasingly important role in industrial investment during the inter-war period; hence more persons of trading background had entered the industry. Merchants, rural rich, qualified professionals, and white colour employees of upper castes were found side by side in many industries in Andhra. In terms of caste background, all of them belonged to the twice-born and Sat-Shudra communities.

In this paper two-related aspects i.e., growth of industries and entrepreneurial response to it is highlighted. The growth of agro-based medium and large industries characterized the evolution of industrialization in colonial Andhra. It was facilitated by changing government polices and economic conditions. The world economic depression and its effects, to a large extent, influenced entrepreneurial response to industrial development. It was found that diversion of surplus profits from commercial agriculture, rural credit, and trade into industrial investment was mediated by merchants and rural rich communities. In the formation of industrial capital and entrepreneurship in Andhra region, a significant role was played by the increasing participation of agrarian capital and the rural rich. Unlike in other parts of India, the traditional merchant communities, viz., Arya Vaishya/Komati did not monopolise investment in the industrial sector. Rather, the capitalist class of Andhra consisted of both the traditional merchants and rich agrarian communities belonging to the dominant peasant castes of Kamma, Naidu, Kapu, Reddy, etc. Thus Bagchi's observation that, "there is little evidence that entrepreneurship in agriculture provided a stepping stone to industry" is not applicable to modern Andhra. It is also interesting to note that landed gentry, like the big Zamindars of Bobbili, Chellapalli etc., did play a notable role in industrial investment. Similarly some of the Brahmin landlords/agrahamdars and professional also participated in industrial enterprises.

There was a clear-cut divergence between caste and occupation as far as the formation of entrepreneurship was concerned. The emergence of industrial entrepreneurs with peasant background was also a proof of this. Yet in caste/community terms entrepreneurial activity was confined to and the preserve of the dominant upper castes Raju, like Brahmin, Vaishyas, Kamma, Kapu, Reddi etc. It meant convergence of caste and class status, i.e., the upper echelons of these castes evolved as an industrial class. Possession of landed property, economic wealth/resources, educational and technical qualifications, access to sources of power and patronage did enable them to evolve as capitalist class. Caste/class convergence is also confirmed by the absence of entrepreneurs drawn from the lower sudra and untouchable caste/communities. In other words, lower caste status, meager landholding, poor economic position and literacy etc., did not provide an opportunity for social mobility and the rise of entrepreneurs from among them; in spite of the fact that caste system was dynamic and undergoing transformation. In this sense, caste was a crucial determinant in the formation of entrepreneurship in colonial Andhra during the period under study.

Caste and Power in Post-Colonial Andhra: An Overview

The peasantry beneath the landlords predominantly belonged to the Sudra varna. The peasant society was differentiated in terms of caste and class. There were rich, middle and poor peasants as well as upper and lower (or forward and backward) castes among the peasants in Andhra. However, compared to the lower caste peasants/ tenants, the peasants/ tenants the peasantry belonging to the upper castes (numerically preponderant Kammas and Reddys) enjoyed certain advantages. Within the constraints of colonial agrarian legislation they were able to secure occupancy rights and were protected from rack-renting and arbitrary eviction. The Kamma, Kapu and Reddi peasantry in Andhra were/are known for their hard-work and enterprising nature. The ryotwari land tenure, the widespread prevalence of peasant proprietorship and the development of irrigation system contributed to the rise of a stable middle level peasantry in coastal Andhra. Furthermore, expansion of commercialization, commodity production and agrarian trade led the emergence of fairly prosperous peasantry. Elsewhere we have explained the process of emergence and crystallization of 'nascent peasant-bourgeoisie' in rural Andhra towards the end of colonial rule. It has also been noted that certain peasant castes such as the Gowaras in Vishakhapatnam district and Kapus, Kammas and Reddies in the delta districts of Krishna, Godavari, Guntur and Nellore were market-oriented, dynamic and acquisitive. Because of their overall dynamic nature, these communities became and assertive social class and set a new trend and direction in rural Andhra.

The emergence of a dynamic social class within the peasantry was manifested in the rise and growth of the Kisan movement in Andhra. These dominant caste peasantry provided leadership to the agrarian movements and challenged the authority of the feudal ladlords. They took active part in the development of the anti-zamindari movement and other agrarian struggles. The growth of the left movement between 1934 and 1947, which weakened the authority of landlords in Andhra also benefited the upper echelons of the peasant proprietors. The anti-feudal struggles in coastal Andhra and Telangana during the 1930's and 1940's successfully eliminated the Zamindari and Jagirdari power in Andhra Pradesh. The post-colonial period witnessed a situation in which the hither to dominant social group viz., the landlords, Jagirdars, Deshmukhs etc. tended to lose their pre-eminent position in the realm of economy and polity in the countryside. Various factors contributed for such a decline. An examination of the changing relationship between caste/ class, land and dominance in A.P. during the post -colonial period indicates a gradual decline of power and authority of the landlord class. The traditionally dominant social groups in the rural society tended to lose their hegemony since the late 1950's. The post-independence agrairian legislation developmental programmes of agricultural modernization etc., contributed for the emergence of Kulak Pattadars belonging to the non-brahman upper castes viz., Reddi, Kamma, Raju, Kapu and Velama. The upper caste peasantry which gradually replaced the feudal landlord class became the main exploiting class caste in the countryside of Andhra Pradesh.

By the end of the colonial rule there emerged a situation in which the hitherto dominant social groups, i.e., the landlords and Brahmins tended to lose their pre-eminent position in the realm of economy and polity in the countryside. Various factors were responsible for such a decline: (i) The abolition of the zamindari system and other land tenure systems. (ii) The shift of landholding from Brahmins to non-Brahmins and migration of Brahmins from rural areas to towns and cities. (iii) The crystallization of a dynamic agrarian entrepreneurial class, which had taken advantage of the new economic opportunities of the post-1947 year and consolidated its position as a dominant social class.

Conclusion

Our analysis of the changing relationship between caste, class and power in rural Andhra during the colonial and the post-colonial periods indicates a gradual decline of the power and authority of landlords as a whole. The traditionally dominant social groups in the rural society, viz., the zamindars and Brahmins (insofar as they were landholders) have lost their hegemony since the post-1956 years i.e. the formation of the State of Andhra Pradesh. During the colonial period, the landlords and the Brahmins formed the dominant political elite. And the emerging rural rich from among the dominant peasant castes were subservient to them. The peasantry belonging to the non-Brahmin upper castes was not able to compete or challenge the entrenched groups during the colonial rule. The Brahmins, because of their landed property, education and employment, occupied pre-eminent position in the Congress Party and colonial bureaucracy while the zamindars, as they were rich and influential in the countryside, dominated (rather monopolized) the higher level of politics. Therefore, there was a clear convergence of control over land and political power. By virtue of the possession of vast estates the landlords (both in the permanently settled and ryotwari areas) exercised dominance and power in the countryside. The vast majority of the peasantry had to acknowledge their supremacy.

Nevertheless, during the late-colonial period and around the beginning of the post-colonial period, there emerged a rural rich peasantry. But they could consolidate their position only after the abolition of the zamindari system. The upper caste peasants, who were the ex-tenants of zamindars, purchased lands from the landlords as well as from the small lower caste peasants to enlarge their landholdings. Moreover, the post-colonial land reforms further strengthened their position by eliminating the intermediaries. The evolution of an agrarian economy during the post-independence period also provided opportunities for the rural rich to emerge as an important economic power in the countryside. Since they became substantial landholders, they could benefit from the changing economic conditions, i.e., growth of commercial farming, internal and external trade in agricultural commodities, etc. While the peasants belonging to Kamma,

Kapu, Velma and Reddy castes emerged as the dominant peasantry, the vast majority of peasants from the lower and backward castes, artisans and Scheduled Castes and tribes remained poor and subservient. In the process of economic transformation the small peasants of the lower castes were expropriated by the rural rich. A substantial section of the backward castes and Dalits today constitutes the rural poor. The upper caste peasants who replaced the feudal landlords have thus became the main exploiting class in the countryside. The contradiction between the rural rich and the rural poor has been manifested in terms of caste conflict and atrocities on Dalits. It clearly demonstrates the fact that the proletarianisation of agrarian social classes cuts across caste lines.

The emergence of rural rich as a dynamic class has brought about a change in the social basis of power structure. The post-independence developments such as adult franchise, pancharyat raj institutions, etc., have enabled the upper caste dominant peasantry to exercise control over the local and regional institutions of power and authority. Thus, there is a shift of power from the landlords to the rural rich. Two factors have contributed to this change in a significant way: (a) the decline of the in-political of the old feudal system, and (b) the growth of an elaborate political machinery which linked the village leadership to the provincial and the national leaderships. This has made it possible for the rural rich to acquire power. The power of the rural rich is based on control over land and their preponderant numerical strength within the village. By and large, these two factors tend to reinforce each other. However, it should be pointed out that although political power has shifted from the landlords to the rich peasants, it has not gone into the hands of the backward sections of Andhra society.

References and Notes

V.I. Lenin (1978), *The Development of Capitalism in Russia,* Coll.Works, Vol. 3, Moscow.

Carol Boyack Upadhyay (1988), "The Farmer-Capitalist of Coastal Andhra Pradesh", in *Economic and Political Weekly*, Vol. XXII, No. 27, July 2, p. 1376.

D.A. Washbrook, *The Emergence of Provincial Politics: The Madras Presidency, 1870-1920 (Delhi, 1976).* (hereafter Wash brook, Provincial Politics); D.A. Washbrook, 'Country Politics; Madras 1880 to 1930', Modern Asian Studies, 7, 3 (1973), pp. 475-531; C.J. Baker, 'Economic Development and Social Stratification in Rural Madras; "The Dry Region", 1878-1929' in Clive Dewey and A.G. Hopkins (eds), TheImperial Impact; Studies in the Ecnomic History of Africa and India (London, 1978), pp. 6882; C.J. Baker, *The Politics of South India, 1920-1937* (Delhi, 1976), (hereafter Baker, The Politics of South India). Also see his *An Indian Rural Economy 1880-1955*, Tamilnadu Countryside (Delhi, 1984); A. Satyanarayana, 'Agrarian Relations under the impact of Colonial Rule in Madras Presidency, 1900-1940; A study of the Andhra districts' (Ph.D. thesis, Heidelberg, 1983) and D. Ludden, Peasant History in South India (Princeton, 1985).

Baker, *The Politics of South India*, pp. 88 and 190.

T. Prakasam (1939), *The Madras Estates Land Act Committiee Report*, Vol. I & II, Madras.

They were the Raja of Panagul 1921-26, The Zamindar of Kumaramangalam (Dr Subbrayan) 1926-30; The Raja of Bobbili 1932-36.

Baker, op.cit., p.155

M Venkatarangaiya, Local Boards, p.67, cited in C J Baker, op.cit., p.112.

For Details See, A. Satyanarayana, Andhra Peasants under British Rule, 1900-1940, Delhi 1991, ch. 5.

See F, No. 3 above

Baker, *The Politics of South India*, pp. 88 and 190.

See F. No. 3 above

G.N. Rao and D. Rajasekhar, 'Agrarian Expansion in Andhra- A Long Term Overview' (mimeo)

'The Ceded Districts are so called because ... they were ceded to the company by the Nizam in 1800,' W. Francis, Anantapur District

Gazetteer (Madras, 1905), p.1. 'Rayalaseema has come to be applied to the tract comprising the ceded or Deccan districts together with the district of Chittoor. The term is meant to convey the idea that this area was the land of the Rayas (kings). The Rayas referred to the rulers of the Vijayanagar Empire who ruled from 1336 AD to 1650 AD.

Dharam Narain (1965), Impact of Price Movements on Area under Selected Crops in India, 1900-1939 (Cambridge). p.40.

Ibid., p. 71

(1900-20), The Rail-borne Trade Statistics of Madras Presidency.

Carol Boyack Upadhyay (1988), "The Farmer-Capitalist of Coastal Andhra Pradesh", in *Economic and Political Weekly*, Vol. XXII, No. 27, July 2, p. 1376.

B.K. Sudhakar Reddy, "Regional Industrialisation: Partial Transformation of a Late Starter", A.P. Economic Association Conference Papers, January 986. pp. 39-62; B. Sarweshwar Rao and V.L. Rao, -Industrial and Commercial Entrepreneurship in the Coastal Region of A.P.", *ICSSR Research Abstracts*, Vol.7, 1978. p. 37.

G.O. Revenue 110, 15.4.1914.

Some South Indian Villages, Vol. I, Madras, 1918.

Baker , Op.cit., 1978, p. 239.

Ibid.

It is interesting to note that the Raja of Bobilli engaged in grain trade since the early 20th century. He was particular in collecting rents in kind on irrigated wet lands, inspite of peasants demand for money rents. He used the grain so collected for the purpose of trade. He was also known as moneylender, because he used to advance loans to fellow zamindars. The Raja of Venkatagiri invested in real estate in Madras city.

G.O. Revenue 1283-84, 11.7.1945.

G.O. Dev, 1927, 16th August 1940; G.O. Dev. 3382, 1st Sep. 1945.

See M. Singer (ed)., *Entrepreneurship and Modernization of Occupational Cultures in South Asia*, Durham 1973; Morris D.Morris, "Values as an Obstacle to Economic Growth in South Asia: An Historical Survey". *The Journal of Economic History*, 27, 1967, p.588-607.

H.A. Gould, "The Adaptive Functions of Caste in Contemporary Indian Society", *Asian Survey*, 3 (9), 1963, p.429.

E.W. Nafziger, Class, caste and Entrepreneurship, Honolulu, 1978, p.47.

They were Ganjam, Vizagapatnam, Eeast Godavari, West Godawari, Krishna, Guntur, Nellore, Bellary, Anantapur, Kurnool, Cuddapah and Chittoor. SeeO.H.K. *Spate, India and Pakistan: A General and Regional Geography*, London 1960, p. 689.

For a detailed discussion on various aspects of the world economic depression see D. Rothermund, *India in the Great Depression*, 1929-39, Delhi 1992;, *The Global Impact of the Great Depression, 1929-39*, London 1997; C.J. Baker, An Indian Rural Economy, 1880-1955, Delhi, 1984.

G.O. Dev. 5426, 3rd Nov. 1948.

G.O. Dev. 2381, 23rd July, 1946.

A.K. Bagachi, Private Investment in India, p.213.

A Satyanarayana, "Agrarian Relations Under the Impact of Colonial Rule in Madras Presidency 1990-1940: A case study of Andhra districts", unpublished Ph. D. Thesis submitted to Heidelberg University, (West Germany) 1983, Chapter V.

In an earlier study it has been shown that the rich peasant class belonging to the non-Brahmin upper castes was mainly responsible for the growth of Kisan Sabha Movement in Coastal Andhra. See A. Satyanarayana "Kisan Movement in Madras Presidency, 1928-42: A study of the Anti-Zamindar Agitation," Jawaharlal Nehru, University, Delhi, 1979, Ch III, IV and V.

2

Implementation of Land Reforms in India

G. Surya Prakasa Rao, K. Rama Chandra Rao

During the colonial period, the British had introduced three main types of tenures in India – the zamindari, ryotwari and mahalwari tenures. Under zamindari tenures, which prevailed over most of Eastern India, land revenue was fixed in perpetuity and land was permanently 'settled' with 'zamindars'. In the other two forms of tenures, the 'settlement' with a class of proprietors was temporary and revenue was periodically revised. In the parts of India, which were under indirect suzerainty of the British and were part of various kingdoms, various forms of feudal tenures prevailed.

In our country, implementation of land reforms which is the responsibility of individual states, has occupied a central stage in the policy debate for long time, given inequality in the distribution of productive assets, especially land, which the country inherited from its colonial masters. Reforms had three main elements namely (i) abolition of intermediaries (zamindars) shortly after independence; (ii) tenancy laws to increase tenure security by sitting tenants by registering them and often imposing restrictions on the amount of rent they had to pay or the scope for new rental transactions (iii) ceiling laws that provided a basis for expropriating land held by any given owner in excess of a state-specific ceiling and subsequently transferring it to poor farmers or landless agricultural workers. While the first of these is considered to have been highly successful, progress on the remainder was initially very slow, accelerating only during the 1970s and slowing down again in the 1980s. Still, both types of intervention resulted in the transfer of rights to almost 10 million hectares of land, an area more than three times what was involved in the well-known land reforms of Japan, Korea, and Taiwan together. With the exception of few states, the political commitment to implement reforms was limited and sometimes outcomes were counter to what had been desired, as with large-scale tenant evictions to prevent them from gaining more permanent land rights in anticipation of tenancy laws.

Land Reform Implementation in India

Table 1 provides summary statistics for the level of land reform implementation, measured as the share of rural population who received land through tenancy reform, the area transferred as a result of ceiling legislation, or the number of ceiling laws, by state based on a summary report that draws together official data from various annual reports by the Ministry of Agriculture (Kaushik 2005). Over and above the large amounts of land affected by zamindari abolition and private initiatives such as donations of land under the Bhoodan movement, direct land distribution affected about 2.5 million hectares under programs to redistribute of ceiling surplus land, and 7.35 million hectares under tenancy reform, implying a direct transfer of 5.45% of the area to about 5.35% of the agricultural population for the country as a whole. Comparing this to what has been involved in other land reforms internationally illustrates the size of India's land reform. Ceiling and tenancy laws together resulted in the redistribution of about 10% of arable land, about the level of the Philippines, Brazil, or Zimbabwe before 2000, but below Asian countries such as Japan, Korea, and Taiwan (33.3%, 27.3%, and 26.9%) or even El Salvador, Bolivia, and Mexico

(27.9%, 32.3%, and 13.5%). In terms of the share of rural households benefiting, India's accomplishment is at the lower end of the scale; while it exceeds what has been accomplished in the pre-1994 period in Kenya, Zimbabwe, and Brazil (1.6%, 3.1%, and 5.4% of the rural population, respectively), it remains considerably below other Asian countries such as the Philippines (24%), Japan (60.9%), and Taiwan (62.5%) or Latin American ones such as Mexico (67.5%), Bolivia (47.5%), and El Salvador (16.8%) (In Table-2)

Table 1
Shares of Rural Households and Arable Land Area Affected by Different Land Reforms in Indian States

	Tenancy Legislation				*Ceiling Legislation*	
State	*Area (%)*	*Popula-tion (%)*	*No. of Laws*	*Avg. age*	*Area (%)*	*Popula-tion (%)*
Andhra Pradesh	3.48	0.75	2	17.0	8.34	3.81
Bihar	0	0	3	18.3	4.42	4
Gujarat	15.0	11.20	2	15.5	1.95	0.31
Haryana	0.51	0.01	0	0	1.26	0.26
H.P	0.16	3.19	-	-	0.06	0.05
Karnataka	15.38	5.29	2	14.5	1.71	0.30
Kerala	8.47	12.49	4	10.8	1.30	1.04
M.P	2.15	0.61	1	24.0	2.69	0.71
Maharashtra	27.01	10.68	1	23.0	7.74	1.08
Orissa	0.15	1.43	3	9.0	2.24	1.28
Punjab	1.89	0.04	1	10.0	1.50	0.25
Rajastan	0.0	0.16	0	0	6.63	0.75
Tamilnadu	3.65	3.23	5	13.6	2.47	1.24
Uttara Pradesh	0.0	0.0	2	14.5	5.81	3.68
West Bengal	6.41	10.80	5	8.2	14.91	19.73
Total	5.45	5.35	2.1	13.03	4.41	2.27

Source: Kaushik (2005), Besley and Burgess (2000).

Comparing the share of beneficiary households to that of the area transferred points towards considerable variation across states. In some cases, e.g. Kerala or West Bengal, 12.5% and 10.8% of the population benefited from transfer of 8.5% and 6.4% of the land area, respectively, plot sizes for land transferred remained considerable below the state average. While some states (e.g. Gujarat or Tamil Nadu) provided beneficiaries with plots of about average size, in most of the states the fact that the share of beneficiaries remains significantly below the area share points towards transfer of above-average plot sizes, as in Maharashtra (27% of area distributed to 10.7% of population), Karnataka (15.4% and 5.3%), Andhra Pradesh and Madhya Pradesh (3.5% and 2.2% to 0.75% and 0.61% of population, respectively).

With 4.4% and 2.3%, the share of area redistributed overall or share of households benefiting from ceiling laws has been below the figures for tenancy reform. Although some states such as Rajasthan, U.P, Bihar, and A.P transferred more land (6.6%, 5.8%, 4.4%, and 8.3%) under ceiling legislation than through tenancy reform, results seem to have been biased towards transfer of above-average sized plots of land, suggesting that even where it was possible to acquire above ceiling land by the state, overcoming political pressures in the distribution of such land may have been difficult. In West Bengal, on the other hand, a state that ranks at or near the top for both measures and that counts with a formidable level of grass-roots level organization, land reform land appears to have been transferred in a very pro-poor fashion.

For the country as a whole, an average of 2.1 land reform laws had been passed per state with the mean law being about 13 years old in 1999. Despite the fact that the highest number of laws was passed in West Bengal where reform-induced transfers were also highest, the correlation between number of laws and the share of area transferred through or of rural households benefiting from reform is, with 0.28, low throughout. This supports the notion that legal provisions alone did not automatically translate into action on the ground, consistent with arguments that there is no *a-priori* reason to expect a positive link between passage of laws-which could be a result of an objective need for land reform and political mobilization or even lack of actual progress- and their actual implementation. In fact, in a number of states, high levels of legal activity appear to have been used to deflect attention from lack of progress on the ground.

While not differentiated in the table, a detailed look at the time dimension of reform measures allows a number of conclusions (Kaushik 2005): After a spurt of land transfers in the 1970s and 1980s, progress has slowed down considerably; in fact between 1995/96 and 2003/04, i.e. for almost a decade, progress in awarding land rights to tenants had come to a complete standstill; the increment in ceiling surplus land transferred during the period amounted to only 10,800 hectares. The latter represents about one-tenth of the land declared ceiling surplus, with the remainder being tied up in litigation. This suggests that, unless there are significant changes in the overall parameters, progress in achieving further redistribution of ceiling land could be slow -it would take almost 90 years to dispose of remaining ceiling surplus cases if the current pace is maintained- but also that, by clogging up the court system and preventing it from quickly dispensing justice in other urgent matters, the ceiling legislation may impose external effects beyond land rental markets (Moog 1997). While broader changes in the legal framework could make much additional land available, they do not seem to be too likely in the current political environment.

Despite considerable interest in the topic at the policy level and a large literature documenting the way land reforms were put in practice at the state level (Yugandhar 1996, Thangaraj 2004), attempts to quantitatively assess their economic impacts at a national scale are surprisingly scant. One study finds that the number of identifiable land reform laws across states is positively related to the extent of poverty reduction but not agricultural productivity (Besley and Burgess 2000). While this could be used to make the case for land reform as a redistributive measure, e.g. through a wage effect, use of a measure only weakly linked to implementation of reforms is a shortcoming. Studies using data on implementation have only been conducted in individual states, mainly West Bengal. District level data point towards a positive impact of land reform on productivity (Banerjee *et al.* 2002), a finding that receives support from household level evidence taking into account other political factors (Bardhan and Mookherjee 2006). However, as the policy environment in West Bengal is likely to be uniquely conducive to land reform, a national assessment of land reform impact based on actual implementation would be very desirable in view of the continued relevance of the topic in India's policy debate.

Table 2

Global Extent and Characteristics of Land Reforms

	Area	*Beneficiary households*				
Country	*Toial area (1000 hect)*	*Share of arable land (%)*	*Number (thou- sands)*	*Share of rural house- holds (%)*	*Area per household (hectares)*	*Implem- entation Period*
Africa						
Egypt	390	15.4	438	10.0	0.89	1952-78
Kenya	403	1.6	34	1.6	11.85	1961-70
Zimbabwe	2371	11.9	40	3.1	59.28	1980-87
Asia						
Japan	2000	33.3	4300	60.9	0.47	1946-49
Korea.Rep	577	27.3	1646	45.5	0.35	1948-58
Philippines	1092	10.8	1511	24.2	0.72	1940-85
Taiwan, China	235	26.9	383	62.5	0.61	1949-53
Central America						
EL Salvador	401	27.9	95	16.8	4.22	1932-89
Mexico	13375	13.5	3044	67.5	4.39	1915-76
Nicaraguna	3186	47.1	172	56.7	18.52	1978-87
South America						
Bolivia	9792	32.3	237	47.5	41.32	1953-70
Brasil	13100	11.3	266	5.4	49.32	1964-94
Chile	9517	60.1	58	12.7	164.09	1973
Peru	8599	28.1	375	30.8	22.93	1969-79

Source: Deininger (2003)

Based on the above review, the implementation of land reforms should be faster and more inclusive. i.e. all sections of farmers like small, marginal, medium farmers and tenants of the rural area. For effective implementation of land reforms in our country the policy makers would utilize institutions like rythu mitra sangalu and self-help groups, which are well established in rural Andhra Pradesh.

References

Appu, P.S. (1997), "*Land Reforms in India: A Survey of Policy, Legislation and Implementation*" New Delhi: Vikas Publishing House.

Banerjee, A.V., P.J. Gertler and M. Ghatak (2002), "Empowerment and Efficiency: Tenancy Reform in West Bengal." *Journal of Political Economy 110* (2): 239-80.

Bardhan, P. and D. Mookherjee (2006), "Land Reform, Decentralized Governance, and Rural Development in West Bengal." Stanford, CA: Paper prepared for the Stanford Center for International Development *Conference on Challenges of Economic Policy Reform in Asia,* May 31-June 3, 2006.

Besley, T. and R. Burgess (2000), "Land Reform, Poverty Reduction, and Growth: Evidence from India." *Quarterly Journal of Economics 115* (2): 389-430.

Deininger, K. (2003), "*Land Policies for Growth and Poverty Reduction* World Bank Policy" Research Report series. Washington, D.C.: World Bank; Oxford and New York: Oxford University Press.

Moog, R.S. (1997), "*Whose Interests are Supreme? Organizational Politics in the Civil Courts in India*" Ann Arbor, Michigan: Association for Asian Studies.

Kaushik, A. (2005), "Nature of Land Market Interventions in India", Institute for Sustainable Development Noida.

Yugandhar, B.N. (1996), "*Land Reforms in India", Volume 3, Andhra Pradesh – People's pressure and administrative innovations*", New Delhi; Thousand Oaks, Calif. and London: Sage Publications.

Government of India (2006b), "*Towards Faster and More Inclusive Growth: An approach to the 11th five-year plan*", New Delhi: Planning Commission, Yojana Bhavan.

3

Agrarian Economy of Andhra Pradesh

K. Kishore Babu, A. Bala Krishna, K. Mahendra Kumar

Andhra Pradesh is one of the India's most agriculturally prosperous and developed state .At the end of the 2001, more than 88 percent of Andhra Pradesh citizens were above the poverty line, 61 percent were literate, 96.71 percent of the six year olds were enrolled in primary schools, and 71 percent of the children fewer than twelve months were immunized. 99 percent of households had access to safe drinking water, and the average life expectancy was 68 years. Its remarkable development record can also be inferred from the fact that it has already achieved, or is well on the track to achieve, most of the millennium development goals. According to India's national human development report, Andhra Pradesh was ranked, 10 in terms of the overall level of human development among the major Indian states. Most citizens of Andhra Pradesh have thus already achieved the level of socio - economic status that the majority of Indian citizens are unlikely to experience in their lifetime. This sums to have been made possible by using the agrarian economy of the State.

Changing Structure of the Agrarian Economy

We look at changing structure in terms of employment and land holdings. The share of agriculture in employment in the

State declined from about 69 per cent in 1961 to about 59 percent by 2001. The diversification to the non arm sector has been slow. Among the agricultural workforce, about 60 percent are registered as agricultural labour and the rest as cultivators. Though there are regional differences, they are not significant. The percentage of cultivators in the agricultural workforce was relatively much higher in north coastal Andhra followed by Telanagana and Rayalaseema, and was lowest in south coastal Andhra. There has been a consistent pattern across all the districts of workers shifting to agricultural labour. Interestingly, the rate of increase was relatively higher in south coastal Andhra.

It is well recognized that the growth of agriculture leads to an increase in the non-farm sector and also employment opportunities. The instance of south coastal Andhra indicates that this is true as the region has the highest share of workforce in non-agricultural activities compared to the other regions. But, between 1971 and 2001 employment in non-agriculture had declined in this region, while it had increased in the other regions in the same period.

Distribution of Land Holdings

The data on land holding structure from 1955-56 to 2005-06 show that operational holdings have become much less concentrated (Table 1). Whereas the absolute number and area covered by large and medium holdings has declined since the mid-1950s there has been a significant increase 'in the shares of marginal and small farmers in the number of holdings and area. The share of marginal farmers in the number of holdings increased from 46 per cent in 1970-71 to 61.6 per cent in 2005-06.

In fact, the share of marginal and small farmers in the number of holdings was more than 80 per cent in 2005-06. Area under marginal and small farmers rose from less than 20 per cent in 1970-71 to around 50 per cent in 2005-06. Many of the operational holdings are being held under tenancy contracts. The changing structure of the agrarian economy in terms of size class of landholding when the average size of holdings declined in A.P. from 2.5 hectares in the early 1970s to 1.20 hectares in 2005-06 also meant that the peasantry was increasingly being marginalized. Within the state, the share of marginal and small holdings, in fact, is relatively higher in South Coastal Andhra. When compared to the other regions. But because of the irrigation facilities, marginal farmers in South Coastal Andhra are relatively better off than in other regions. tenancy contracts.

Land Reforms in Andhra Pradesh

Agrarian relations and landholding structure play an important role in the performance of the agricultural sector. Land reforms have been on the national agenda since independence to improve the performance of agriculture as well as for rural re-construction. In addition, creating greater access to land for the landless rural poor is an important component of poverty alleviation programmes. Land reforms, in spite of all the limitations in implementation, did play an important role in changing the agrarian structure in Andhra Pradesh. The early land reform measures in the state were a combination of two administrative histories, of the Andhra region and the Telangana region which had formerly been under the Nizam. Following the pattern at the all-India level, the land reforms in Andhra Pradesh had three components: abolition of intermediaries, tenancy reforms, ceiling legislation and the other government initiatives. Legislative measures were also initiated following Article 46 of the Constitution that made it obligatory for the states to promote the interests of Scheduled Castes and Scheduled Tribes and to protect them from social injustice and all forms of exploitation. State governments have accepted the policy of prohibiting the transfer of land from tribals to non-tribals and the restoration of alienated tribal lands to tribals. In 1977, the government of Andhra Pradesh enacted the Assigned Land Prohibition Act which ruled that land that had been 'assigned' by the government to the landless and tribals could not be resold and used for purposes other than agriculture. To improve women's access to land and landed property Andhra Pradesh along with Karnataka and Tamil Nadu amended the Hindu Succession Act, 1956, to legally protect the right of women to property including land.

The Madras Estates (Abolition and Conversion into Ryotwari) Act 1948 was the first legislation after Independence which removed intermediaries. It brought all land in Andhra area under Ryotwari system. In the Telangana region the Jagirdari Tenurial system ended with the Abolition of Jagirdari Act of 1949 (GOI, 2004). With respect to tenancy, the Hyderabad Tenancy and Agricultural Lands Act was enacted in 1950 which gave protection to nearly six lakh tenants who held over 75 lakh acres of land, constituting 33 per cent of the total cultivated area. This was considered one of the progressive acts of legislation in the state. The AP (Andhra Area) Tenancy Act 1956 was passed to ensure that a tenant was not evicted from his/her holding except by going to court. This legislation has given mixed results it often led to concealed tenancy (Reddy, 2006).

Legislation on ceilings on agricultural holdings was enacted in two phases, 1955-72 and 1972 to the present. The Andhra Pradesh Land Reforms (Ceiling on Agriculture Holdings) Acts were passed in 1961 and 1973. As in most states, the first round of legislation in 1961 was a miserable failure but the second one in 1973 had some impact. Against an estimated surplus land of 20 lakh acres, only 7.9 Lakh acres were declared surplus, of which 6.47 Lakh acres were taken possession by the government and 5.82 lakh acres were distributed among 4.79 lakh beneficiaries till August 2004 (GOAP, 2004). This amounted to about 4 per cent of the net sown area. Of the beneficiaries, 42 per cent were SCs who were assigned 39 percent of the land, while STs constituted 14 per cent of the beneficiaries and received 20 per cent of the land. A major step in land distribution in the state was the assignment of government land to the landless poor, which accounted for 12.5 per cent of the net sown area. By the end of 2002, an area of 43.21 lakh acres of government land was assigned to 23.98 lakh beneficiaries of whom 24 per cent were SCs and 28 per cent were STs (GOAP, 2004).

Though the ceiling legislation was not effective in the redistribution of land, it did act as a constraint on the acquisition of more land by the rich. In addition, the political mobilization of rural masses inspired by the radical political parties and the Naxalite movement arrested the process of acquiring more land by the rich. The rich peasantry began to sell their land and shift to other vocations in non-agricultural activities in urban areas. As a result, on the one hand, the surplus land under land ceiling and government wasteland was distributed to SCs and other rural poor. On the other, land was acquired for cultivation by communities, which had been involved in off-farm activities earlier. Subsequently the concentration of land in a few hands and large holdings declined. In the process, the power of the dominant cultivating castes in agrarian society has declined while backward communities have more control over land.

While land-reform legislation remained active, land policies in more recent decades have focused less on land reform and more on land development and administration. Land policy in India has undergone broadly four phases since Independence. Land reforms were in the forefront in the first and longest phase (1950-72). During the second phase (1972-85) attention shifted to bringing uncultivated land under cultivation. In the third phase (1985-95) water and soil conservation was given more importance through Watershed Development, Drought- Prone Area Development (DPAP) and Desert-Area Development Programmes (DADP). A central government Wasteland Development Agency was established to focus on wasteland and degraded land. The fourth and current phase of policy (1995 onwards) centers on debates about the necessity to continue with land legislation and efforts to improve land revenue administration and, in particular, clarity in land records.

Changes in Land and Water Resources

It is a matter of great concern that land and water resources available for agriculture in Andhra Pradesh have declined over a period especially during the 1990s. Area under cultivation (net area sown) declined from 110.42 lakh hectares at the beginning of the 1990s to 100.87 lakh hectares by the triennium ending 2004-05, indicating a decline of about 10 lakh hectares or 8.65 percent (Table 2). In fact, during the triennium ending 1957-58 net sown area had been about 112.3 lakh hectares. Despite the improvement in cropping intensity, there has been a significant fall in the gross cropped area (GCA), which declined by about 6.4 lakh hectares or 5.3 per cent of GCA during the same period. The GCA was about 122.5 lakh hectares in 1957-58 and increased to 127.9 by 1990-91, but declined to 121.5 by the triennium ending 2004- 05. Multiple cropping could not lead to a proportionate increase in agricultural production because productivity is lower for crops grown after the first crop. In addition, there has been an increase in instability in the area under cultivation.

The decline in net area sown is observed across almost all the districts in the state except two, Anantapur and Nellore where, in fact, it has increased (see Table 3). Four districts - Mahabunagar, Nalgonda, Chittoor and Karimnagar - accounted for about 54 per cent of the decline in net sown area in the state. Another four districts - Nizamabad, Prakasam, Khammam and Rangareddy - contributed to almost one-fourth of the decline. Of these eight districts six are located in Telangana region.

There has also been a decline in irrigated area. The state had an irrigated area of about 27.8 lakh hectares in the mid-1950s, which increased, to 43.5 lakh hectares, an increase of about 56.5 per cent, by the end of the 1980s. During this period (mid-fifties to eighties), out of the total increase (15.7 lakh hectares) of irrigated land, about 6.7 lakh hectares was added in the first 23 years (i.e. late 1950s to late 1970s) and 9.0 lakh hectares in the next 10 years (in the 1980s). As a matter of fact, the addition in the 1980s was mostly due to expansion of area under groundwater which is highly vulnerable to fluctuations in rainfall.

During the 1990s, the irrigated area declined to 37.1 lakh hectares, which was almost equal to the level in 1980-81. Similarly, the gross irrigated area, which had increased by

10.1 lakh hectares in the 1980s declined by 6.5 lakh hectares in the 1990s and after. Irrigated area, which was 33.2 lakh hectares in the late 1950s, increased to 54.2 lakh hectares in the late 1980s but declined significantly during and after the 1990s and had come down to 47.7 lakh hectares in 2004-05. The highest increase in irrigated area happened in the 1980s and the lowest in the 1990s. While the growth rate of gross irrigated area declined from its highest level of 1.81 in the 1980s to 0.31 percent in the 1990s, it became negative for net irrigated area from 2.0 to -0.49 per cent during the same period.

Production and Productivity of Crops

The compound growth rates of area, production and yield of important crops are shown in table-3. It is observed from the table that Rice production recorded an higher growth rate of 6.12 percent per annum during 1990's, when compared to earlier decades. The annual compound growth rate of Rice production after 2000 declined to 0.83 percent. While the annual compound growth rate of area under Rice between 1971-72 to 1980-81 was 1.70 percent, it has declined to 0.54 percent between 1981-82 to 1990-91. After 1990-91 the growth rate in the area under Rice is stagnant, around 0.75 percent. The growth rate in yield of Rice declined after 1991-92, the total area under rice being 30 percent the cropped area, the decline in growth rates of production productivity and area indicate the distress performance of Andhra Pradesh agriculture.

The area under course Cereals like Jower, Bazra and Ragi showing a continues decline indicates that these crops has been replaced by other commercial crops like Cotton, Sugercane, Chillies. Maize also recorded a significant growth in area and production with a declining productivity. Shift in favor of commercial crops represent more risk in agriculture.

Among pulses Bengal gram recorded highest growth rate with a declining growth rate in productivity after 1990's. Other pulses like Horsgram, Blackgram and Greengram declined in terms of area and production, and it has been replaced by

Redgram and Bengalgram. The overall trend in the growth rate of area and production of pulces fluctuating for the last 50 years. Among Oilseeds, the growth rate of Groundnut area has recorded a continuous decline after 1991. The annual growth rate in production and productivity of Groundnut shows a continuous decline.

The annual growth rate in production and productivity of cotton is highest (Productivity 8.32 percent and Production 11.41 percent) between 1971-72 to 1980-81. The average annual growth rate in production and productivity of cotton has declined to 5.29 percent and 1.93 percent between 1981-82 to 1990-91. Between 1991-92 to 2000-01 growth in productivity is negative for cotton. While the growth rate in cotton production is stagnant after 1990's, the growth rate in area under cotton is highest between 1991-92 to 2000-01, it is negative after 2001-02. The average annual growth in production was negative during 199192 to 2000-01, it is about 5.76 percent between 2001-02 to 2006-07. The productivity of cotton increased due to the introduction of Bt- cotton in this period.

Sugarcane is another impotent commercial crop, for which the growth rate in productivity is positive after 1991-92, while it was negative before 1991-92. Another important commercial crop is Chillies, the annual average compound growth rate in production and productivity of Chillies between 1956-57 to 2006-07 is 3.87 and 3.49 percent.

The overall growth rate of area production and productivity of important crops for the period 1956-57 to 2006-07 indicate that the Rice which is an important crop in terms of proportion of area in the cropped area has recorded 2.52 percent growth in production, 1.9 percent growth in productivity and 0.62 percent growth in area per annum. Then the important commercial crops cotton recorded high annual growth rate of 5.75 percent in production, 3.87 percent in productivity and 1.78 percent in area. Among the course cereals Maize recorded highest growth rate in production and productivity after cotton. While area under Jower Bajra and Ragi was continuously declined and become an unimportant crops.

Among Pulses, Bengal gram recorded a highest growth in production, productivity and area, while the growth rate in the area of other pulses declined. The Sugarcane crop recorded contradicting results, while the annual growth rate in area is 2.49 percent, the annual growth rate in production is at declining trend, the growth rate in productivity is marginal. So the decline in production is due to decline in productivity.

Other important commercial crop Chillies recorded 3.49 percent growth in productivity, 3.87 growth rate in production and 0.37 percent growth rate in the area during the 50 years. The overall picture reveals that except Cotton, Rice, Maize and Bengalgram there is a negative growth in production. While the growth rate in area under some crops is stagnant, in majority cases the area is declining.

Except few crops the growth rate in production is also stagnant. But overall comparison of growth rate in productivity, it is also stagnant. But the comparison of growth rates for different periods shows that Andhra Pradesh agriculture is facing a problem of stagnation in production, productivity after 1990's. The slow down in growth of different crops had a negative impact on the income, employment of the farmers as well as agricultural laborers. The area under different crops almost reached to the maximum possible level. Any increase in the area of particular crop will result in decline of another crop. In this way the overall picture of Andhra Pradesh agriculture is in a state of stagnancy.

Agrarian Distress and Farmers' Suicides

The agrarian economy of Andhra Pradesh has been in distress since the 1990s. The state is one of those states with highest number of farmers' suicides in the country. The agrarian distress in the state coincided with the period in which reforms were initiated. The agricultural crisis and farmers' suicides were mainly due to inadequate agricultural services, including extension, reliable seed supply, quality pesticides, machinery, proper soil survey testing, soil conservation, market information and market intelligence. The failure of extension services, the mushrooming of spurious seed and pesticide companies, and the relegation of the Agricultural University and the Andhra Pradesh Seeds Corporation to an insignificant role in the research, development and propagation of seeds of non-food crops, are all the consequences of deliberate policy changes in the state. There was also an attempt to privatize extension services.

Irrigation, a critical infrastructure for agriculture in the state, had also suffered. A decline in public surface irrigation (canal and tanks) resulted in the emergence of private groundwater as the single largest source with all the attendant ecological problems. Lack of access to institutional credit is another problem for farmers, particularly small and marginal farmers. Farm gate prices of most agricultural commodities fall steeply at harvest time. It is known that many poor farmers sell their output at harvest time because of their poor retention capacity. Because of these uncertain conditions, about 40 percent of the farmers across the country have stated that they would like to quit farming if there was a choice.

The reforms in agriculture resulted in an increase in electricity charges, growing dependence on high cost groundwater resources, increased irrigation charges and high degree of dependence on credit at high interest rates provided by the informal credit market. The recent NSS survey shows that about 82 percent of farmer households are in debt, which is the highest incidence of indebtedness in the country. Further, institutional sources in the state account for only 30 percent of the loans, which is the lowest for the country.

According to a judicial commission appointed by the State Government, between May 14, 2004 and November 10, 2005 alone 1068 farmers had committed suicide, and in addition there were 277 starvation deaths of weavers in the same period (Nagesh Kumar 2005). The Commission also brought out the fact which shocked the state that 26 debt-ridden farmers of Guntur district had sold their kidneys.

Most of the suicides are by male members in the age group of less than 40 years. By and large the incidence of suicides has been higher among small-marginal farmers moving from subsistence agriculture to the high value crops with a strong motivation to improve their social land economic status. With a few exceptions, the majority belong to Backward Communities or Scheduled Castes or Scheduled Tribes. Barring the ST households, most have had some schooling.

The agrarian crisis has not only continued but has spread to different regions and to a number of high value crops other than cotton. Any commercial or high risk crop can put a farmer under stress and make him vulnerable to suicide. The trigger in these cases again is the failure of water resources particularly groundwater.

Conclusions and Policy Implications

This Paper examined changes in agrarian structure, issues in land reforms, performance in agriculture and farmers' suicides, it is well known that the agrarian structure in terms of operational holdings has undergone significant changes in the last 50 years. More than 80 per cent of the holdings belong to small and marginal farmers now. Land reforms through redistribution of land, tenancy reforms and recording of land titles etc. are relevant and important in A.P. Except few crops the growth rate in production is also stagnant. But overall comparison of growth rate in productivity, it is also stagnant. But the comparison of growth rates for different periods shows that Andhra Pradesh agriculture is facing a problem of stagnation in production, productivity after 1990's. The slow down in growth of different crops had a negative impact on the income, employment of the farmers as well as agricultural laborers. The area under different crops almost reached to the maximum possible level. Any increase in the area of particular crop will result in decline of another crop. In this way the overall picture of Andhra Pradesh agriculture is in a state of stagnancy. Another important aspect is the high level of indebtedness. One of the major factors for high indebtedness is investment in wells and frequent failures. There is no insurance against this investment and most of this investment is financed by informal sources. The co-operative sector, which is active in other states, plays a negligible role in the state. It is desirable to regulate investment in groundwater and extend insurance coverage for it. The present government is rightly giving importance to irrigation but it has to take a holistic view of agriculture rather than concentrating only on irrigation. Short term and long term measures are required to come out of the agrarian crisis and prevent suicides by farmers.

Land relations in Andhra Pradesh are extremely complicated which have led to serious problems for actual cultivators. Unregistered cultivators, tenants, and tribal cultivators all face difficulties in accessing institutional credit and other facilities available to farmers with land titles. Among others, the Farmers Welfare Commission (GOI, 2004) made the following three recommendations on land issues.

(a) There is a need to record and register actual cultivators including tenants and women cultivators, and provide passbooks to them, to ensure that they gain access to institutional credit and other inputs;

(b) The land rights of tribals in the agency areas must be protected; and

(c) Considerable scope exists for further land redistribution particularly when waste and cultivable lands are taken into account. In order to develop the lands, complementary inputs for cultivation (initial land development, input minikits, credit, etc.) should be provided to all assignees. The future assignments of land should be in the name of women.

Table 1

Changing Structure of the Agrarian Economy in Andhra Pradesh: The Prcentage Distribution of Operational Holdings by Size Class, 1956-2006

	Share in Number of Holding					*Share in Operated Area*					
Year	*Marginal*	*Small*	*Semi-Medium*	*Medium*	*Large*	*Marginal*	*Small*	*Semi-Medium*	*Medium*	*Large*	*Avg-size*
1955-56	38.6	18.3	17.7	16.7	8.7	7.9	9.7	16.1	28.1	38.2	2.43
1970-71	46.0	18.5	17.4	12.7	4.3	8.0	11.3	19.2	30.8	30.7	2.43
1976-77	46.6	20.3	17.4	12.2	3.4	9.3	12.8	20.8	32.3	24.8	
1980-81		20.9	16.0	9.12	2.1	13.1	16.2	23.3	28.7	18.7	1.94
1985-86	54.2	20.8	15.2	8.0	1.8	14.5	17.3	24.0	27.3	16.3	
1990-91	56.0	21.2	14.5	6.9	1.3	16.4	19.6	25.2	26.1	12.8	1.50
2000-01	60.9	21.8	12.4	4.3	0.6	21.6	24.8	26.4	19.8	7.5	1.25
2005-06	61.6	21.91	12.0	4.0	0.5	22.7	25.8	26.5	19.0	6.1	1.20

Note :

1. Marginal – 0 to 1 hectare; Small – 1 to 2 hectare; Semi-medium – 2 to 4 hectare; Medium – 4 to 10 hectare; and Large – 10 and above hectare;
2. Avg - Average Size of the Holding is given in hectares

Source: Directorate of Economics and Statistics, Government of Andhra Pradsh

Table2

Changes in Cropped and Irrigated Area in Andhra Pradesh

Area	*1957-58*	*1980-81*	*1990-91*	*2004-2005*
1	*3*	*4*	*5*	*6*
Net Area Sown	12.3	108.7	110.4	100.9
Gross Area Sown	122.5	125.6	127.9	121.5
Cropping Intensity	1.09	1.16	1.16	1.20
Net Area Irrigated	27.8	34.5	43.5	37.1
Gross Area Irrigated	33.2	44.3	54.2	47.7
Irrigation Intensity	1.19	1.28	1.25	1.29

Note: Figures presented are in lakh hectares.
Source: Directorate of Economics and Statistics, Government of Andhra Pradsh

Table 3

Growth Rate of Area Production and Productivity of Crops in Andhra Pradesh

Year	1956-57to 1960-61			1961-62 to 1970-70			1971-72 to 1980-81		
	Area	Production	Productivity	Area	Production	Productivity	Area	Production	Productivity
Rice	0.29	1.81	1.57	0.37	0.58	0.22	1.70	4.04	2.53
Bajra	0.37	-0.17	-0.62	-0.4	-3.96	-3.55	-2.07	-0.52	1.59
Black gram	-0.43	3.28	-2.05	-1.51	-2.11	-0.62	-0.13	3.95	4.08
Maize	-0.81	10.23	11.24	2.25	1.58	2.52	1.71	9.45	7.63
Green gram	-1.17	0.37	1.62	-2.3	-3.79	-1.52	-0.72	-0.78	-0.07
Ground nut	-11.9	-13.9	-1.37	1.77	7.4	1.02	2.18	3.24	1.06
Jowar	2.09	5.18	3.03	2.95	8.72	5.71	2.23	3.48	1.11
Red gram	-2.12	10.02	12.26	1.35	-1.48	-3.01	2.01	0.47	-1.56
Horse gram	-2.26	-4.14	-1.83	-2.18	0.77	1.33	-3.55	-5.64	-2.27
Tobacco	-2.77	4.55	-1.49	-2.01	2.92	3.72	-7.87	-4.03	-2.85
Castor	-3.31	-3.23	0.39	7.18	8.86	1.55	-2.31	-4.13	-1.86
Ragi	4.06	0.68	-4.19	0	1.87	1.9	-1.81	-7.39	-5.6
Sugar cane	-4.09	6.63	2.1	-0.04	1.65	1.59	3.74	-2.27	1.36
Cotton	-4.8	-2.54	2.94	-0.93	-5.05	-2.34	2.26	11.41	8.32
Bengal gram	-5.74	-7.35	-1.52	3.2	1.26	-1.89	-3.37	-2.21	1.18
Sesa-mum	-6.56	-10.5	-6.31	2.26	1.83	-0.27	3.75	-1.24	-2.3
Chillies	-9.01	-7.55	1.56	6.56	6.59	-0.34	-2.18	0.7	2.98
Bengal gram	-5.74	-7.35	-1.52	3.2	1.26	-1.89	-3.37	-2.21	1.18
Sesa-mum	-6.56	-10.5	-6.31	2.26	1.83	-0.27	3.75	-1.24	-2.3
Chillies	-9.01	-7.55	1.56	6.56	6.59	-0.34	-2.18	0.7	2.98

Contd.

1981-82 to -1990-91			1991-92 to 2000-01			2001-02 to 2006-07			1956-57 to 2006-07		
Area	Production	Productivity	Area	Production	Productivity	Area	Production	Productivity	Area	Production	Productivity
0.54	2.07	1.51	0.75	6.14	2.04	0.79	0.83	0.04	0.62	2.52	1.9
-6.02	-4.4	1.74	-4.45	-0.52	3.89	-7.92	-8.3	-0.82	-3.5	-1.96	1.55

-8.21	10.21	-1.13	-2.81	0.92	3.72	-7.89	-7.91	0.13	-4.5	-3.63	0.91
-0.69	0.22	0.91	5.23	9.55	4.12	6.74	11.06	-0.06	2.32	6.51	3.68
-4.47	-3.99	0.51	-3.81	-3.99	1.49	-6.37	-9.08	-3.3	-3.21	-2.98	0.25
-1.37	-4.14	-2.85	0.12	-1.73	-1.83	-3.71	-12..3	2.23	0.13	0.36	1.41
9.44	15.06	5.2	-0.14	1.38	1.51	-4.5	-43..5	2.84	2.96	-0.55	2.07
3.39	2.12	-1.26	4.23	6.29	1.95	-0.46	-3.05	-2.24	-0.92	2.68	0.78
5.4	9.04	3.56	12.12	17.16	4.5	16.13	12.46	-3.12	3.38	6.15	2.71
5.4	-4.16	4.02	-4.93	-9.46	-4.49	-4.36	-5.11	-0.79	-4	-2.17	1.93
5.13	8.86	-0.44	-2.77	-0.04	2.82	-4.63	-9.88	-5.5	0	-0.99	-0.99
2.37	4.32	1.9	1.79	4.06	2.6	-6.59	0.95	7.97	-1.04	0.58	1.65
-0.29	1.3	1.65	-0.05	-1.02	-0.84	-2.89	1.44	4.71	-1.67	-1.2	0.3
3.31	5.29	1.93	3.77	2.5	-1.18	-2.59	3.05	5.76	1.78	5.75	3.87
-0.96	-0.32	0.64	-12..8	11..31	4.29	N/A	1.61	1.86	-0.49	0.6	1.07
0.31	2.17	-2.25	4.92	1.73	1	-7.41	-1.97	2.04	2.49	-1.85	0.18
2.85	7.72	4.74	0.65	7.3	-6.21	-1	5.32	6.35	0.37	3.87	3.49

Source: Directorate of Economics and Statistics, Government of Andhra Pradesh

4

Modernization-Mobilization: A Means of Development

P.P. Satyanarayana Rao

Till very recently, development was defined only in economic terms and measured in terms of Gross National Product. The government and planners might have felt that the people will come forward spontaneously to take active participation in the developmental process. Even after sixty years of Independence, the increased growth rates have only made the rich richer and the poor and poorer. The growing gap between the more progressive and traditional segments of the society leads to social unrest, which seriously effected, other systems in the society. It was when the elaborate programme of planned development had failed to register impressive gains that the need was felt to look for new strategies of development. As a result, development came to be defined in terms of Gross National Welfare along with Gross National Product. Especially, in the third world countries, the development should mean the growth and active participation of the people in such a growth. People's participation or people's centered development is empowering the people as engines of their own development by enabling them to express their ideas, concepts, needs, necessities, their capacities and capabilities as their concern in the development planning and in its implementation. If the people are not involved in a right place at a right time, the all-round development cannot be achieved and the majority of the people is impoverished and cannot enjoy the fruits of development.

Development now needs to be defined in terms of people and the people's choice of development or growth rate will enhance the people's livelihood, besides secure to livelihood, overall quality of life, better nutritious food, health and hygienic conditions, portable water, housing, education, security against crime and violence and real freedom in social, political, cultural, economic and other spheres of life. In the developmental process, the people will play a central role in mainly determining the path and the level of development.

The new Nations had been striving with all intensity of purpose to achieve all-round development that would enable them to get out of the rut of 'backwardness'. Various studies on development problems of third world countries acknowledge that a close relationship exists between the effectiveness of development policies in the economic field and prevailing attitudes and institutions. Cairncross has stated that 'Development is not governed in any country by economic forces alone and the more backward the country the more this is true. The key development lies in the men's minds, in the institutions in which their thinking finds expressions and in the play of opportunity on ideas and institutions'. Further Mishra (1981) has pointed out that 'the concept of development refers to a relatively stable, long range increase in real national income that is accompanied by a change in the attitudes of the people, their motivation, institutional set-up, production techniques etc.,' The current indicators of development include both economic and non-economic factors. Material means of production refers to the economic factor in the development whereas the enrichment of human capital refers to the non-economic factors such as the social, political, ethnic or educational background of the people who participate in the developmental tasks.

Development cannot be achieved without involving the people since, the prime benefactor of development outcomes are for the people; the people's involvement in the development process should be a primary target. Involving the people in the development process implies dealing with generation of men and women-alteration of the way of life of these people in the development direction. If there is a lag between the developmental efforts on the one hand and the attitudes and mental preparedness of the people on the other, it will result in the stalling of these programmes. The realization of nation's aspiration is to correct the lag between the developmental efforts and the attitudinal and mental preparedness of the people in bringing change in the knowledge, skills, interests and values of the people as a whole for National Development. Unless the change is accomplished, the social and economic revolution necessary to make India a modern and progressive country is being postponed. While the development of physical resources is a means to an end, development of human resources is an end itself and without it, even the adequate development of physical resources is not possible.

It is clear that the most powerful thrusts of the planners can be stalled without the involvement of masses. Involving the masses in the developmental process implies the mobilization of a generation of men and women. This means the development requires the very transformation or modernization of the nature of man-a transformation that is both a means to the developmental goals and at the same time one of the greatest ends itself of the development process. Modernization of man thus becomes at once the means to development and the goal of development because the modern man not only facilitates development but also ensures sustained development. The modernization of man thus becomes at once the means of development and the goal of development also.

Modernization stands for rational approach to all aspects of human life. The term modernization is often used as a synonym for economic growth, since modernization calls for directed change in the system of attitudes, beliefs, values and also in the institutional complex. While economic development is certainly one of the goals of modernization, it has another goals like social and political development. Therefore, Modernization is a means, at the end of which is, National Development and as such, it is a process, which involves change in the social, political, economic and in other systems.

Black defines Modernization as a process by which historically evolved institutions are adapted to the rapidly changing functions that reflect the unprecedented increase in man's knowledge permitting control over his environment that accompanied the scientific revolution. This means that modernization refers to the dynamic form that the age-old process of innovation has assumed as a result of the explosive proliferation of knowledge in recent centuries. It owes its special significance both to its dynamic character and to the universality of its impact on human affairs. It stems initially from an attitude, a belief that society can and should be transformed, that change is desirable for human development. And human development mainly enlarges the people's choices and open avenues for wider opportunities if sound policies are suitably formulated and implemented the targeted (people's oriented) programmes effectively in a strategic way.

Eisenstadt (1969) characterizes modernization as a process of transformation involving both social mobilization and social differentiation. Social mobilization stands for a psycho-social, qualitative transformation and is the process, where by commitments to traditional economic, political and social roles are loosened and the individual is made susceptible to new values, new socialization patterns and new commitments. Social differentiation refers to the structural aspects of modernization and denotes a high degree of specialization and differentiation of individual activities and institutional structures, which are characterized by the specificity of roles and allocation of roles on the basis of achievement criteria. The above definition of modernization points out that there are two levels at which modernization studies can be made.

One could be at the societal level and the other at the individual level. The former would focus on patterns of social organization while the latter would be a social-psychological approach to modernization treating it as a process of change in ways of perceiving, expressing and valuing. The former approach is concerned more with the institution and, as such, is more sociological. The latter, being concerned more with the individual, is more social and psychological which denotes a set of values, attitudes and ways of behavior, which better fit men in life in modern society.

For any programme or project or for welfare schemes, people's active participation is necessary for its successful implementation to get the effective outcomes and the people's active participation will be possible with strategic mobilization. People's mobilization mainly deals with their emotional motivation and their psycho-social spurring towards communal needs and goals. Mobilization of the people is the process of involving and bringing them together as a unit to increase their level of awareness on their needs and objectives in order to achieve them for better quality of life. Akindele has stated that '............... mobilization must be seen in terms of involving the people in taking part actually and freely in discussions and decisions affecting their general welfare................ It should aim at increasing people's level of awareness or cognition of political and other issues, so that they can apply their energies positively and participate actively in the social and political life of the country'. Mobilization will sensitize the situation, develops cognition, consciousness, emotion and efficacy on their beliefs, values, attitudes, behavior and in institutional complex for their development, which is a holistic object of the government.

American Development Foundation (a U.S. non-profit private voluntary organization) working on Community Mobilization and Development has expressed that 'Community mobilization ensures citizens participation as stakeholders in decision-making processes – in partnership with local government where possible – to work together to develop their communities. This increased citizen participation in political and economic decision-making depends heavily on community openness to being active participants and partners with government in improving local conditions. It is enhanced when citizens gain practical experience in working together to improve local conditions. When people feel that they are powerless to bring about change, or when they do not know how to organize themselves and work across sectors to effect change, then citizen participation remains low. ADF's approach to Community Mobilization and Development focuses on raising awareness within the community on the critical nature of civic participation, facilitating the creation of mechanisms through which the community can plan and manage local initiatives, building dialogue and cooperation with local government authorities and structures, and providing support that complements local resources to improve local conditions'.

Modernization and mobilization should begin upon tradition and issue forth from it. It is an additive process and not a substitutive process to developmental direction. It is a process of becoming modern-the process of change in values, attitudes and behavior that is required for people's active participation in the developmental process especially in modern/modernizing society.

Inkels in an effort to provide an empirical basis for defining modern man conducted a survey of people in six nations and concludes that the modern man is characterized by certain traits. He is change oriented, less suspicious of novelty, he is more present and future oriented rather than backward looking and bound to tradition. He casts off fatalistic attitudes prevalent in the more traditional societies and acquires a faith that he can dominate his environment. He also tends to hold opinions over a range of issues reaching beyond local matters.

Rudolph and Rudolph have explained modernity assumes that 'local ties and parochial perspectives give way to universal commitments and cosmopolitan attitudes, that the truths of utility, calculation and science takes precedence over those of emotions, the sacred and the non-rational, that the individual rather than the group be the primary unit of society and politics, that the associations in which men live and work be based on choice not by birth, that mastery rather than fatalism, orient their attitudes towards the material and human environment, that identity be chosen and achieved not ascribed and affirmed, that work be separated from family, residence and community, in bureaucratic organizations that manhood be delayed while youth prepares for its task and responsibilities, that age even when it is prolonged surrenders much of its authority to youth and men some of theirs to women, that mankind cease to live as race apart from recognizing in society and politics its common humanity; that government cease to be a manifestation of powers beyond man and out of reach of common men by basing itself on participation, consent and public accountability'.

In the context of development, modernization is the most liberal instrument for development of human resources, which involve changes in the knowledge, skills, values, and attitudes of the people. Modernization parallels at the individual level, what development represents at the national level. It is a process of individual change in ways of perceiving, expressing and valuing and refers to the acquisition of a set of values, attitudes and ways of behavior, which better fit men for life in modern societies. Especially, the rural and tribal poor are found to be conservative and resistant to change because their cognitive orientations are conditioned by the past when such attitudes and values were effective in daily living and as these cognitive orientations change very slowly in comparison with the rapidly modernizing world around them they are found to be out of tune with reality. This is the reason why they behave in ways that seem irrational or ignorant to those better attuned to reality. Therefore, modernization act as an accelerating agent in bringing change in their cognitive orientation and adaptation making them more modernized in their attitudes and behavior at individual level being looked upon as a means for National Development.

The basic challenge of modernization is the infusion of a 'rationalistic and positive spirit' (Lerner, 1964) among the people. The effective functioning of a modern society requires that citizens have certain qualities, attitudes, values, habits and disposition. It requires of its citizens a readiness for new experience and an acceptance of innovation, a concern with public issues at the community and national levels, a sense of efficacy that encourages and support various developmental programmes of social change. Contemporary writers have envisioned psychosocial modernity as a determinant of social and economic development. If not sufficient, modernity is defined as at least a necessary condition for these societal goals.

Inkels study of modernity at the individual level has identified the modern man as innovative, knowledgeable and opinionated, future oriented, committed to planning and believing in the calculability and controllability of events by means of Science and Technology. Further, modern man sees his roles in social process as efficacious; he is tolerant of difference, a believer in distributive justice and holds the dignity of man in high value.

Modern man develops through improved access to knowledge, skills and changes in attitudes and perspectives. The result, the modern man is change-oriented, less suspicious of novelty, more present and future oriented rather than bound to tradition. The modern man casts off fatalistic attitudes and acquires a faith that he can dominate his environment; he also tends to hold opinions over a range of issues in solving the problems he is facing in his day-to-day life in the development direction.

Modernization is not an end in itself but a means, in one case, for economic and political development and in the other for social and cultural transformation. Modernization promotes development with multi-dimensional outcomes embracing with sustainability in their livelihood, self-esteem with better quality and equality in the life style, social and political consciousness for all-round development. It enables the individual to gain knowledge about himself, his environment, the society in which he lives thereby enables him to lead a meaningful and richer life by participating more effectively in the developmental process. Modernization of man thus becomes at once the means to development and the goal of development because the 'modern man' not only facilitates development but also ensures sustained development.

References

Akindele, S.T. (2004), 'Political Mobilization for Rural Development and a Stable Nigerian Democratic Republic: An Indepth Examination of the Role of Local Governments', Kamla-Raj 2004, *J.Hum. Ecol.16* (2).

Black, C.E. (1966), "*The Dynamics of Modernization: A Study in Comparative History*", Harpert Row, New York.

Cairncross, A.K. (1961), 'International Trade and Economic Development', ECONOMICA Vol. XXVIII, No. 109, Feb., p.250.

Dubell, Folke (1980), 'Mobilization of Human Resources for Development', *The Portugal Project Document No. VII.*

Eisenstadt, S.N. (1969), "*Modernization: Protest and Change*", Prentice Hall of India Private Ltd., New Delhi, p-2-3.

Hans-Gert Braun (2003), 'A Possible Means of Encouraging Development: Mobilization of Savings Capital in Third World Countries', "*Priorities*", *No.1 (7)*, reprinted in April.

Inkeles, Alex (1966), "The Modernization of Man", in *Modernization, ed.* Myron Weiner, Basic Books, New York.

Inkeles, Alex (1968), "Making Men Modern": On the Causes and consequences of Individual Change in Six Developing Countries", (paper presented in the Annual meeting of the AAAS, Dallas).

Inkeles, Alex (1969), 'Making Men Modern: On the Causes and Consequences of Individual Change in Six Developing Countries', American Journal of Sociology, Vol.75, Sept, p.208-225.

Lerner, Daniel (1964), "*The Passing of Traditional Society: Modernizing in the Middle East*". The Free Press of Glencoe, p.45.

Mishra, Rajeswar (1981), 'Literacy and Development', Indian Journal of Adult Education, Vol. 42, No. 9, Sept.

National Human Development Report (2006), Liberian on 'Mobilization Capacity for Reconstruction and Development.

Report of the Conference of FAO (in its Fifteenth session) held on 8-12 November 1969, originated by Knowledge and Communication Department.

Rudolph, L.I. and Susanna Rudolph (1967), "Tradition of Modernity", Orient Longmans Ltd., Bombay, p.3.

5

Dry Land Farming in India: Constraints and Opportunities

D. Pulla Rao

The Need

The main aim of any agricultural development programmes is to maintain sustainable growth in agricultural production for ensuring food security to the growing population and also to generate adequate surplus for exports. Besides, it is expected to generate sufficient employment opportunities to the teening millions. When the demand for food products increases, with the limited land resources, there will be degradation of land fertility causing great environmental degradation. Thus, eradication of rural poverty is associated with environmental degradation. During the last three decades, there has been a substantial increase in agricultural production, especially food grains, mainly wheat and rice. Most of the gains in increased agricultural production were realized due to increase in agricultural productivity with interaction of seed-irrigation-fertilizer technology and farmers' initiatives rather than due to area expansion. However, this growth in agricultural production remained concentrated mostly in high production environments with developed infrastructure, irrigation facilities and assured rainfall. A large tract of cultivable land is dependent on rain fall with out assured irrigation facilities. And such lands are kept out of the so called green revolution. It needs separate strategy to bring in the dry land farming under high yielding variety technology.

The Dimension of Dry Land Farming

Rain fed farming, more popularly known as "dry land agriculture" means raising crops mainly with rainwater is spread in four continents covering almost 48 countries. Worldwide, about 6, 510 million hectares (mha) of land is under rain fed agriculture of which approximately 60 per cent are in the developing countries. India ranks first among the dry land agricultural countries in terms of both extent and value of produce. Out of every three hectares of cultivated land in India, nearly two hectares are under the influence of rain fed agriculture. Out of a total 142.1 million hectares of cultivated area in India, dry land accounts for 91.0 million hectares and in the foreseeable future also nearly 60 per cent of our population will still continue to depend on dry land agriculture.

Dry lands across the world are estimated to be supporting 38 per cent of the world's population. In India, it is estimated that about 410 million people live on the dry land farming. Many of these people also constitute the 'poverty geography' of the country. Other than the arid zones where even rain fed farming is quite difficult, the heart of the dry lands is in the semi-arid zones. Dry lands in this country constitute more than 70 per cent of the cultivable lands and despite several odds stacked against them, produce about 42 per cent of the country's food. It is reported that nearly 83 per cent of sorghum, 81 per cent of pulses and 90 per cent of oilseeds grown in the country come from these areas.

Neglected Dry Lands

Dry lands are home to an enormous wealth of biodiversity. The adaptability and resilience of the dry land livelihood systems are well noted. Rural livelihood systems in dry lands have, by their persistence over several decades, demonstrated a resilience which runs counter to some predictions of imminent irreversible degradation or collapse. However, the positive features of dry lands were ignored with heavy concentration of agricultural resources on the green revolution belts. The Green Revolution though ensured national food security for the country and increased the production and productivity of various crops, it has also created serious regional imbalances in terms of resource allocation and incomes.

Much of the technologies, subsidies and public support systems provided under this undifferentiated agriculture policy by passed the needs or problems of dry land agriculture, thus promoted inequitable distribution of essential inputs like irrigation, fertilizers and seeds. A similar tendency is visible in terms of agriculture research priorities, technology development and investments.

Characteristics of Dry Land Agriculture

Some of the important characteristics of dry land agriculture are projected in Table-1. It is revealed that, dry land is less densely populated compared to irrigated areas but the proportion of landless households and agricultural labourers is quite high. These dry land regions have limited irrigation, that is, about 15 per cent compared to 48 per cent in irrigated regions. The land and labour productivity are considerably low in dry land regions. Due to low opportunities and higher population of landless households and agricultural labourers as well as low productivity of land and labour, poverty is concentrated in these regions. These are the regions, which have low infrastructure facilities like markets and roads. Per capita consumption expenditure on food grains in the dry land regions is almost half the level of consumption expenditure in irrigated areas.

All these indicators clearly show that dry land areas have remained neglected even after 60 years of independence. However, dry land is not a homogenous region and varies in terms of soil type, rainfall, cropping pattern, literacy, land

and labour productivity, etc. It is always not true that all the dry land regions are much inferior in terms of productivity and infrastructure or level of development, but in general, this is true.

Table 1
Some Important Characteristics of Dry land and Irrigated Regions in India

Particular	*DRY Regions (29)*	*WET Regions (29)*	*ALL Regions (58)*
Population density (Persons per sq kms)	163	297	230
Proportion of agricultural labour (%)	30	28	29
Proportion of small farms (%)	52	76	69
Proportion of landless households (%)	43	44	44
Literacy- male (%)	47	47	47
Proportion of irrigated area (%)	15	48	32
Poverty ratio, Headcount (%)	37	33	35
Land productivity (Rs./ha)	5716	8017	6867
Labour productivity (Rs./ha)	6842	9830	8336
Per capita consumption (Kg/year) of:			
Cereals	240	459	350
Pulses	20	12	16
Total Food grains	260	471	365
Per capita monthly consumption expenses (Rs)	279	297	288
Share of Food in total consumption (%)	65	62	63
Real wage rate for men (Rs./day)	25	27	26
Market density	2.86	3.69	3.28
Road density	3.79	6.99	5.89
Gini ratio in consumption	0.25	0.27	0.26
Bank credit (Rs./ha)	1050	1650	1350
Cooperative credit (Rs./ha)	816	1038	925
Social development Index	0.43	0.44	0.43
Infrastructure Development Index	0.30	0.40	0.35

Major Constraints of Dry Land Farming

It is our contention that the dry land agriculture policy be conceived in a framework germane to its own constraints, opportunities and ecological prerequisites. Some defining conditions for dry land agriculture are:

- Uncertainty of weather conditions imposing multiple risks during the crop growing season;
- Low water (surface or ground) potential;
- Low levels of fertility of the soil and increasing desertification;

- High intensity of livelihood dependence ('livelihood load') on the system, particularly of those who are below or near the poverty line;
- Low levels of private investment in land improvement and cultivation;
- Uncertain, ill-.distributed and limited annual rainfall;
- Occurrence of extensive climatic hazards like drought, flood etc;
- Undulating soil surface;
- Occurrence of extensive and large holdings;
- Practice of extensive agriculture i.e. prevalence of monocropping etc;
- Relatively large size of fields;
- Similarity in types of crops raised by almost all the farmers of a particular region;
- Very low crop yield;
- Poor market facility for the produce;
- Poor economy of the farmers; and
- Poor health of cattle as well as farmers.

Special Strategies for Dry Land Farming

The range and diversity of the dry lands presents a qualitatively complex set of constraints which needs a more delicate mode of handling. We must give up the one-size-fits-all approach and focus on fine-tuning and matching our interventions to the subtle variations in local contexts.

At the outset, we must realize the crucial role that the state has to play in a positive reshaping of the dry land landscape. In the current context of liberalization and dominance of anti-state sentiments (shared, paradoxically, by the staunchest of neo-liberals as well as the purest among radicals), this point needs strong emphasis. In particular, the key role of kick starting the growth process in the forsaken dry lands has to be played by public investment. The dry lands are caught in a low-level equilibrium trap. Public investment is required to enable them to break out of this trap. The endemic process of natural resource degradation needs to be checked. Public investment in dry lands has to be substantially increased and sustained over a long period of time. The state has to step up its investment in the dry lands substantially. All these call for special strategies to help the poor farming communities that are eking out their lives on dry lands.

Conclusion

Even after utilizing all the available water resources, about 50 per cent of our cultivable area is still dependent on rains. Therefore, our agricultural scientists, policy formulators and the politicians should appropriately realize the magnitude of role that rain fed agriculture or dry land farming can play in the national economy. They should thoroughly examine the problems of dry land agriculture from different view points and evolve appropriate technologies, crop varieties, etc. for these areas to better the economic position of the dry land farmers. Dry farming needs a greater attention of the nation.

Farmers should utilize well in time whatever improved technology and varieties suitable for dry farming are available. They should be extra careful about the utilization of available rain water, selection of crops and protection of crops from different harmful physiological or biological agencies. And only then they can make dry farming as profitable as irrigated farming itself.

References

Kerr, J.M, Ganesh Pangare and Vasudha Pangare (2002), *Watershed Development Projects in India: An Evaluation*, International Food Policy Research Institute, Washington, D.C.

Lakshmikanthamma, S. (1997), *Sustainability of Dry Land Agriculture in India–A Case study of Watershed Development Approach*, M.D.Publications Pvt. Ltd., New Delhi.

Mihir Shah, D. Banerji, P.S. Vijayshankar and Pramathesh Ambasta. (1998), *India's Dry lands: Tribal Societies and Development through Environmental Regeneration*, Oxford University Press, New Delhi.

Philip Dobie (2001), *Poverty and Dry Lands, UNDP*, Dry Land Development Centre, Nairobi.

Reddy, Y.V.R. and Pandurangaiah, K. (1988), *Status Report on Economics and Adoption Levels of Dry Land Technology in Model watershed* at Mittemari Central Research Institute for Dry Land Agriculture, Hyderabad.

6

Challenge of Food Security in India

P. Kothandarami Reddy

Introduction:

A nation may acquire self-sufficiency in food at a point of time but the concept of food security necessities that, timely reliable and nutritionally adequate supply of food should be available on a long-term basis. Poverty reduction has been a major goal of development policy in India since the country became independent and the achievement of a minimum standard of living for all within a reasonable period has been the implicit or explicit objective of all socio-economic endeavors initiated under various five year plans. This was sought to be achieved by attaining higher growth; raising purchasing power of the poor through the endowment of land and non-land assets and generating employment opportunities; and through public intervention for consumption smoothening by understanding large scale food-for-work programmes. The Indian planners right from the beginning realized the need to attain self-sufficiency in foodgrains as one of the important goals of planning. Even though self-sufficiency of food production has been achieved, the population still lacks access to balanced food. It is a matter of concern that even though cereal production has kept pace with the increasing requirements and average per capita intakes of cereals have remained satisfactory, there have been a fall in the per capita consumption of pulses. Well laid down procedures are in place to identify the poor; to measure income poverty, to monitor changes over time and across space and to evaluate the impact and outcomes of different policies and programmes. There is extensive literature on different aspects of poverty reduction and better understanding of the efficacy of different policies.

Food Security at Global Level

World Development Report (1986) defined food security as access by all people at all times to enough food for an active, healthy life. FAO (1983) defined food security as ensuring that all people at all times have both physical and economic access to basic food they need. The key agents that play a significant role in achieving sustainable food security system are population, food supplies, economic access, apart from environmental aspects of pollution and resource exhaustion. In spite of the success of the population stabilizing efforts of many countries, as per the International Food Policy Research Institution's (IFPRI's) food policy report (Vision 2020) the world population is expected to reach 7.5 billion by 2020. Much of population growth will occur in the cities of developing countries. Per capita incomes are also expected to increase in all major developing countries of the world. With the increase in population and income, there shall be an increase in the demand for food and change in the food composition in favour of animal and fish products. As per the IFPRI's study reports, in order to meet this increased demand, world farmers have to produce 40 per cent more grain than now by 2020. The studies also projected that for the required increase in cereal production, the expansion in area can contribute only up to 20 percent, and the remaining has to come from productivity increase. But unfortunately many countries in the world have been experiencing either stagnation or decline in yields. With the policies and approaches now being pursued in most developing countries and international organizations, there is no possibility of achieving food security for all even by 2020 (IFPRI Report).

Food Security : Indian Scenario

In India before the introduction of High Yielding Variety (HYV) technology there were famines and the possibility of achieving a balance between population and food supplies was almost nil. The green revolution in the seventies and eighties reversed this trend and helped a lot to achieve balance between population growth and population supporting capacity of the eco-system. In 1983, Government of India declared that the country achieved food security (self sufficiency in food production). How ever this favourable situation for food security did not continue for a long time. In the nineties, the country experienced significant shifts in the cropping pattern from food crops to non-food crops, depletion of water resources, soil erosion, and stagnation or decline in the crop yields. These broad trends continued in the country even after 2000 and they are likely to pose severe problems for food security. The present situation of high levels of poverty, especially among women, children, SC & ST population and disturbing trends in nutritional status stands as a testimony to it. Recognizing this threat to the food security, a target of producing additional two crore tones of food grains is set in the Eleventh Plan. For achieving this target the National Food Security Commission has been constituted recently.

Food security has also been a major goal of development policy in India since the beginning of planning. Food availability and price stability were considered good measures of food security till the seventies and the achievement of self-sufficiency was accorded high priority in the food policy. India achieved self-sufficiency in food grains in the mid 70's and sustained it since then. The achievement of macro food grain security at the national level did not percolate down to the household level and the level of chronic food insecurity in India is high. According to the FAO over 225 million Indians remain chronically undernourished. This is due to the fact that a substantial proportion of the people are too poor to buy enough food and also exposed to diseases. Against this back ground it is proposed here to discuss some issues relating to poverty and food consumption levels in the country.

Profiles of the Poor

The composition of the poor is changing and rural poverty is getting concentrated in households belonging to agricultural labour and artisans and urban poverty in casual labour households. The share of agricultural labour households accounted for 41 per cent of rural poor in 1993-94 and increased to 47 per cent of rural poor in 1999-00. The increase in the relative size of agricultural labour households was due to the rise in the dependence of rural households on agriculture for livelihood from 28 to 31 percent as well as higher incidence of poverty among agricultural labour households 40 per cent in 1999-00 in contrast to 26 per cent in all rural households.

The casual labour households constituted 32 per cent of urban poor in 1999-00 compared with only 25 per cent in 1993-94. This was due to their increased dependence on urban labour market from 25 per cent in 1993-94 to 32 per cent in 1999-00 as well as higher incidence of poverty among urban casual labour households. It needs to be recognized on the casual labour market exposes them to market risks and tends to increase transient poverty. Among the social groups Scheduled castes, Scheduled tribes and Backward castes accounted for half of the rural population in 1999-00 which they accounted for a greater percentage of the rural poor. The percentage share of Scheduled tribe population among the rural poor has increased rapidly from 14.8 per cent in 1993-94 to 17.5 per cent in 1999-00 which was mainly due to comparatively slower reduction in the incidence of poverty.

Chronic Poverty

How can chronically poor households be identified among the poor? The sub-category of poor persons who are below the poverty line for a long duration, usually five years, constitutes the chronic poor. A poor household with a malnourished child is considered as chronically poor. The standard of living index data revealed that in the case of children belonging to poor households, 57 per cent of those in rural areas and 50 per cent in urban areas were studied. The incidence of chronic poverty has been estimated by multiplying the percentage of malnourished among the poor with the proportion of poor and the estimates are presented in Table.1.

Table 1
Under Nutrition Among Poor and Incidence of Chronic Poverty: 1997-98

	Rural		*Urban*	
Area	*% of Stunted Children Among Poor*	*% of Chronically Poor*	*% of Stunted children Among Poor*	*% of Chronically Poor*
A.P	49.6	5.2	34.3	13.8
Karnataka	56.5	9.6	49.7	13.9
Kerala	32.4	3.1	30.9	6.5
Tamil Nadu	41.6	3.4	46.5	9.4
Gujarat	49.5	6.1	51.2	7.3
Punjab	56.9	3.4	46.4	3.1
U.P	63.1	19.6	59.6	19.4
West Bengal	60.0	19.0	53.5	8.8
Jammu Kashmir	59.9	2.8	51.6	1.2
Rajasthan	60.1	8.1	57.2	11.7
Orissa	51.1	24.4	49.1	22.2
Bihar	57.5	25.3	63.0	21.1
All India	57.1	15.1	49.6	13.7

Source : Radhakrishna et.al, Chronic Poverty and Malnutrition in India, CPRC, p.48

The percentage of chronically poor in rural areas is estimated to be 15 per cent and 14 per cent in urban areas. The percentage of chronically poor is quite high in Bihar (25.3 per cent in rural and 21.1 per cent in urban), Orissa (24.4 per cent in rural and 21.4 per cent in urban) and Uttar

Pradesh (19.6 per cent in rural and 10.4 per cent in urban). Rural areas of Assam and West Bengal have high incidence while it is very low in Jammu & Kashmir and Kerala.

Food Consumption and Calorie Intake

Per capita cereal expenditure at constant prices declined both in rural and urban areas throughout this period (1970-98) for all the expenditure classes, except for the bottom 30 per cent for urban areas during the last decade (Table 2). During 1990's the decline was more in rural areas. The fall in cereal

Table 2
Growth Rates of Per Capita Food Expenditure, Calorie Intake and Total Expenditure

Item	*Year*	*Bottom 30%*	*Middle 40%*	*Top 30%*	*All Classes*
		Rural			
Per capitaCereal exp.	1970-89	0.10	-0.55	-1.26	-0.67
	1989-01	-1.38	-2.04	-2.26	-2.04
Per capitaFood exp.	1970-89	1.11	0.72	0.58	0.73
	1989-01	-0.29	-0.56	-0.36	-0.42
Per capitaCal.intake	1970-89	0.16	0.15	0.40	0.23
	1990-98	-0.96	-1.63	-1.76	-1.53
Per capitaTotal exp.	1970-89	1.73	1.48	1.65	1.60
	1989-01	1.48	1.31	1.03	1.20
		Urban			
Per capita Cereal exp.	1970-89	0.08	-0.32	-0.18	-0.17
	1989-01	-0.93	-0.91	-0.34	-0.72
Per capita food exp.	1970-89	1.15	1.05	0.60	0.86
	1989-01	0.18	0.21	0.24	0.22
Per capita Cal.intake	1970-89	0.31	0.05	0.32	0.21
	1990-98	-0.58	-0.74	-0.05	-0.44
Per capita Total exp.	1970-89	1.75	1.38	1.99	1.92
	1989-01	2.32	2.33	3.29	3.01

Note: Cal - caloric, exp.- expenditure
Source: Radhakrishna et.al. op. cit. p.20

consumption was more than compensated by the increased consumption of non-cereal food items and as a result the per capita calorie intake increased at 0.2 per cent per annum during this period. However this did not continue during

1990's when the per capita calorie intake fall by about 1.5 per cent per annum in rural areas and by 0.4 per cent in urban areas. For the bottom 30 per cent of the population the per capita cereal expenditure at constant prices was stagnant during 1970-89 but declined during 1990's which indicates that the improvements in income growth did not translate into a higher consumption of cereals.

There is a substantial variation in energy intake among different expenditure segments of the population (Table 3) while the top 30 per cent of the population is adequately fed the middle 40 per cent gets barely close to the nutritional requirement. The per capita calorie intake of the bottom 30 per cent in 1999-00 was very low at 1696 k.cal per day in rural areas and 1715 k.cal per day in urban areas. This section of the population was largely deprived of nutritionally adequate diet. Another important equally disquieting is the large year-to-year variation in food energy intake. The trend in increase in the real price of food items in the recent period is a cause of concern for all.

Table 3
Average Per Capita Calorie Intake and Its Growth Rates in India

	K. Calories per day				
	Rural				*Growth Rate (%)*
Expenditure Classes	*1972-73*	*1977-78*	*1993-94*	*1999-00*	*1972-00*
Bottom 30%	1504	1630	1678	1696	0.6
Middle 40%	2170	2296	2119	2116	-0.1
Top 30%	3161	3190	2672	2646	-0.8
All groups	2268	2364	2152	2149	-0.3
		Urban			
Bottom 30%	1579	1701	1701	1715	0.4
Middle 40%	2154	2154	2438	2136	-0.0
Top 30%	2572	2979	2405	2622	0.1
All groups	2107	2379	2071	2156	0.1

Source: Radhakrishna et.al. op. cit. p.49

Conclusion:

Reduction of poverty has been a major goal of development policy in India since the beginning of planning era and achievement of a maximum standard of living by providing food security for all has been the objective of all five year plans. Achievement of food grain security at national level did not percolate down to the bottom level. The incidence of poverty is very high in rural areas particularly in house holds belonging to agricultural labour and artisans. Among the social groups SCs, STs and BCs accounted for half of the rural population and they accounted for a greater percentage of rural poor. The percentage of chronically poor is high at 15 per cent in rural areas compared with 14 per cent in urban areas. Per capita cereal expenditure has declined both in rural and urban areas during the period under study. Wide variations are found in energy intake among different expenditure segments of the population. The problem of under nutrition among poor is also very high both in rural and urban areas. The governments at different levels should try to strengthen the existing programmes like food for work programme, public distribution system etc. and also immediate steps are to be taken to provide food security to the target groups by introducing new programmes in the country.

References

Govt.of India, 9th & 10th Five Year Plans

World Bank (1986), World Development Report.

R. Radhakrishna et.al. : Chronic Poverty and Malnutrition in India, CPRC.

Govt. of India (2002-03), Economic Survey.

IFPRI: Vision 2020- Food Policy Report, Washington, DC

M.S. Swaminathan (2001), Food Security and Sustainable Development, "*Current Science*", Vol. 81, October.

7

Land Reforms and Agrarian Conditions in Andhra Pradesh During Post Independent Era

M. Venkata Ramanaiah, B. Parameswara Reddy, G. Ranganath

Introduction

Among the four factors of production, the land is a principal factor which determines economic, social, cultural and political conditions in a particular society. As per Srinivas, a great Anthropologist, land plays a key role to occupy dominant position in all aforesaid aspects. It decides political, economic and social statues of human beings in India. In simple terms it is said to be all in one. From ancient times to modern era, different doctrines, thesis, synthesis are coming with new face which explain that the all sorrows, pains, tragedies, disasters and misfortune of the people are the resulting factors of the land.

In pre-independence period, there were many attempts to make land reforms, but in vain. The British and indigenous rulers have plundered peasants in many ways. After independence also, our visionaries did not give enough importance to land reforms. Due to many pressure groups and for political interests government could not escape from land reforms. Land reforms facilitate the society to reduce power concentration at a particular group of people.

Land reforms and agrarian relations are closely related to each other. Agrarian relations and landholding structure play an important role in the performance of the agricultural sector. Land reforms have been on the national agenda since Independence to improve the performance of agriculture as well as for rural re-construction. In addition, creating greater access to land for the landless rural poor is an important component of poverty alleviation programmes. Land reforms, in spite of all the limitations in implementation, did play an important role in changing the agrarian structure in Andhra Pradesh. In this paper, an earnest attempt is made to study the land reforms and agrarian conditions in Andhra Pradesh during post independence period. The entire study has divided into three sections. In the first section, initiatives taken by the government relating to land reforms during post independence was discussed. In the second section, the present agrarian conditions are examined. In the last section, the results of land reforms attributed to S.C, S.T and B.C, who have downtrodden for centuries together, have studied.

Section - I

Land Reforms in Andhra Pradesh

By recognizing the importance of land reforms for reconstruction of agrarian relations, there are some provisions in our constitution. These provisions are facilitating to achieve democratic social structure, elimination of exploitation in unequal distribution of land and increasing agricultural productivity.

The landholding structure plays an important role in the performance of the agricultural sector. Land reforms have been on the national agenda since Independence to improve the performance of agriculture as well as for rural re-construction. In addition, creating greater access to land for the landless rural poor, particularly S.C, S.T and other backward classes, is an important component of poverty alleviation programmes. Though there are number of limitations in implementation, land reforms played an important role in changing the agrarian structure in Andhra Pradesh. The early land reform measures in the state were a combination of two administrative histories, of the Andhra region and the Telangana region which had formerly been under the British and Nizam respectively. Following the pattern at the All-India level, the land reforms in Andhra Pradesh had three components: abolition of intermediaries, tenancy reforms, ceiling legislation and the other government initiatives.

Abolition of Intermediaries: Land reforms included abolition of Zamindari system and all intermediaries since the beginning of the fifties. The Madras Estates (Abolition and Conversion into Ryotwari) Act 1948 was the first legislation after Independence which removed intermediaries. It brought all land in Andhra area under Ryotwari system. In the Telangana region the Jagirdari tenurial system ended with the Abolition of Jagirdari Act of 1949 (GOI, 2004).

Tenancy Reforms: Tenancy reforms were intended to abolish or regulate tenancy to ensure fixed tenures and a fair rent. After tenancy reforms initiated, farmers have established direct relations with the government. With respect to tenancy, the Hyderabad Tenancy and Agricultural Lands Act was enacted in 1950 which gave protection to nearly six lakh tenants who held over 75 lakh acres of land, constituting 33 per cent of the total cultivated area. This was considered one of the progressive acts of legislation in the state. The AP (Andhra Area) Tenancy Act 1956 was passed to ensure that a tenant was not evicted from his/her holding except by going to court. This act had come into force from 1956 which has the following main provisions.

Due to these reforms, in total, nearly 2 crores of tenants turn into title-holders of land. As per tenancy reforms act, the rate of tenancy should not fix the will and wish of landlord. The landlords have no right to remove tenants from the land as long as they are cultivating the land. If any landlord wants to sale his/her land, the first preference has to given to the tenant only. In addition to that, if any development of land initiated by tenant, the owner of land has to compensate the same.

Ceiling legislation

Legislation on ceilings on agricultural holdings was enacted in two phases, 1955-72 and 1972 to the present. The Andhra Pradesh Land Reforms (Ceiling on Agriculture Holdings) Acts were passed in 1961 and 1973. As in most states, the first round of legislation in 1961 was a miserable failure but the second one in 1973 had some impact. Against an estimated surplus land of 20 lakh acres, only 7.9 Lakh acres were declared surplus, of which 6.47 Lakh acres were taken possession by the government and 5.82 lakh acres were distributed among 4.79 lakh beneficiaries till August 2004 (GOAP, 2004). This amounted to about 4 per cent of the net sown area. A major step in land distribution in the state was the assignment of government land to the landless poor, which accounted for 12.5 per cent of the net sown area. By the end of 2002, an area of 43.21 lakh acres of government land was assigned to 23.98 lakh beneficiaries.

Instead of the above results, big landlords had not declared their excess land, and where they had, it was fallow land. Whatever be the intention of the government of the day, even the Assigned Land Act has been observed only in the breach. There are numerous instances of assigned land being purchased from the poor at cheap prices by the rich.

Though the ceiling legislation was not effective in the redistribution of land, it did act as a constraint on the acquisition of more land by the rich. In addition, the political mobilization of rural masses inspired by the radical political parties and the Naxalite movement arrested the process of acquiring more land by the rich. The rich peasantry began to sell their land and shift to other vocations in non-agricultural activities in urban areas. As a result, on the one hand, the surplus land under land ceiling and government wasteland was distributed to SC, ST and other rural poor. On the other, land was acquired for cultivation by communities which had been involved in off-farm activities earlier. Subsequently the concentration of land in a few hands and large holdings declined. In the process, the power of the dominant cultivating castes in agrarian society has declined while backward communities have more control over land.

Structure of land holding in A.P

The share of agriculture in employment in the State declined from about 69 per cent in 1961 to about 59 per cent by 2001. Among the agricultural workforce, about 60 per cent are registered as agricultural labour and the rest as cultivators. Though there are regional differences, they are not significant. The percentage of cultivators in the agricultural workforce was relatively much higher in north coastal Andhra followed by Telangana and Rayalaseema, and was lowest in south coastal Andhra. There has been a consistent pattern across all the districts of workers shifting to agricultural labour. Interestingly, the rate of increase was relatively higher in south coastal Andhra.

The data shows that in 1991, there were 92 lakh 90 thousand landholdings whereas this have increased to 1 crore 15 lakh in 2001. At the same time, the cultivatable land in 1990-91 was 1 crore 44 lakh and 60 thousands hectors. First it was decreased to 1 crore 43 lakh and 73 thousands hectors in 1995-96 and later it gradually increased to 1 crore 43 lakh and 99 thousands hectors. Since the variation between the said periods is very slight and the changes in the pattern of landholdings is said to be more or less constant. It indicates that the dependents on agriculture are gradually increasing whereas the land constant. At the same time, the process of shifting from agriculture sector to other sectors is very slow. In this juncture, one point is to be identified that the unequal distribution of landholdings among the peasants still continuing with great extent. The following table shows the picture of total structure and distribution of operational land holdings.

Table 1

The Structure and Distribution of Operational Landholdings in Andhra Pradesh During 1956-2006

	Share in Number of Holding					*Share in Operated Area*					
Year	*Marginal*	*Small*	*Semi-Medium*	*Medium*	*Large*	*Marginal*	*Small*	*Semi-Medium*	*Medium*	*Large*	*Avg. Size*
1955-56	38.60	18.30	17.70	16.70	8.70	7.90	9.70	16.10	28.10	38.20	2.43
1970-71	46.00	18.50	17.40	12.70	4.30	8.00	11.30	19.20	30.80	30.70	2.51
1976-77	46.60	20.30	17.40	12.20	3.40	9.30	12.80	20.80	32.30	24.80	-
1980-81	49.30	20.90	16.00	9.10	2.10	13.10	16.20	23.30	28.70	18.70	1.94
1985-86	54.20	20.80	15.20	8.00	1.80	14.50	17.30	24.00	27.30	16.30	-
1990-91	56.00	21.20	14.50	6.90	1.30	16.40	19.60	25.20	26.10	12.80	1.50
2000-01	60.90	21.80	12.40	4.30	0.60	21.60	24.80	26.40	19.80	7.50	1.25
2005-06	61.60	21.90	12.00	4.00	0.50	22.70	25.80	26.50	19.00	6.10	1.20

Note:

1. Marginal – 0 to 1 hectare; Small – 1 to 2 hectares; Semi-medium – 2 to 4 hectare; Medium – 4 to 10 hectare; and Large – 10 and above hectare;
2. Avg - Average Size of the Holding is given in hectares.

Source: Directorate of Economics and Statistics (DES), Hyderabad.

For the purpose of study, the entire period was divided into two phases, 1955-71 and 1972 to the present. During the first phase land reforms were not fruitful up to the level of expectation of government due to many loopholes in the law. In the second phase more initiatives were taken by the government with much political will. During this period of time, in Andhra Pradesh, new land reforms acts come into force in addition to old laws. The data on landholding structure shows that share in number of holding of marginal and small farmers accounted for 56.9 percent during 1955-56 whereas share in operational area accounted for only 25.8 per cent. During 1976-77, there was up trend in both of the divisions. Share in number of holdings increased to 64.5 per cent from 56.9 per cent and share in operational area increased to 30.5 per cent from 25.8 per cent. At the same time, the share of semi-medium, medium and large farmers accounted for 43.1 per cent during 1955-56 regarding number of holdings whereas the same group occupied 82.4 per cent altogether in operated area. It explains how the land was concentrated at a few farmers.

In second phase, during 1976-77, the share of marginal and small farmers in landholdings and area accounted for 66.9 per cent and 22.1 per cent respectively. During 2005-06, the share of same group has grown up by 83.5 per cent and 48.5 per cent respectively. On other hand, there was a decline in the share of semi-medium, medium and large farmers in landholdings and area occupied with 33 per cent and 77.9 per cent respectively, compared with the first phase. Further it was slipped down to 16.5 per cent and 51.6 per cent respectively during 2005-06.

Regarding to average size of landholding during 1956-57 was 2.43 hectares where it is reduced to 1.2 hectares at present by 2005-06. This state of condition says that the increase of heavy pressure on land. Further, it is obvious that still more than 50 per cent of land is concentrated at a few landlords where they are accounted for only 16.5 per cent of total farmers' community. It calls attention to further land reforms for equal distribution of land and more agricultural productivity.

Section - II

Agrarian Conditions in Andhra Pradesh

Andhra Pradesh is known as treasury of food grains for the rest of country. Agriculture plays a pivotal role in generating employment, food security to the ever increasing population and contribution to the GSDP. To know the present agrarian conditions in the state one has to examine different elements from different dimensions.

Performance and Growth of Agriculture

The GSDP/NSDP is the first and foremost component to measure the performance of agriculture sector. In Andhra Pradesh, the annual growth rate of agriculture increased from 2.3 per cent during 1980-81 to 1992-93 to 2.7 percent during 1993-94 to 2005-06, which was due mainly to the extraordinary performance of the livestock component during this period. The livestock sector achieved a high growth rate of 8.4 per cent per annum between 1993-94 and 2005-06 whereas the growth rate of value of output in the crop sector was very low at 0.59 per cent. Moreover the share of livestock in agriculture increased from 18.1 percent in 1993-94 to 34.7 percent in 2005-06. The share of agriculture in NSDP in terms of the crop sector, excluding all allied activities, declined sharply from 26.7 per cent in 1983 to 14.12 percent in 2005-06, relegating agriculture almost to insignificance. Therefore, the growth of agriculture will not properly reflect the ongoing crisis referred to as agrarian distress in the crop sector.

To understand in detail the performance of agriculture during the last fifteen years, it is observed that the deceleration in growth was mild till 2001-02. Between 1990-91 and 2001-02 the growth rate was 2.39 per cent per annum .But in the last three years the growth rate has fallen very sharply. The year-to-year movement of the value of agricultural output remained almost constant till the mid nineties without much fluctuation and thereafter it grew at a high rate till 2000-01. In the next four years (2001-02 to 2004-05), or the post-reform period, the performance is very poor as compared to any pre-reform period.

Prices of Agricultural Commodities

Stability in prices of agricultural commodities is very important for the survival of cultivation. Though it is not profitable but not slaughters the lives of farmers. One hand low productivity is a severe problem on other hand there is no guarantee to get feasible price for their sweat. The price received by the farmers is relatively very low compared with the prices they pay for consumer goods.

The aggregate price index grew at an annual rate of 4.83 per cent per annum between the periods 1991-92 to 2004-05. The prices of all the coarse cereals have grown at less than 4 per cent per annum. While the price of maize, which is an important crop in the drought prone areas of the state, grew at 3.99 per cent, the shortfall in the relative price was more than 12 per cent. The growth rate in prices of pulses was higher than the average of all the commodities while the price of rice has grown at a rate lower than the average of all the commodities. The growth in prices of cotton, sesame and groundnut was observed to be relatively lower than that of other agricultural commodities.

Trade liberalization with respect to agriculture has led to destabilization in some crops in A.P. The two major crops after rice viz., groundnut and cotton are known to have suffered in the state because of trade liberalization. The import duty on cotton has been reduced to almost zero, thus depressing cotton prices. Similarly, the import of palm oil has affected the profitability of groundnut in Andhra Pradesh.

High Indebtedness

'Farmers in India are born in debt growing in debt and dying in debt'. This quotation is said to be a mirror image of socio economic conditions in India. In A.P also the same condition is prevailed. Indebtedness is the rigorous problem on the face of rural economy. The amount of loan outstanding per farmer is Rs.24000 which is nearly double the all-India figure. The position of the small farmer is the worst among all classes of farmers, and the outstanding loan is Rs. 33000 per farmer in the state as against Rs. 14000 at the national level. Since most of the loans are borrowed from private moneylenders and traders, the implicit rate of interest is very high.

Inadequate expansion of formal credit facilities and poor access to these has made the farmers, especially small and marginal ones, to resort to informal credit agencies. An NSSO survey reveals that about 68.6 per cent of the total loans taken by farmers in Andhra Pradesh are from the informal credit market. This is much higher than the corresponding figure at the national level as well as in other south Indian states.

Decelerated Capital Formation

The trend rate of growth in Gross Fixed Capital Formation (GFCF) in agriculture in Andhra Pradesh shows that the growth rate in the state slipped from a high value of 6.9 per cent during the 1980s to 1.1 percent in the 1990s whereas at the national level it recovered from negative growth during the 1980s. In A.P., the growth rates of both public and private investment have declined. The growth rate of public investment declined from 7.6 to 3.9 and that of private investment declined from 5.2 per cent in 1980s to (-) 1.7 per cent in 1990s. The available data shows that the state experienced a decline in capital formation in agriculture in the post reform period, even in absolute terms, basically on account of a decline in capital formation by the private sector, at a time when there was a significant increase in private sector capital formation in this sector for the country as a whole.

Agrarian Distress and Farmers Subside:

The distress in the agrarian economy in A.P has been since 1990s. The state has become suicide zone with high number of suicides in the country next to Maharastra. As noted above, there was a sharp fall down in the growth rate of agricultural output since the 1990s as compared to the 1980s. The growth rate of investment in agriculture slashed down from 6 percent in the 1980s to just 1.5 percent per annum in the 1990s. There has been a systematic decline in the budgetary expenditure on agriculture and allied activities in the name of fiscal constraint. Research and extension have been neglected. Government investment in agricultural research and education in the state was lower than for the other three southern states and was just around half the all-India figure (0.49 percent or center and states together). Public expenditure on extension, which is borne by the state government, declined in absolute terms in the nineties. It was only 0.02 percent of the state's GSDP during 1992-94, as against the all-India average of 0.15 percent.

The agricultural crisis and farmers' suicides were mainly due to inadequate agricultural services, including extension, reliable seed supply, quality pesticides, machinery, proper soil survey testing, soil conservation, market information and market intelligence. The failure of extension services, the mushrooming of spurious seed and pesticide companies, and the relegation of the Agricultural University and the Andhra Pradesh Seeds Corporation to an insignificant role in the research, development and propagation of seeds of non-food crops, are all the consequences of deliberate policy changes in the state. There was also an attempt to privatize extension services.

Irrigation, a critical infrastructure for agriculture in the state, had also suffered. A decline in public surface irrigation (canal and tanks) resulted in the emergence of private groundwater as the single largest source with all the attendant ecological problems. Lack of access to institutional credit is another problem for farmers, particularly small and marginal farmers. Farm gate prices of most agricultural commodities fall steeply at harvest time. It is known that many poor farmers sell their output at harvest time because of their poor retention capacity.

In addition, farmers are opting for high value crops like cotton, face serious problems of spurious and unregulated seed supply, undue reliance on disproportionate use of pesticides due to lack of proper extension information, and face high risks of losing the entire crop. The other high cost risk is the investment made in wells and tube-wells, which often fail because of overexploitation of groundwater or lack of recharge of groundwater due to prolonged drought conditions.

According to a source there were 16,770 farmers' suicides between 1997 and 2005 in the state. According to a judicial commission appointed by the State Government, between May 14, 2004 and November 10, 2005 alone 1068 farmers had committed suicide.

By and large the incidence of suicides has been higher among small-marginal farmers moving from subsistence agriculture to the high value crops with a strong motivation to improve their social and economic status. With a few exceptions, the majority belong to Backward Communities or Scheduled Castes or Scheduled Tribes. The major cause reported by most of the victims' households is accumulated debt for digging or deepening of wells and repeated crop losses or the failure of the bore-wells. Inadequate credit availability from institutional sources had forced them to resort to informal credit sources.

The number suicides of farmers that published in various news papers were collected. It reveals that the total number of suicides of farmers happened in the year 1998 was 253. This figure in 1999 was 63 and 169 in 2,000. This number has increased to 196 in 2001 whereas it was decreased to 169 in 2002. From 2003, the number of suicides reached 206 with drastic increase. By 2004 it was reached to 1709.

During the said period, Telangana region was the main victim of farmer suicides where it was accounted for 1699 suicides. Coastal region accounts for 451 lives in total whereas Rayalaseema region alone was accounted for 556 suicides. The Telangana was in the first place with 62.79 per cent. Rayalaseema was in the second place with 20.55 per cent and Coastal was stand in last place with 16.67 per cent farmer suicides. Nearly 75 per cent of the farmers were taken their lives due to failure of cotton crop. Most of the suicides happened in Rayalaseema due to failure of groundnut crop. Anantapuram alone accounted for above 60 per cent farmers suicides. The costal belt was some what better compared with the rest of A.P. Among nine districts in Costal Andhra, Guntur district was the premier sufferer with 36.81 per cent suicides.

All this shows that state policy and actions which have no sensitivity to the regional specificities of agriculture, likely to put disproportionately high pressure on the livelihood of farmers in dry land areas where there is no canal irrigation but the entire burden of developing water resources through wells or bore-wells is on the shoulders of farmers. In addition, there has been rising pressure on farmers in terms of meeting their needs for basic social services like education and health which are increasingly privatized, and have become a significant component of household expenditure. A combination of these stress factors have been at the back of the crisis in the farming sector which has been manifested into widespread suicides, particularly since 1997.

Small-marginal farmers constitute almost 80 per cent of the farming communities in the country and many of them operate in dry and drought prone conditions and are the most vulnerable. It is the apathy of government that has been forcing these farmers to shoulder all the costs and risks of high investment, including land and water resource development with borrowed capital at usurious interest rates.

Section - III

Land Reforms and Downtrodden People

Many Legislative measures were initiated following Articles 38, 39 and 46 of the Constitution that made it obligatory for the states to promote the interests of Scheduled Castes and Scheduled Tribes and to protect them from social injustice and all forms of exploitation. Theses articles act as safeguards to poor people from concentrating land and factors of production at few people. State governments have accepted the policy of prohibiting the transfer of land from tribals to non-tribals and the restoration of alienated tribal lands to tribals. In 1977, the government of Andhra Pradesh enacted the Assigned Land Prohibition Act which ruled that land that had been 'assigned' by the government to the landless and tribals could not be resold and used for purposes other than agriculture. To improve women's access to land and landed property Andhra Pradesh along with Karnataka and Tamil Nadu amended the Hindu Succession Act, 1956, to legally protect the right of women to property including land.

As per data available, share in number of holdings and operated area of Scheduled Caste in Andhra Pradesh were 11 lakh 83 thousand and 10 lakh 82 thousand hectares respectively during 1990-91. In next four years of time (1990-91 to 1995-96) the number of holdings increased to 12 lakh 85 thousand and the operated area decreased to 10 lakh 66 thousand hectares. Further, by 2000-01, the number of land holdings and operated area increased to 13 lakh 67 thousand and 11 lakh 34 thousand hectares respectively. Though, there is a slight increase in operated area, this change may be due to increase in number of holdings. The average size of land holdings by S.Cs during 1995-96 was 0.83 hectares, still the same position is continuing.

Regarding to Scheduled Tribes, share in number of holdings and operated area was very interesting. There were 6 lakh 38 thousand landholdings and 10 lakh 45 thousand hectares of land in custody of S.Ts by 1990-91. It was increased to 7 lakh 54 thousand and 10 lakh 87 thousand hectares respectively. Further, it increased to 8 lakh 62 thousand and 11 lakh 86 thousand hectares respectively. However, this is not evenly increased where the increase in number of holdings is very less than that of operated area. This may be one of the reasons to slip down the average size of land holdings to 1.37 hectares from 1.44 hectares.

The picture of landholdings and share in operated area of S.C and S.Ts is shown below.

By analyzing the above table one can conclude that the landholding position of SC and S.Ts is not in good track, moreover, most of the marginal and small farmers are in this segment. The fruits of sixty years of independence not yet reached to so call downtrodden, exploited and broken families.

Group	Land Holdings(in Lakhs)			Operated Area (Lakhs of Hectares)		
	1990-91	1995-96	2000-01	1990-91	1995-96	2000-01
S.Cs	11.83 (12.7 %)	12.85 (12.1%)	13.67 (11.9%)	10.82 (7.5%)	10.66 (7.4%)	11.34 (7.9%)
S.Ts	6.38 (6.9 %)	7.54 (7.2%)	8.62 (7.5%)	10.45 (7.2%)	10.87 (7.3%)	11.86 (8.2%)
Others	74.68 (80.4%)	-	93.01 (80.6%)	123.33 (85.3%)	-	120.8 (83.9%)

Source: Directorate of Economics and Statistics (DES), Hyderabad.

Recommendations Made by Farmers Welfare Commission

The Commission on Farmers' Welfare has deliberated on the problem of the agrarian crisis in A.P. and held discussions with a large number of farmers during its field visits and has also consulted experts in various relevant fields. While the issues are complex and require detailed investigation of each area, they generally reflect structural conditions and especially the collapse of public institutions that affect farmers and farming. The Commission feels that solutions to the current crisis require interventions in six important areas, which would do the following:

- Correct spatial inequalities in access to irrigation and work towards sustainable water management;
- Bring all cultivators, including tenant farmers, into the ambit of institutional credit;
- Shift policies to focus on dry land farming through technology, extension, price and other incentives;
- Encourage cheaper and more sustainable input use, with greater public provision and regulation of private input supply and more research and extension support;
- Protect farmers from high volatility in output prices; emphasize rural economic diversification to more value-added activities and non-agricultural activities.

The commission on land reforms made the following three recommendations on land issues:

- There is a need to record and register actual cultivators including tenants and women cultivators, and provide passbooks to them, to ensure that they gain access to institutional credit and other inputs;
- The land rights of tribals in the agency areas must be protected; and
- Considerable scope exists for further land redistribution particularly when waste and cultivable lands are taken into account. In order to develop the lands, complementary inputs for cultivation (initial

land development, input mini kits, Credit, etc.) should be provided to all assignees. The future assignments of land should be in the name of women.

Conclusion

To attain golden age for the farming and turn into the reality that farmer is king, the misery and gloom of the farmers should be removed. It needs a strong political will. To make it possible, all of these problems have to be tackled at different levels and require intervention by various institutions over the short as well as medium term. The new role envisaged for the state government will require a substantial increase in public expenditure. Therefore, at least, public expenditure on agriculture and allied activities should reach 5 per cent of GSDP in the next budget. In addition to this, there is a need for further land reforms with strong political will. The spirit of land reforms not yet materialized in all the way. Finally, the political will have to translate them into government policy and on the ground-level implementation.

References

Human Development Report (2007), Government of Andhra Pradesh

Mahendra Dev and et.all (2007), "Poverty in Andhra Pradesh: Measurement, Identification and Policy imperatives", paper presented at Human Development, A.N. Sinha Institute of Social Studies and Asian Development Research Institute.

Vandana Shiva (2004), "The Suicides and Economy of Corporate Globalization".

Chadrasekhara Rao. N. (2004), "Suicides of Farmers and Cotton Cultivation in India", *Journal of Applied Economics,* ICFAI, September 2004.

T. Sri Ram Prasad (2006), 'Agrarian Distress- A Micro Study in Guntur District, A.P." *Research Thesis,* Nagarjuna University, Guntur, June 2006, pp. 57

M. Venkata Ramanaiah and et.all (2008), " Agrarian Suicides in India with a Special Reference to Andhra Pradesh", *Vision,* Vol.XXVIII.No.1

8

Area, Production and Productivity of Agriculture With Special Reference To Rice in Andhra Pradesh

D. Pulla Rao

Introduction

Agriculture is the largest sector of economic activity in India. The significance of agriculture in India arises also from the fact that the development in agriculture is an essential condition for the development of the national economy. It provides not only food and raw materials but also employment to a very large proportion of population. It is clear, that agriculture is the backbone of the Indian economy and prosperity of agriculture can also largely stand for the prosperity of the Indian economy. Agricultural growth has direct impact on poverty eradication. Agricultural growth is also an important factor in containing inflation, raising agricultural wages and for employment generation. But after independence our agriculture was in a hopeless and deplorable condition. Our farmers were in heavy debt to the private moneylenders. They were having small and scattered holdings. They had neither the money nor the knowledge to buy and use proper equipment, good seeds and chemical fertilizers. Most of our agriculture was dependent upon rainfall and upon the vagaries of the monsoons. Productivity of land as well as of labour had been declining and was at a very low level. In spite of the fact that nearly 70 per cent of our working population was engaged in cultivation, the country was not self-sufficient in food grains. Rapid growth of agriculture is, therefore, essential to achieve the multi-pronged objectives of the Indian planning system. These include self-reliance at the national level, food security to individual households, equitable distribution of income and wealth, rapid reduction of poverty levels, absorbing the growing labour force, facilitating export growth, to achieve balance of payments equilibrium in the economy, and so on.

Agriculture and Economic Development

There are different views regarding the role of agriculture in economic development. According to some economists, if economic development begins with agriculture it cannot lead to a self sustained growth due to the following reasons: (1). There will not be sufficient capital formation. (2). It will not create the necessary climate for industrialization, and (3). It cannot generate forces of expansion.

According to Nurkse, economic development consists in transferring population from agriculture to industries. But, some economists like Arthur Lewis do not completely agree with this view. According to Lewis, in France, prior to 1944, industrialization was slow because agriculture was stagnant. Agricultural development is a necessary condition for economic development due to the following reasons:

1. Developing agriculture must first create the necessary conditions for industrialization.
2. Food grains for the growing population have to come from agriculture.
3. Raw materials for the industries have to come from agriculture.
4. Developing agriculture can create marketable surplus, which is necessary for economic development.

5. The capital- output ratio in agriculture is low and hence a low capital investment will bring large output.
6. The ratio of savings and investment can be increased if the rate of savings and investment are high in agriculture.
7. Foreign exchange is not very much necessary for agricultural development.
8. Agriculture contributes nearly 34 per cent to national income. Unless there is development in agriculture, per capita income cannot be increased, and
9. Imports are not very much necessary for agricultural development.

Therefore agricultural development should be given first priority in India. The neglect of agriculture in the second plan created several problems.

No economic reform will be successful without a steady growth in agriculture. It is estimated that if we want to achieve 5 per cent growth rate of the economy, the growth rate of agriculture should be at least 4 per cent. To achieve this growth rate in agriculture investment in the agricultural sector should be about 25 to 35 per cent of G.D.P. Thus, agricultural development is a precondition for economic development, especially in a predominantly agricultural country like India. If agriculture is not developed industrialization will be slow.

New Agricultural Strategy

The Government of India has taken several measures to increase agricultural production and productivity. These measures are responsible for the agricultural revolution called "The Green Revolution". Since the mid - 1960's the traditional agricultural practices are gradually being replaced by modern technology and farm practices in India. Initially, the new technology was tried in 1960-61 as a pilot project in seven districts.

The new agricultural strategy goes by the names of IADP and High Yielding Variety Programme (HYVP). The new agricultural strategy consists of (a). Introduction of new and high yielding varieties of improved seeds (b). Short duration crops and multiple cropping (c). Increased use of fertilizers and pesticides (d). Soil conservation methods (e). Extension of irrigational facilities (f). Adequate supply of agricultural credit and other inputs. (g). Using modern machinery and equipment (h). Increased provision of storage, marketing and processing facilities. (i). Institutional changes like land reforms (j). Development of infrastructural facilities, and (k). Agricultural price- support.

High Yielding Variety Seeds

The Green Revolution was mainly due to hybrid seeds, which raised agricultural yields. In Mexico, Prof. Norman Borlaug developed new varieties of wheat, which were high yielding, disease-resistant and early maturing during 1960. These varieties were imported and planted in selected regions in India, which have adequate irrigation facilities. The yield from these Mexican varieties of wheat was more than 25 to 100 per cent compared to the old varieties. Encouraged by the results the government launched a programme of developing hybrid seeds suitable to Indian conditions. The Indian Council of Agricultural Research, Punjab Agricultural University, G.B. Pant Agricultural University etc., developed new seeds. Production of improved and high-yielding variety of seeds was also encouraged in Central and State government farms. As a result, several high-yielding variety seeds are developed. Regarding wheat we have the Mexican varieties Lerma Rojo, Sonara-64, and hybrid varieties Kalyan, P.V.18, Sharbati sona, Pusa Lerma. In rice we have TN-1, I.R.-8, Timen-3, ADT-17, Jaya, Padma etc, for maize Vijay and for bajra H.B.-1.

Introduction of such high-yielding varieties requires adequate supply of water, fertilizes, pesticides, insecticides etc. Therefore, they have to be introduced in areas where there are adequate institutional facilities under a "Package Programme" which provides adequate supply of fertilizers, pesticides and insecticides. Areas, which are under Intensive Agricultural Area Programme (IAAP) and other areas, which are suitable are selected for introducing High yielding

Varieties Programme (HYVP). In addition to the High Yielding Variety Programme (HYVP) the Government has taken several steps to increase agricultural production and remove the bottlenecks in agricultural progress. It has adopted a new agricultural strategy. The other aspects include short duration crops, multiple cropping, farm machinery, extension of irrigation, price support, processing, storage and marketing facilities, improved credit facilities, institutional changes, production of supplementary food products etc.

Thus, the new Agricultural strategy, which has led to revolutionary changes in agriculture, has broken agricultural stagnation in India and resulted in higher productivity that lead to higher production. The Green Revolution is a technological break through in Indian agriculture.

Andhra Pradesh is an important agricultural state of the country and it mirrors Indian agricultural sector because it has all types of soils and crops available elsewhere in the country. Andhra Pradesh accounts for 8.34 per cent of country's geographical area, for 7.37 per cent of India's population. The state accounts for 7.54 per cent of country's net sown area and 7.42 per cent of India's food grain production. 62.3 per cent of the state's population depends on agriculture (at national level it is 56.2 per cent). Similarly, the share of Agriculture to state GDP is 28.6 per cent which is higher than All India level (24.0%). The state is one of the largest producer of rice in India and leading producer of cash crops like ground nut, tobacco, turmeric, cotton, sugarcane, oil seeds, mango, grapes, banana, papaya and guava. In fact the state was called the granary of Southern India a decade back. But in the recent years decelerating agricultural growth becoming cause of concern. Added to this, agriculture is exposed to global competition, climatic variation, market fluctuations and declining public investment and shrinking resources base in agricultural sector during past two decades. If this scenario continues further, it will have severe adverse effect on states's overall economic growth rate in the era of liberalisation and economic reforms and there will be social imbalances also.

With this background in view, there is an urgent need for reforming present agricultural extension system by encouraging innovations in technology dissemination, involvement of private sector in agricultural extension, group approach, gender concerns, IT support to extension, market linkages, multi agency extension strategies and convergence of line departments.

With these new approaches under Extension Reforms Scheme introduced by Government of India, there will be definite impact on agricultural sector in Andhra Pradesh. These reforms can accelerate agricultural growth rate to 5-6 per cent every year, making it more productive, competitive, and sustainable rise to global standards in agricultural produce for exports.

An attempt is made in the present paper to analyse the trends in the area of cultivable land, production and productivity of agricultural production with special reference to rice in Andhra Pradesh. The study is confined to five decades i.e., from 1956-57 to 2005-06. The entire study period is divided into two phases. Phase I is before Green Revolution related to 1956-57 and 1965-66. Phase II is after Green Revolution related to 1978-79, 1987-88 and 2005-06. In order to estimate the growth of important food grain production by area, crop wise production and yield, the annual compound growth rates were calculated for each crop for both the periods separately and also to the total period. And also we estimated the annual compound growth rates of production and productivity of rice as a whole from 1956-57 to 2005-06 and also estimated the annual compound growth rates of productivity of rice / hectare by district in the state for a period of two decades i.e., from 1985-86 to 2005-06.

Area under Important Crops in Andhra Pradesh

There has been a rise in the size of the cultivable area in Andhra Pradesh. In 1956-57 the total amount of cultivable land for total food grains was 89.1 lakh hectares and it decreased to 71.7 lakh hectares in 2005-06. The annual compound growth rate of cultivable land for total food grains in Phase I is -0.11

Table 1
Area under Important Crops in Andhra Pradesh

(In lakh hectares)

Crop	Phase I (Before Green Revolution) 1956-57	1965-66	Annual Compound Growth Rate 1956-57 to 1965-66)	Phase II (After Green Revolution) 1978-79	1987-88	2005-06	Annual Compound Growth Rate (1978-79 to 2005-06	Annual Compound Growth Rate (1956-57 to 2005-06)
Total Food Grains	89.1	88.2	-0.11	96.5	75.7	71.7	-1.09	-0.44
Rice	29.3	31.4	0.77	39.8	32.1	39.8	0.0	0.63
Jowar	25.1	24.5	-0.27	23.4	17.3	4.4	-6.0	-3.49
Maize	1.9	2.2	1.64	3.2	3.0	7.6	3.26	2.87
Red gram	1.6	1.8	1.32	2.1	3.4	4.9	3.19	2.31
Green gram	3.7	4.5	2.19	5.2	4.9	3.8	-1.15	0.05
Black gram	1.2	1.4	1.73	2.3	3.9	4.2	2.26	2.59
Ground nut	13.4	12.4	-0.86	12.8	19.1	18.8	1.43	0.69
Castor	3.4	2.7	-2.53	2.5	3.1	3.4	1.14	0.0
Sugarcane	0.8	1.4	6.42	1.6	1.8	4.3	3.73	3.49
Chillies	1.8	1.4	-2.75	1.5	1.7	1.7	0.46	-0.12
Cotton	4.0	2.8	-3.89	3.8	5.7	10.3	3.76	1.95

Source: Directorate of Economics and Statistics Government of Andhra Pradesh, Hyderabad.

and Phase II is -1.09 and it is -0.44 for the total study period. The annual compound growth rate of cultivable land for rice, maize, red gram, green gram, black gram and sugarcane registered positive while jowar, ground nut, castor, chillies and cotton registered negative growth in Phase I. And in Phase II, the annual compound growth rate of cultivable land registered positive except for jowar, green gram which registered negative growth (Table-1).

Production of Important Crops

Food grain production occupies the most dominant position in agriculture. Since beginning of the Green Revolution in the mid 1960s, the State has shown quite impressive growth in food grain production except 1987-88. With the population growing and accelerating income growth, demand for food is continuously growing in the State. The food grain production has also been increasing rapidly over the years in the state of Andhra Pradesh. The annual compound growth rate of the production of rice, maize, red gram, black gram and sugarcane registered positive while that of jowar, green gram, ground nut, castor, chillies and cotton registered negative in Phase I. And in Phase II, the annual compound growth rate of all crops has shown positive except in the case of Jowar (Table-2).

Productivity (yield) of Important Crops in Andhra Pradesh

Yield of important crops / hectare of net sown area also increased substantially except Ground nut and Sugar cane during our study period. As shown in Table - 3 the annual compound growth rate of yield for all crops decreased in the Phase I except for rice, maize and red gram. The annual compound growth rates of yield for all crops increased in Phase II except for the ground nut. And in the total study period, the annual compound growth rate of yield has increased except in the case of ground nut and sugar cane.

Table 2
Production of Important Crops in Andhra Pradesh

(Lakh tonnes)

	Phase I (Before Green Revolution)			*Phase II (After Green Revolution)*				
Crop	*1956-57*	*1965-66*	*Annual Compound Growth Rate (1956-57 to 1965-66)*	*1978-79*	*1987-88*	*2005-06*	*Annual Compound Growth Rate (1978-79 to 2005-06)*	*Annual Compound Growth Rate (1956-57 to 2005-06)*
Total Food Grains	58.9	61.0	0.39	106.7	99.0	169.5	1.73	2.18
Rice	34.1	39.6	1.68	74.3	71	117	1.69	2.55
Jowar	11.1	10.1	-1.04	14.2	11.5	5.9	-3.20	-1.28
Maize	1.1	1.8	5.62	3.6	5.3	30.9	8.29	7.04
Red gram	0.4	0.7	6.42	0.4	0.5	3.0	7.75	4.19
Green gram	0.7	0.6	-1.69	1.5	2.3	1.6	0.24	1.70
Black gram	0.3	0.4	3.25	0.9	3.0	2.5	3.86	4.42
Ground nut	12.3	6.3	-7.16	11.6	19.1	13.7	0.62	0.22
Castor	0.7	0.4	-6.03	0.4	0.7	1.4	4.75	1.42
Sugarcane	6.1	10.6	6.33	10.1	9.5	18.6	2.29	2.30
Chillies	1.2	0.8	-4.41	2	2.5	5.4	3.75	3.12
Cotton	1.3	0.8	-5.25	3.3	5.4	21.1	7.11	5.85

Source: Directorate of Economics and Statistics, Government of Andhra Pradesh, .Hyderabad.

Table 3
Productivity (kg/ha) of Important Crops in Andhra Pradesh

	Phase I (Before Green Revolution)			*Phase II (After Green Revolution)*				
Crop	*1956-57*	*1965-66*	*Annual Compound Growth Rate (1956-57 to 1965-66)*	*1978-79*	*1987-88*	*2005-06*	*Annual Compound Growth Rate (1978-79 to 2005-06)*	*Annual Compound Growth Rate (1956-57 to 2005-06)*
Rice	1164	1262	0.90	1907	2258	2939	1.61	1.90
Jowar	445	414	-0.79	605	662	1324	2.94	2.25
Maize	559	853	4.8	1141	1756	4073	4.83	4.14
Red gram	274	370	3.39	217	135	608	3.89	1.64
Green gram	181	135	-3.21	289	460	429	1.47	1.78
Black gram	250	217	-1.56	429	771	593	1.21	1.78
Ground nut	923	512	-6.34	909	997	728	-0.82	-0.48
Castor	190	145	-2.96	172	233	407	3.24	1.57
Sugarcane	8185	8157	-0.04	7067	6902	8110	0.51	-0.02
Chillies	669	617	-0.89	1378	1475	3136	3.09	3.20
Cotton	56	53	-0.61	154	159	347	3.05	3.79

Source: Directorate of Economics and Statistics, Government of Andhra Pradesh, .Hyderabad.

Trends in the Area, Production and Productivity of Rice in Andhra Pradesh

Rice occupies the enviably prime place among the food crops cultivate around the world. It is grown in 147 million hectares with a production of 525 million tonnes. India has the largest area among the rice growing countries enjoying the second rank in rice production, the first one being China. India produces 109.5 million hectares with a productivity of 2.62 tonnes / hectare. Rice is the most important and staple food crop for more than two thirds of the population of India. The slogan 'Rice is Life' is most appropriate for India as this crop plays a vital role in our national food security and is a means of livelihood for millions of rural households. By increasing productivity, part of rice area can be made available to other crops. Therefore, efforts to enhance rice productivity must receive top priority. Andhra Pradesh - rice bowl of India is not at the top in productivity and hence the concern to enhance the same in this most important State. Andhra Pradesh has contributed many high yielding varieties like Swarna, BPT 5204, MTU 1010 etc., with high quality grain which have become popular at the national level and improved the economic status of the farming community. Intensity of rice crop is so high in some areas that it is often cultivated twice or thrice a year. For cultivation of rice moderate to high temperature is ideal. The minimum temperature should not be below 15^0 C as germination cannot take place below this temperature. Paddy is a rain loving plant. It needs plenty of water for its growth. The annual water requirement is nearly 175 to 300 cm. It can grow well in fertile river line alluvial soils, clayey loan soils in monsoon lands and in fact in all those fertile soils where there is plenty of water. Rice cultivation is labour intensive activity, which is apt for a State like Andhra Pradesh to fight the problem of unemployment.

Trends in the area, production and productivity of rice in Andhra Pradesh are shown in Table - 4. It is evident from the table that the area under rice cultivation in Andhra Pradesh increased from 29.27 lakh hectares in 1956-57 to 39.82 lakh hectares in 2005-06, i.e., at an annual compound growth rate of 0.63 per cent. Production of rice in Andhra Pradesh increased from 34.07 lakh tonnes in 1956-57 to 117.04 lakh tonnes in 2005-06 with the annual compound growth rate of 2.55 per cent. The peak level of rice production i.e., 117.04 lakh tonnes reached by the year 2005-06. The yield / hectare of rice in Andhra Pradesh increased from 1163 Kg in 1956-57 to 2939 KG in 2005-06, i.e., at an annual compound growth rate of 1.90 per cent. The peak level of 2978 Kg / hectare of yield for rice was reached in the year 2001-02 and later it decreased to 2939 Kg / hectare in 2005-06.

Table 4
Trends in the Area, Production and Yield of Rice in Andhra Pradesh

Year	*Area(In lakh hectares)*	*Production(lakh Tonnes)*	*Yield(Kg/ hectare)*
1956-57	29.27	34.07	1163
1961-62	33.92	45.15	1329
1966-67	33.23	44.15	1328
1971-72	30.41	47.17	1551
1976-77	35.65	49.3	1410
1981-82	38.24	78.68	2102
1986-87	34.59	65.91	1951
1991-92	39.36	92.49	2400
1996-97	41:1	106.86	2654
2001-02	38.25	113.9	2978
2005-06	39.82	117.04	2939
Annual Compound Growth Rate	0.63	2.55	1.9

Source: Directorate of Economics and Statistics, Government of Andhra Pradesh, .Hyderabad.

Productivity of Rice by District in Andhra Pradesh

Productivity of rice in the different districts of the state for the period of 1985-86, 1995-96 and 2005-06 is shown in Table–5. It is evident that productivity of rice varied from district to district, with the lowest level of 1434 Kg / hectare in Vizianagaram District to the highest level of 3702 Kg / hectare in Nellore District in 2005-06. There are also inter-district variations in the annual compound growth rates of productivity of rice in Andhra Pradesh. Among the 23 districts of the state, only 5 districts, i.e., Warangal, Adilabad, Rangareddy, Mahbubnagar and Medak have shown the highest annual compound growth rates in the State. Srikakulam and Vizianagaram districts experienced a significant decline in rice productivity. The annual compound growth rates of productivity of rice in Srikakulam and Vizianagaram Districts have shown negative values. Productivity of rice has shown considerable fluctuations in different districts of the State.

Table: 5
District-Wise Productivity of Rice in Andhra Pradesh

(Kg / hectare)

District	*1985-86*	*1995-96*	*2005-06*	*Annual Compound Growth Rate (1985-86 to 2005-06)*
Srikakulam	2219	1975	1785	-1.08
Vizianagaram	1773	2420	1434	-1.06
Visakhapatnam	954	1823	1490	2.25
East Godavari	2537	2924	2967	0.78
West Godavari	2693	2856	3057	0.64
Krishna	2668	2864	3080	0.72
Guntur	2859	3123	3135	0.46
Prakasam	2261	1780	3248	1.82
Nellore	2280	2597	3702	2.45
Chittoor	2184	2307	2794	1.23
Kadapa	2110	2942	2122	0.03
Anantapur	2255	2366	2608	0.73
Kurnool	2051	2569	3301	2.41
Mahbubnagar	1266	2134	2501	3.46
Rangareddy	1361	2319	2786	3.64
Medak	1520	2076	2900	3.28
Nizamabad	1907	2116	3384	2.90
Adilabad	1226	2122	2550	3.73
Karimnagar	2059	3096	3425	2.57
Warangal	1528	2402	3201	3.77
Khammam	1765	2409	2654	2.06
Nalgonda	2330	2931	3021	1.30
Andhra Pradesh	2264	2441	2939	1.31

Source: Government of Andhra Pradesh, Season and Crop Report, various issues.
Note: Hyderabad district is purely treated as urban district.

Conclusions

Agriculture is the largest sector of economic activity in India. The significance of agriculture in India arises also from the fact that the development in agriculture is an essential condition for the development of the national economy. It provides not only food and raw materials but also employment to a very large proportion of population. It is clear, that agriculture is the backbone of the Indian economy and prosperity of agriculture can also largely stand for the prosperity of the Indian economy. Majority of the people in India depend on agriculture sector directly or indirectly. Agriculture in the state of Andhra Pradesh is basically related to small farm cultivation. The cultivable area for total food grains has decreased from 89.1 lakh hectares to 71.7 lakh hectares in 2005-06, but the production of total food grains increased from 58.9 lakh tones to 169.5 tonnes in 2005-06.

Rice is the most important among the principal crops of the State of Andhra Pradesh. Production of rice in the state increased from 34.07 lakh tones in 1956-57 to 117.04 lakh tones in 2005-06 i.e., at an annual compound growth rate of 2.55 per cent. Increase in the productivity of rice contributed significantly to the substantial increase in the rice production in the State. However, instability in the productivity of rice is the main cause for the instability in the production of rice in Andhra Pradesh. There are inter-district variations in the productivity of rice in the State with the lowest level of 1434 Kg / hectare in Vizianagaram District and the highest level of 3702 Kg / hectare in Nellore District in 2005-06. Among all districts only five districts have shown the highest growth rates in the productivity of rice in the State. As productivity of rice play a very important role in increasing rice production in the state, immediate steps have to be taken by the Govt. to reduce the inter-district variations in the growth rates of the productivity of rice and the high degree of instability in the productivity of rice, which mainly arise due to the healthy dependence on erratic monsoons. Most of the cultivated land in Andhra Pradesh is still under dry farming because they do not have irrigated facilities. Construction of minor-irrigation projects, scientific and optimum use of available water resources in these areas, development of new methods of water utilization etc. are some of the steps required to extend green revolution to dry areas as well.

References

Bhalla, G.S. and Singh Gurmail. (2001), *Indian Agriculture-Four decades of Development*, Sage Publications, New Delhi.

Bilgrami, S.A.R. (2000), *An Introduction to Agricultural Economics*, Mumbai, Himalayan Publishing House.

Geetha Mohan (2005), Crop Diversification in Andhra Pradesh (A District-wise Analysis), *M.Phil Dissertation*. (Submitted to Andhra University), p.3 & p.87.

Government of Andhra Pradesh (1999), *Andhra Pradesh: Vision 2020*, State Secretariat, Hyderabad.

Government of Andhra Pradesh (2003-04): *Economic Survey*, Planning Department, A.P. Secretariat, Hyderabad.

Government of India. (2001), "National Agricultural Policy", *Yojana*, Vol. 45, No.1, 4-11.

Handbook of Statistics on Indian Economy (2001), Reserve Bank of India, Ministry of Agriculture, Government of India, New Delhi.

Hanumanta Rao, C.H. and S. Mahendra Dev (2003), "Economic Reforms and Challenges Ahead" (ed.) in Andhra Pradesh Development, Centre for Economic and Social Studies, Hyderabad.

Iqbal, C. (1979), "High Yielding Varieties of Seeds and their Impact on Agricultural Development", in A. Mohammad (ed.) *Dynamics of Agricultural Development in India*, Concept Publications, New Delhi, India, 71-80.

Mohammad, A. (1979), *Dynamics of Agricultural Development in India*, Concept Publications, New Delhi, India.

Rao. C.H.H. (2001), "Technological Change in Indian Agriculture: Emerging Trends and Perspectives", in K.S. Dhindsa and A.Sharma, (ed.), *Dynamics of Agricultural Development*, Concept Publications, New Delhi. Vol. 2, 31-49.

Singh, K.K., Khan, M. and Shekhawat, M.S. (2000), "Green Revolution - How Green it is?" , *Yojana,* Vol. 44, No. 6, 26-28.

Subrahmanyam, S. (2003), "Agricultural Growth: Regional Disparities: Causes and Remedies", in C.H. Hanumanta Rao and S. Mahendradev (eds), *Andhra Pradesh Development: Economic Reforms and Policies Ahead,* C E S S, Hyderabad.

Tilak, J.B.G. (1993), "Education and Agricultural Productivity in Asia: A Review", *Indian Journal of Agricultural Economics,* Vol.48, No. 2, 187-200.

9

Progress of Foodgrains Production In Andhra Pradesh: An Analysis of Post Reform Period

A. Vamsi Krushna, S. Marulu Reddy, K. Kiran

Introduction

Agriculture is the largest sector of economic activity and has a crucial role to play in the country's economic development by providing food and raw materials. In fact, development of agriculture is virtual precondition of sectoral diversification and hence of development itself. Agricultural production has two components namely food grains and non-food grains. The former contributes approximately two-thirds of total agricultural production.

Of all the food articles, food grain constitutes the most significant part of the Indian diet. Nearby 60 per cent of an average Indian's food expenditure gets spent on food grains. The demand for food grains in India, as in most developing countries is increasing rapidly, because of population growth and rising income. As per estimates of Paroda, there is a need to double the food production so agricultural production would hence, be primarily focused on food grains.

Globalisation and Changing Cropping Patterns

New economic policy initiated by the Government of India in 1991 has the following components such as: (a) liberalization (b) privatization (c) globalization. Among them, globalization extends its area of influence vastly encompassing all the spheres of agriculture. The European Commission defined globalization as "the process by which markets and productions in different countries are becoming increasingly interdependent due to the dynamics of trade in goods and services, flows of capital, and technology".

Cropping patterns are determined in large measure by agro-climatic factors. Generally, agro-climatic factors are fairly stable over time, while demographic, social and economic factors are less. Thus, while agro-climatic factors determine the conditions under which crops are grown, farmers are increasingly inclined to change cropping patterns in response to changes in economic factors, technological factors, institutional factors and policy-induced factors.

In the 1970s and 1980s the policy of food self-sufficiency was pursued vigorously, and incentives were provided to the food grains production. During that period area under commercial crops stagnated. But soon this phase was over and from the mid 1970s gradual increase in the area under commercial crops began. With the globalization of the economy, and the agriculture playing an important part in exports, incentive for rising commercial crops also improved.

In the crop composition a major change has taken place due to globalization. Within the crops sector three major changes have taken place. (1) The share of non-food crops has increased in terms of area devoted to as well as value generated from these crops. (2) Among the non-food grains, other food crops i.e., sugar, oilseeds, spices and condiments and fruits and vegetables etc., are acquiring greater importance. They are now occupying a larger part of the cultivated area and account for larger share in value of agricultural production. (3) The third important change has taken place in the share of so-called superior cereals among the food grains such as rice, wheat.

The reason for concentrating on food grains is that major technological breakthroughs, so far, have taken place only in the case of food grains, an exception has been cotton. The relative importance of food grains will increase because of the acceptance of food self-sufficiency as an important goal of agricultural development.

The present study was undertaken to analyze the growth pace in food grain production in Andhra Pradesh during the period 1990-91 to 2004-05 with the objectives of:

Objectives

(1) To study the growth of area of major food crops.

(2) To examine the trends in the production of major food crops.

(3) To analyze the trends in the yield of major food crops.

Methodology

The study is based on the secondary data for the periods of 1990-91 to 2004-05. The data are collected from the Centre for Monitoring Indian Economy (CMIE) special bulletin on Agriculture, March, 2006.

To analyze the trends in the growth of area, production and yield of major food crops in the state during the study period exponential growth rates were estimated. The following exponential function is fitted for the time series data.

$$Y_t = AB^t$$

Results

During the study period the trends in the area, production and yield of Arfhar, Bajra, Gram, Jowar, Maize, Ragi, Rice, Wheat, Food Grains both Kharif and Rabi Food Grains are observed.

For all the crops above mentioned the total cultivated area of them are shown in Table-1. From the Table-1 it is clearly understand that the cultivated area of Arhar, Gram, and Maize shows an increasing trend, and the remaining crops witnessed decreasing trend.

Table 1

Cultivated Area of Selected Food Crops During the Period 1990-91 to 2004-05

('000 hectares)

Year	*Rice*	*Jowar*	*Bajra*	*Maize*	*Ragi*	*Wheat*	*Gram*	*Arhar*	*Food-grains*	*Kharif Food grins*	*Rabi Food-grains*
1990-91	4035.9	1190.2	231.4	309.4	164.1	10.0	88.4	345.7	7761.8	5363.0	2398.8
1991-92	3936.1	1066.7	192.0	317.4	145.8	8.2	64.0	339.0	7431.4	5148.5	2282.9
1992-93	3604.1	1051.9	170.8	321.9	144.7	10.0	60.0	313.5	7001.7	4652.5	2349.1
1993-94	3546.8	1053.2	143.2	304.0	140.3	11.1	88.7	306.7	6870.9	4365.7	2509.3
1994-95	3638.0	944.4	137.3	320.6	129.9	11.0	168.2	298.9	6879.3	4246.7	2631.6
1995-96	3692.1	887.6	133.3	333.1	126.8	10.7	112.9	327.8	6893.7	4369.6	2524.1
1996-97	4109.0	852.7	132.4	360.7	119.9	12.5	105.5	359.3	7309.0	4630.9	2678.0
1997-98	3500.3	788.8	95.60	395.9	97.7	11.0	146.8	318.8	6520.5	3988.7	2531.8
1998-99	4316.0	752.0	127.0	399.0	103.2	12.0	146.0	394.0	7370.2	4603.0	2767.1
1999-00	4014.2	735.9	116.6	452.1	96.8	13.5	163.0	432.2	7138.0	4682.2	2455.8
2000-01	4243.0	677.0	143.0	528.0	99.2	14.3	201.0	513.5	7673.9	5077.0	2596.9
2001-02	3824.7	639.3	92.00	429.0	82.0	14.0	285.2	419.8	7056.1	4158.5	2897.6
2002-03	2822.1	623.8	87.00	525.6	71.3	11.0	390.1	431.6	6288.9	3892.9	2396.0
2003-04	2974.6	648.0	138.00	721.0	78.0	11.9	422.0	520.7	6807.0	4303.0	2504.0
2004-05	3086.0	500.0	94.00	657.0	69.0	9.0	341.0	480.0	6266.0	3991.0	2275.0

Source: Centre for Monitoring Indian Economy (CMIE), March, 2006.

As this study is mainly focused on food grains the cultivated area under food grains witnessed a decreasing trend. The area under food grains has decreased from 7761.8 thousand hectares in 1990-91 to 6266.0 thousand hectares in 2004-05.

The productions of above listed crops are presented in Table-2. An increasing trend was observed for Maize, Gram, Arhar, Total food grains and Rabi food grains.

The Yield or Productivity of selected food crops were shown in Table-3. It is very interesting to notice that except wheat all the crops witnessed an increasing trend during the study period.

The exponential percentage growth rate estimated for the selected crops have been shown in Table-4. In the case of cultivated area and production similar results were obtained. The highest growth rate was noticed for Gram, (12.9% &17.4%) followed by Maize, (5.79% & 8.7%) and Arhar (3.5% & 7.3%). And the lowest growth rate was observed for Ragi, (-6% & -5.4%) followed by Jowar, (-5.4% & -2.4%) and Bajra (-4.8% & -0.2%).

In the case of Yield highest growth rate was noticed for Gram (4.4%) followed by Arhar, (3.7%) Jowar (2.9%) and Maize (2.9%). As in the case of yield Wheat (-1.2%) is the only crop having a negative growth rate during the study period.

Conclusions and Suggestions

As per the study, the cultivated area under food grains declined from 7761.8 hectares in 1990-91 to 6266.0 thousand hectares in 2004-05. It is accounted for a negative growth rate of -0.007. Production increased slightly from 12329.6 thousand tones to 13394.0 thousand tones and yield increased marginally from 1588 to 2138 during the same period. In absolute terms production and yield indicators witnessed an increasing trend. But when we observed the growth rates during the study period they are as 0.011 for production and 0.018 for yield.

Table 2
Production of Selected Food Crops During the Period 1990-91 to 2004-05

('000 tns)

Year	Rice	Jowar	Bajra	Maize	Ragi	Wheat	Gram	Arhar	Food-grains	Kharif Food grins	Rabi Food-grains
1990-91	9654.0	851.2	167.7	645.6	191.3	9.0	56.9	73.8	12329.6	8593.8	3735.8
1991-92	9246.4	665.5	135.2	635.2	152.2	6.8	47.0	119.3	11705.5	8154.8	3550.6
1992-93	8792.2	908.7	128.6	856.1	159.6	7.6	28.1	74.7	11658.1	8022.3	3635.8
1993-94	9561.9	872.2	110.6	776.5	163.3	5.9	64.8	104.3	12253.5	8032.6	4221.0
1994-95	9276.7	642.1	107.1	858.5	171.4	8.4	136.1	98.8	11783.4	7473.2	4310.2
1995-96	9014.2	648.6	127.2	876.8	148.0	7.8	71.1	101.0	11666.7	7549.3	4117.4
1996-97	10686.1	626.8	122.1	1189.8	148.0	8.9	89.7	138.2	13681.6	8522.1	5159.4
1997-98	8510.0	514.9	66.7	1083.5	89.5	6.0	58.4	57.0	10822.1	6573.7	4248.4
1998-99	11878.0	523.0	119.0	1383.0	122.2	6.0	130.0	170.0	14905.4	8898.9	6007.2
1999-00	10637.8	535.7	97.4	1472.7	110.6	9.1	95.1	154.8	13696.2	9022.6	4673.6
2000-01	12458.0	619.0	149.0	1581.0	120.2	8.1	230.0	219.2	16027.8	10334.6	5693.2
2001-02	11389.8	634.1	714.0	1459.0	103.0	9.0	363.1	188.3	14836.6	8303.4	6533.2
2002-03	7326.8	607.5	57.5	1485.7	76.9	14.9	381.8	150.4	10655.5	6653.3	4002.2
2003-04	8952.8	742.0	148.0	2477.0	101.0	6.7	457.0	217.9	13697.0	8649.0	5048.0
2004-05	9601.0	516.0	81.0	2064.0	87.0	5.0	345.0	219.0	13394.0	8397.0	4997.0

Source: Centre for Monitoring Indian Economy (CMIE), March, 2006.

Table 3
Yield of Various Food Crops During the Period 1990-91 to 2004-05

(Kg/ha)

Year	Rice	Jowar	Bajra	Maize	Ragi	Wheat	Gram	Arhar	Food-grains	Kharif Food grins	Rabi Food-grains
1990-91	2392	715	725	2087	1166	900	644	214	1588	1602	1557
1991-92	2349	624	704	2001	1044	824	734	352	1575	1584	1555
1992-93	2440	864	753	2660	1103	764	469	238	1665	1724	1548
1993-94	2696	828	772	2554	1164	534	730	340	1783	1840	1682
1994-95	2550	680	780	2678	1320	764	809	330	1713	1760	1638
1995-96	2442	731	954	2632	1167	729	630	308	1692	1728	1631
1996-97	2601	735	922	3299	1234	715	850	385	1872	1840	1927
1997-98	2431	653	698	2737	916	546	398	179	1660	1648	1678
1998-99	2752	696	937	3466	1184	500	890	432	2022	1933	2171
1999-00	2650	728	836	3258	1143	670	584	358	1919	1927	1903
2000-01	2936	914	1042	2994	1212	570	1144	427	2089	2036	2192
2001-02	2978	992	772	3401	1256	643	1273	449	2103	1997	2255
2002-03	2596	974	661	2826	1079	1349	979	348	1694	1709	1670
2003-04	3010	1145	1072	3436	1295	565	1083	418	2012	2010	2016
2004-05	3111	1032	862	3142	1261	556	1012	456	2138	2104	2196

Source: Centre for Monitoring Indian Economy (CMIE), March, 2006.

Table 4
Exponential Method Results

Crop/Values	Area					
	a	B	*Sig T*	R^2	F	*Growth Rate (%)*
Arhar	285.72	0.03	0.0001	0.70	30.92	3.5
Bajra	192.83	-0.04	0.0005	0.61	20.73	-4.8
Foodgrains	7426.81	-0.07	0.053	0.25	4.52	-7.32
Gram	54.59	0.12	0.000	0.86	80.90	12.9
Jowar	1241.22	-0.05	0.000	0.96	388.64	-5.4
KharifFoodgrains	4958.36	-0.01	0.020	0.34	6.92	-1.2
Maize	257.12	0.057	0.000	0.86	80.50	5.79
RabiFoodGrains	2457.77	0.002	0.507	0.03	0.46	0.2
Ragi	174.59	-0.06	0.000	0.95	311.67	-6.00
Rice	4082.35	-0.01	0.074	0.22	3.74	-1.3
Wheat	9.97	0.01	0.116	0.17	2.82	1.4

Contd.

Production						Yield					
a	*b*	*Sig T*	R^2	F	*Growth Rate (%)*	*a*	*b*	*Sig T*	R^2	F	*Growth Rate (%)*
71.34	0.07	0.0009	0.58	18.32	7.3	249.82	0.03	0.018	0.36	7.32	3.7
128.04	-0.002	0.945	0.00	0.004	-0.2	741.13	0.01	0.145	0.15	2.40	1.3
11678.23	0.01	0.124	0.17	2.69	1.1	1572.18	0.01	0.0006	0.60	19.93	1.8
29.81	0.17	0.000	0.78	48.18	17.4	546.12	0.04	0.018	0.35	7.19	4.4
789.05	-0.02	0.023	0.33	6.63	-2.4	635.75	0.02	0.002	0.51	13.61	2.9
7986.51	0.00	0.708	0.01	0.14	0.2	1610.59	0.01	0.001	0.57	17.91	1.5
575.12	0.08	0.000	0.92	158.14	8.7	2236.79	0.02	0.0005	0.61	20.77	2.9
3689.32	0.02	0.008	0.42	9.72	2.7	1501.03	0.02	0.0008	0.59	18.74	2.4
193.76	-0.05	0.000	0.77	43.59	-5.4	1109.84	0.00	0.296	0.08	1.18	0.6
9470.82	0.00	0.720	0.01	0.13	0.3	2320.10	0.01	0.0002	0.67	26.84	1.6
7.53	0.00	0.887	0.00	0.02	0.2	755.95	-0.01	0.443	0.04	0.62	-1.2

This situation is not good for the state having a large population. And also to meet the goal of food self-sufficiency as stated by the Government of India as well as the State Government increasing food grains production and yield with this momentum is not enough. To attain food self-sufficiency and to arrest the health obstacles such as malnutrition among children the Governments both at the Centre and State level must draw attention towards increasing food grains production by giving incentives to farmers who are cultivating food grains.

10

Impact of Five Year Plans on Rural Industries

V. Divya Thejomoorthy, I. Narendra Kumar

The Indian economy consists of a whole collection of farmers, factories, workshops, mines, shops, railways, offices, banks, schools, theatres, hospitals etc; which help to produce goods and services. The essential processes are functions of the Indian economy are: Production, consumption and growth. The Indian economy produces all types of goods and services; it enables people to consume these goods and services; and it grows and becomes richer. In the world there are all types of economics. The United States of America, England, Sweden, West Germany, Japan and other countries are highly developed and advanced countries. Their agriculture, Industry, mining etc, are very developed. Their land, labour and other resources are used in the best possible manner. Naturally, they produce very efficiently and provide their people with abundant goods and services. In other words, people in these countries have a high standard of living. The Indian economy consists of agriculture, animal husbandry, dairying, forestry and fisheries etc. These occupations are primary sector because they are the first and oldest of occupations known to man. In this sector, nature is dominant and powerful in production, man works with nature to produce goods. Under the secondary sector, we include small scale and large-scale manufacturing industries. Small-scale industries may be divided in to two types, namely, Small-Scale enterprises and cottage industries. These industries use very little of capital but give employment to more people.

Cottage industries are mainly household enterprises (like handloom, cotton and silk weakling) and employ little or no hired labour. India was once famous for its small-scale industries its cotton and silk goods were world famous. Handloom cloths, beedis, toys pottery etc., are made by thousands of people in their homes or is small workshops and factories. Agriculture has a dominant role in the Indian economy contributing nearly 36.86 percent of the national income, providing employment to about 70% of the working population and accounting for a sizable share of the country foreign exchange earnings. Agriculture provides the food grains to large population 85 crores of this country. Besides, it provides fodder of equally large cattle population.

Indian agriculture was in a depressed and deplorable condition. Farmers were generally in heavy debts to the profession of moneylenders and agriculturist moneylenders. Mostly agriculture was dependent upon rainfall and the vagaries of the monsoons. The productivity of land as well as of labour had been declining and was the lowest in the world.

The planning commission at the centre makes a comprehensive survey of the available human and economic resources in the country, determines the Socio-economic objectives to be followed in the short period as well as in the long period and the growth potentialities of economy, the level of savings and investment in the country, the volume of resources that can be raised with in the country/ out side the country. In other words, through planning the government attempts to bring about growth with justice through the non-farm sectors consist of the occupation of dairy development, poultry, Fishery, Sheep rearing, Horticulture etc, and including different traditional occupations which come under the Rural Industries or under the IBS sectors (Integrated Small Industries Board).

Importance of Rural Industries

India is rich in mineral resources and Hydro-electric power. Many factories are being set up. They process products derived from farms, forests and mines. India possesses numerous textiles, mills, sugar factories and iron and steel plants. Machines and Transport equipment are also produced. Textiles, sugar, Vegetables oil, tobacco, paper and rubber are some of the industries depending upon agriculture. Iron and steel, ship building, automobile, air-crafts, fertilizers, cement, chemical, electronic and oil refining are some of the modern industries.Since times immemorial, village and small industries (VSI) have been playing on important role in the rural economy of India. In the past, village artisans and craftsmen contributed richly in terms of goods and support services for achieving a self-sufficient village economy.

India developed a system of specialized artisan's concentration throughout the country, where the entire village was a workshop and handloom and handicrafts, apart from other rural enterprises dominated the scene, occupied a pride of place in this production set-up. This system was later destroyed due to foreign rule and the industrial revolution in England. However, due to strong historical and cultural roots, a part of the giant rural industrial structure could survive and make a significant contribution to overall rural development. In the rural development strategy with focus on betterment of the weaker sections, a faster rate of rural industrialization becomes very crucial. Rural industrialization embraces different kinds of village and small industries. After attaining independence in 1947, the government of India realizing the importance of cottage industries, small scale industries and Ancillary industries as the chief means of livelihood for a large number of people and to provide economic security Indian economy rural industrialization embraces different kinds of "cottage industry", village industry and small scale industries. The terms cottage industries carried on in the house of workers where the scale of operation is small and there is but little organization and capable of supply only local needs. The important cottage industries are pottery, carpentry, basket malting, dairy, poultry, wooden toys, Ghani industries rope-weaving and rope making etc. The industrial Policy Statement laid before the parliament by the then union industries Minister, on the 23 rd December 1977 evolved another sector called "tiny sector" within the small-scale sector.

The new industrial policy statement made by the union Industries minister in July, 1980 laid emphasis on the need for rapid growth of small scale industry. In order to boost the development of small-scale industries, the government decided.

- To increase the limit of investment in the case of tiny units from Rs.1 lakh to 2 lakhs and below with a capital invest in plant and machinery, which are localized either in villages or in semi-urban areas.
- To increase the limit investment in the case of small-scale units from Rs. 10 lakhs to Rs. 20 lakhs and below with a capital investment in plant and machines, power and certain modern techniques in the process of production.
- To increase the limit of investment in the case of ancillaries from Rs. 15 lakhs to Rs. 25 lakhs are classified as ancillary industries eg. rice mills, match industry, Soap works, stone crushing and certain engineering and chemical industries etc.

Rural Industrial Development Under Plans

The relative backwardens of industrial development in India may be Judged from the fact that, the industrial output in 1948-49 accounted for only about 6.6 percent of the total national income and that the total labour force engaged was only about 2.4 million. When the first five-year plant was implemented, the emphasis for industrial development in India was more on consumer good industries rather than on producer goods industries. To make good the deficiencies is various shores; high rate of industrial advancement has become necessary.

First Five Year Plan (April 1951-March 1956)

The year 1951 was a land mark in the history of the Indian economy since the era of planning stated form April, 1951. The first plan assigned priority to agriculture development. No big efforts were made for the industrialization. Nevertheless, emphasis was to set up basic industries which would provide power and irrigation potentialities. The plan also provided for the completion of the various industries already under implementation by the central and state governments. However, about Rs. 30 crores were allotted for the development of village small-scale industries and six All-India Boards were set up during the first plan period. These were

- The All-India Handloom Board set up in October, 1952.
- The All-India Handicraft Board Set up in November, 1952.
- The Silk Board set up in 1949 and reorganizes in 1952.
- The coir Board set up in July 1954.
- Small scale industries Board set up in November, 1954.
- All India khadi and Village Industries Board set up in 1953 and reorganized as an Autonomous commission in April 1957.

Second Five Year Plan (April 1956-March 1961)

The second Five-year plan accorded a high priority to industrialization and especially to the development of basic and heavy industries. In the light of the industrial policy Resolution of 1956 the pattern of industrial development during this plan was conceived is terms of the following priorities.

- Modernization and requirement of important national industries, which have already come into existence, such as jute, cotton textiles and sugar.
- Fuller utilization of existing installed capacity in industries where there are wide gap between capacity and production.

The whole of the proposed outlay on the Agro-based industries was intended for the development of rural industries such as paper, newsprint and security paper, sugar, cotton, Jute, woolen and silk yarn and cloth, yarn and staple fiber and others, the overall investment exceeded by 206.8 crores.

Third Five Year Plan (April 1961-March 1966)

The industrial plan for the period 1961-66 was envisaged to be governed by the over riding need to lay the foundations for rapid industrialization over the next 15 years if long term objectives in regard the national income and employment were to be attained.The emphasis to be attained to industrial programmes and projects in the third plan was in accordance to increased production from domestic industries of commodities required to meet essential needs like essential drugs, paper, cloth, sugar, vegetable oils and housing materials.

The Annual Plans (April 1966-March 1967)

The fourth five-year plan was to start on the 1st of April, 1966, soon after the completion of the third plan on the 31st of March, 1966. But because of many difficulties in financing the ambitious projects, aimed to be taken up during the plan, it was postponed becomes of the conflicts with China in 1962 and with Pakistan in 1965. As such, annual plans were adopted for three years-1966-67, 1967-68, 1968-69. This period was considered as plan holiday. During the annual plans, and outlay of Rs. 1449 crores was envisaged for the development of overall industries.

Fourth Plan (April 1969 March 1974)

The fourth plan forms an integral part of the 12 years perspective programme, i.e. up to 1980-81. The board approach to industrial development in the fourth plan is to rapid increase in non-form employment opportunities by increasing the tempo of industrialization. The fourth plan provided for a substantial step-up of investment on industrial and mineral programmes accounting to Rs. 3,050 crores in the public sector and Rs. 2,250 crores in the private and cooperative sectors.

Fifth Five Year Plan (April 1974-March 1979)

In January 1973, the planning commission issued a document "Approach to Fifth Five year plan" which has drawn pointed attention to the declining rate of growth in industrial production during the first three years of the fourth plan. The draft Fifth five year plan envisaged a total outlay of Rs. 53, 250 crores over the five year period 1974-79. The plan envisaged an average rate of growth of 5.5 percent in Cross-National product. The national development council approved the revised Fifth plan, on the 24th September, 1976, which envisaged a total outlay of Rs. 69, 303 crores as against the draft plan provision of 53,250 crores. An outlay of Rs. 307 crores of the investment spend on agro-based industries such as paper and newsprint, textiles during the Fifth plan. Under the Fifth plan (1974-79) the centrally sponsored 20 point programme initiated in the year July 1, 1975 and Distinct industries centres (Dics) programme launched in 1978 provides a focal points at distinct level and national level for promotion of handicrafts, handloom, tiny, small and village industries all facilities to grown and to update their technology.

Rolling Plans

With the coming of the Janata party into power in March 1977, there had been some rethinking on the pattern of planning in the country. This government thought that the adoption of the five-year plans was not in tune with the prevailing times. With a view to allow more flexibility in the planning framework in accordance with the changing times, the planning commission decided to switch over to "Rolling plans" on annual basis along with a long-term perspective plan. Fixed five year planning systems has been in practice in India since 1951with the exception of three annual plans from 1966 to 1969, its working has yielded mixed results. It has resulted in economic growth and has built capital goods, technological transport and communication infrastructure basis. In the changed political atmosphere in the country, the then Janata government adopted the "Rolling Plan" system as a new approach within capacity for adjustment.

Sixth Five Year Plan (1980-1985)

The sixth plan main adjective in addition to the conventional strategies of aiming at optimum utilization of existing capacities and improvement of productivity, certain other elements of policy become necessary in the medium term perspective. The sixth plan envisages an average growth rate of 5 percent during the sixth plan period with the possibility of a higher growth of 5.3 percent per annum. Its total outlay is of Rs. 1, 72, 210 crores out of which Rs. 97, 500 crores is in the public sector and the remaining Rs. 74,710 crores is in private sector. An outlay of Rs. 1,05,800 will be the investment in Argo-based industries such as agricultural, forestry and logging, fishing, manufacturing, construction, Textiles, paper, and newsprint, sugar etc. during the sixth plan period.

Seventh Five-Year Plan (1985-1990)

Under the seventh plan (1985-1990) in respect of the centre and State and Union territories stands at Rs. 2, 752.74 crores, the target of the plan regarding employment generation for 400 lakhs persons by village and small scale industries. The target for exports was Rs. 7,443.90 crores by 1989-90 as against Rs. 4,557.56 crores on village and small-scale industries.

Eight Five Year Plan (1992-97)

Under the Eight Five-year plans (1990-95) the rural industries are renamed as village and small scale industries (VSI). Under the scheme of Integrated Infrastructure Development Centres (II DCs), infrastructure facilities are being developed in backward rural areas. During the plan under khadi village industries (KVI) the production of khadi cloths increased from 1.5 million square meters in 1995-96 to 125 square metrics in 1996-97; in monetary terms increased from Rs 3,504 crores in

1995-96 to Rs 4,120 crores in 1996-97. The employment through (KVI) sector increased from 57 lakhs persons in 1995-96 to 58 lakhs persons in 1996-97.

Ninth Five-Year Plan (1997-2002)

Under the Ninth Five year plan Integrated infrastructure development centres (IIDCs) would be extended to uncover areas and the target of the production for (VSI) has been kept at Rs. 7, 260 crores and provide employment to the extent of 23 lakhs more persons in the ninth plan. The coir industry receives due attention and the export of coir products is targeted at Rs 400 crores as against the worth of Rs. 215.58 crores in 1996.With the goal of strengthening export promotion of handicraft items, Non-government organizations (NGOs) and cooperative societies drafted for training purpose in this area. The special schemes have been identified for the benefit of SC and STs, special employment scheme for women have been initiated to provide employment excessively to woman.

Tenth Five Year Plan (2002-07)

Under the five-year plan (2002-07) with the liberalization and globalization of the economy and the removal of quantitative restrictions, the small units of the Agro & Rural industries of the khadi and village industry sector are facing stiff competition. A large portion of India's population live in the villages where illiteracy still prevails and large industry is not in a position to absorb the work force from rural areas. In view of this, it is necessary to create more employment opportunities in villages by utilizing local resources and skills so that rural people can get work in the villages itself. The main strategies of the khadi and village industries sector for the Tenth plan;

- To provide employment to rural people in villages.
- To produce saleable/marketable products.
- Creating self-reliance amongst people and building up of a strong rural community.

- More emphasis on "No loss" instead of "No Profit" by khadi and village industries organizations/ institutions.

The Agro & Rural Development of Khadi and Village Industries expenditure of outlay for the Tenth plan of Rs. 2,085 crores. In the areas of research and development (R&D), various sponsored projects were taken up and funded by the khadi and village industries commission (KVIC) from the science and Technology. The Jamanlal Bajaj central Research Institute (JBCRI), wardha, one of the prominent rural development institutes under KVIC, is in the Process of being revamped. It is proposed to upgrade JBCRI to the National Institute of Rural Industrialization (NIRI), involving an estimated expenditure of Rs. 8 crores. Some of the technologies developed by the R&D institutions under the KVIC are:

- High productive 6, 8 and 12 spindle all steel new model charkha (NMC).
- Production system for 500 and 600 counts muslin khadi.
- New shades of herbal dyes.
- Production of portable Ghani for vegetable oil extraction.
- Isolation and naturalising of bitter aspect from neem.
- Isolation of various components from sunflower cake.
- Development of LYMPO bricks from ash of rice husk and broken brick lumps.
- Formulation of new herbal formulations and herbal soaps.
- Development of bio-manure, bio pesticides and bio insecticides.
- Use of non-edible oils in soap formulations.
- Use of cashew nut liquid in rubber manufacturing.
- Use of different fibers in hand made paper.
- Decorticators for oil seeds and pulses.

- Development of paddy de-huskers and rice polishers
- Improvement of the potter wheel.
- Neera preservation.

CONCLUSION

When the Indian agricultural was backward and depressed, by the impact of five year plans the rural industries (include cottage industries, small scale industries) were more rapid development and accounting for a sizable share of Indian economy through foreign exchange earnings as well as provide employment for surplus of manpower of agriculture sector due to lack of opportunities for employment and income in rural areas, on the one hand, sure of employment, higher income and possibility to create urban facilities on the other hand. The rural industrialization has augmented the demand for additional food grains, milk, eggs, fish etc. The growth of rural industries such as dairy, poultry, rope making, Ghani industry have widened the market and increased demand has given a better price to the producers. The effort of planning commission has prepared the Five year plans and implemented in order to achieve the development of rapid increase in national income, rapid economic development and increase in employment, reduction of inequality of incomes and establishment of a Socialist society will naturally lead to the removal of poverty and misery and rise in the standard of living of the people in India.

11

Land Reforms and Agrarian Relations

G. Gangadhar Hugar

Agrarian Change, Gender and Land Rights

The past two decades have witnessed significant shifts in international development agendas and policies, marked by a resurgence of laissez-faire orthodoxies and a marked ambivalence, if not outright hostility, towards the developmental state. The debt crises of the early 1980s and the subsequent multilateral lending programmes provided a decisive opening for the international financial institutions to impose a neo-liberal agenda of fiscal restraint, open trade and capital accounts, and privatization on indebted developing countries.

Issues of agrarian change and rural development have been a palpable part of these policy shifts. The neoliberal attack on the post-World War Two consensus was built on a deep aversion to state-led import substituting industrialization, while agriculture featured as the centerpiece of the narrative, especially in national economies where agriculture formed a high proportion of GDP. Alleged "urban bias" was to be corrected by "getting prices right" for agriculture through various measures, such as exchange rate devaluation, abolishing export taxes, and reducing trade barriers, while tenure insecurity was to be tackled through land titling. These standard measures, it was argued, would restore agricultural export growth and improve rural incomes and livelihoods. At the same time, cutbacks in public expenditure outlays on agricultural input subsidies, marketing boards, and research and extension services (representing an inflow of resources into agriculture that was largely ignored by proponents of "urban bias") were prescribed and justified on the grounds that the benefits were either captured by big farmers or squandered by state officials. Ironically, these public expenditure outlays were eroded at a time when they were most needed-when developing countries were being urged to open up their economies to global agricultural markets by intensifying their export thrust and exposing themselves to imports from countries that often provide generous agricultural subsidies to their farming sectors.

In the 1980s, the gender critique of neoliberalism pointed to the ways in which the "reproductive" economy was ignored by stabilization and structural adjustment policies. The cutbacks in public expenditure and the deterioration in social programmes in many countries implicitly assumed an infinitely elastic supply of female labour that would compensate for the shortfalls in state-financed social services. In the 1990s, however, especially given the growing concerns about the lack of agricultural supply response in sub-Saharan Africa, attention has shifted to women's role in the sphere of agricultural production. Using neo-classical micro-economic analytical tools, it is being argued that gender inequalities in intra-household resource allocation are leading to "allocative inefficiencies" and a muted agricultural supply response. It is also being suggested that the absence of a market in land, and women's inadequate land rights in particular, are leading to inefficiencies in resource use. Despite its many weaknesses, this genre of analysis has been taken up by mainstream policy institutions because it fits well with the overall orthodox, neo-classical position on African agriculture.

The 1990s have also been a period of monumental political transformations. The collapse of authoritarian regimes in the Soviet Union and Eastern Europe, Latin America and sub-Saharan Africa, has given issues of rights and democracy a major impulse. The decades saw the growing size and influence of an international women's movement, linked through sub-regional, regional and international networks and able to collaborate on issues of policy and agenda setting. This has coincided with the revival of national women's movements, which in post-authoritarian settings in particular have found themselves in a position to press for political and legal reforms. An important component of these broader processes of democratization, have been political and institutional reforms such as decentralization, which have revived and strengthened the institutions of local governance. While in some countries this has brought more women into government structures, questions remain as to how local and indeed national, power relations feed into these local and community-based structures.

Inspired by these democratising impulses, a wide range of feminist groups and networks operating at national, regional and international levels, and influenced by the increasing use of rights language and instruments, have drawn attention to unequal land rights as an important mechanism through which female poverty and subordination is sustained and reproduced. Whether in the context of national debates on land tenure reform, rural social movement activism, or the political dynamics associated with decentralization and the competing claims over resources that this has given rise to, women's interests in land have emerged as a contested issue, often exposing tensions and divisions within civil society ranks. In some contexts, however, the debate has become polarized with one side pushing for women's unambiguous rights to land as a "good" policy intervention (because it is presumed to enhance their intra-household bargaining power irrespective of context), while the other side opposes women's land rights categorically because it is seen as the thin wedge that is being used by pro-liberalization lobbies to open up indigenous systems of land tenure to market forces and foreign commercial interests. This is a dangerous dichotomy, which precludes the kind of nuanced and contextualized analysis that is needed to identify situations where inadequate access to land constitutes a serious constraint on women's agricultural enterprises. Nor can it facilitate appropriated policy suggestions to enhance greater justice with respect to resource allocation for rural women-both as wives/daughters within male-dominated households and as members of vulnerable social classes and communities that face the risk of entitlement failure in the context of economic liberalization.

The contributions to this project critically reflect on the broad set of issues that have been raised in both the academic literature as well as in policy debates on the interface between gender and land. Different aspects of the gender and land question are explored by the research team. The analysis that they bring to bear on the subject is informed by different understandings of gender relations and the most important arenas within which those relations operate. Yet despite their crucial conceptual and methodological variations, and their different entry points, together they constitute a strong statement on the importance of taking the contextual specificities of the gender and land question seriously.

Gender and Social Policy

The past decade has witnessed a renewed interest in social policies, and some governments have increased social spending to soften the impacts of economic reform. These changes have come in the wake of widespread realization of the failure of the neoliberal economic model to generate economic growth and dynamism, and to eradicate poverty. At the same time, processed of political liberalization have opened spaces for social movements in many parts of the world to articulate demands for more effective social policies that mitigate the effects of market failures and reduce inequalities.

These contestations have coincided with a rediscovery of "the social" in the policy oriented literature, widely understood to embrace the cluster of social and political institutions, norms, and relationships that define the boundaries of market exchange, reduce transaction costs and enhance social and political stability. However despite the movement away from the standard neoliberal approach of the 1980s, and the increasing recognition given to institutions and the state, there is little agreement on a number of critical issues. These include the scope of social policy (universalism versus residualism and targeting); the appropriate interface between social and economic policy; the role of the state (not just as regulator but also as a provider of social welfare); and the values underpinning public policy, in particular core values of equality (and redistribution) which seem to have been displaced by the emphasis on poverty.

A gender perspective on social policies in the South, as in the North until quite recently, has remained on the margins of these debates. This project attempts to move the gender analytical framework closer to the centre of social policy thinking. From their different regional perspectives, the research papers prepared for the project map out the complex ways in which social policies are filtered through social institutions-families and communities; markets; care arrangement; health and education systems; the public sector-that are "bearers of gender". Attention to gender also reveals the extent to which inequalities (of class, gender and region) are being intensified as a consequence of shifts in the global economy, and processes of privatization and commercialization taking place within countries. Women's unpaid care work continues to form the bedrock on which social protection is subsidised, with erosions in state provisioning impacting most strongly on women. Despite women's increasing participation in paid work, labour markets continue to reproduce gender-based segmentations and inequalities in wages/income, work-related social benefits, and social security.

12

Eleventh Five Year Plan - A Vision for Faster and Inclusive Growth

K. Janardana Rao

The goals of social and economic policy are prescribed in the Directive Principles of the Constitution. The Five Year Plan represents the first attempt on the part of the Central Government and all the States to translate those principles into a national programme based upon the assessment of needs and resources. It is now the task of public administration to carry out this programme in cooperation with the people. India has entered the Eleventh Plan period with an impressive record of economic growth. After a modest performance in the 9th Plan period (1997-98 to 2001-02), when GDP grew at only 5.5% per annum, the economy accelerated in the Tenth Plan period (2002-03 to 2006-07) to record an average growth of 7.6%, the highest in any Plan period so far. Besides, there was acceleration even within the Tenth Plan period and the growth rate in the last 4 years of the Plan has averaged 8.6% making India one of the fastest growing economies in the world.

Brief History of Planning in India

The Planning Commission was set up by a Resolution of the Government of India in March 1950 in pursuance of declared objectives of the Government to promote a rapid rise in the standard of living of the people by efficient exploitation of the resources of the country, increasing production and offering opportunities to all for employment in the service of the community. The Planning Commission was charged with the responsibility of making assessment of all resources of the country, augmenting deficient resources, formulating plans for the most effective and balanced utilization of resources and determining priorities. Jawaharlal Nehru was the first Chairman of the Planning Commission.

In defining the objectives, priorities and techniques of planning in India, it is necessary to bear in mind the scale and dimensions of the problem as well as the basic values which must find expression in the economic and social pattern to be evolved. Maximum production, full employment, the attainment of economic equality and social justice which constitute the accepted objectives of planning under present-day conditions are not really so many different ideas but a series of related aims which the country must work for. None of these objectives can be pursued to the exclusion of others; a plan of development must place balanced emphasis on all of these. For instance, even the limited objective of increased production cannot be attained unless the wider objectives of social policy are constantly kept in mind and steadily pursued. On the other hand, equality and social justice will have little content unless the production potential of the community is substantially raised. Development, thus conceived, is a process which calls for effort and sacrifice on the part of the entire body of citizens. For such effort and sacrifice to come forth psychological conditions have to be created which provide an incentive for all to give of their best.

Eleventh Five Year Plan (2007-2012)

On the eve of the 11th Plan, our economy was in a much stronger position than it was a few years ago. After slowing down to an average growth rate of about 5.5% in the 9th Plan period (1997-98 to 2001-02), it has accelerated significantly in recent years. The average growth rate in the last four years of 10th Plan period (2003-04 to 2006-07) is likely to be a little over 8%, making the growth rate 7.2% for the entire 10th Plan period. Though, this is below the 10th Plan target of 8%, it is the highest growth rate achieved in any plan period. This performance reflects the strength of our economy and the dynamism of the private sector in many areas. Yet, it is also true that economic growth has failed to be sufficiently inclusive, particularly after the mid-1990s. Agriculture lost its growth momentum from that point on and subsequently entered a near crisis situation. Jobs in the organized sector have not increased despite faster growth. The percentage of our population below the poverty line is declining but only at a modest pace. Malnutrition levels also appear to be declining, but the magnitude of the problem continues to be very high. Far too many people still lack access to basic services such as health, education, clean drinking water and sanitation facilities without which they cannot claim their share in the benefits of growth. Women have increased their participation in the labour force as individuals, but continue to face discrimination and are subject to increasing violence, one stark example of which is the declining child sex ratio.

The 11th Plan provides an opportunity to restructure policies to achieve a new vision based on faster, more broad-based and inclusive growth. It is designed to reduce poverty and focus on bridging the various divides that continue to fragment our society. The 11th Plan aim is to put the economy on a sustainable growth trajectory with a growth rate of approximately 10 per cent by the end of the Plan period. It will create productive employment at a faster pace than before, and target robust agriculture growth at 4% per year. It seeks to reduce disparities across regions and communities by ensuring access to basic physical infrastructure as well as health and education services to all. It recognizes gender as a cross-cutting theme across all sectors and commit to respect and promote the rights of the common person. The first steps in this direction were initiated in the middle of the 10th Plan based on the National Common Minimum Programme adopted by the government. These steps were further strengthened and consolidated into a strategy for the 11th Plan.

Vision for the 11th Plan

- The central vision of the Eleventh Plan is to build on our strengths to trigger a development process which ensures broad based improvement in the quality of life of the people, especially the poor, SCs/STs, OBCs, minorities and women. The National Development Council, in approving the Approach to the Eleventh Plan, endorsed a target of 9 percent GDP growth for the country as a whole. This growth is to be achieved in an environment in which the economy is much more integrated into the global economy, an integration that has yielded many benefits but also poses many challenges. If this is achieved, it would mean that per capita GDP would grow at about 7.5 percent per year to double in 9 years. However the target is not just faster growth but also inclusive growth, i.e. a growth process which yields broad based benefits and ensures equality of opportunity for all.
- This broad vision of the Eleventh Plan includes several inter related components: rapid growth that reduces poverty and creates employment opportunities, access to essential services in health and education especially for the poor, equality of opportunity, empowerment through education and skill development, employment opportunities underpinned by the National Rural Employment Guarantee, environmental sustainability, recognition of women's agency and good governance.

Background to the 11th Plan

The Eleventh Plan was prepared on the basis of following directions/guidelines given to all Central Ministries/ Departments for the preparation of the plan proposals:

(i) Every Ministry/Deptt. should outline their "Core Plan" and sectoral priorities keeping in view the priorities and objectives outlined in National Common Minimum Programme (NCMP), so that the available resources could be used in the most judicious and economically efficient manner.

(ii) ZBB exercise for all schemes should be given utmost importance by every Central Ministry/Department. This is necessary to prevent a mismatch between the requirement of funds and the Plan allocations and to focus on achievement of desired physical target rather than financial allocation.

(iii) To improve the quality of implementation of development programmes, emphasiswas laid on converting financial outlays into outcomes. The target of intermediate output/outcome of the Plan programmes/schemes implemented by Ministry/Department may be worked out and assessment of the achievement of the targets with respect to quantifiable deliverables as given in the outcome budget may be provided.

(iv) Every Ministry/Deptt. should include the proposed/likely EAPs in its Annual Plan proposal, in order to integrate Externally Aided Projects (EAPs) and direct funded projects (i.e. outside the budgetary flows) with the planning process and the allocation of budgetary resources.

(v) In pursuance to Prime Minister's initiative for the North-Eastern region, all Central Ministries/Departments were required to earmark at last 10% of the budget for the North-East (except those specifically exempted).

(vi) There is a need to encourage public-private partnership in promoting infrastructure to leverage public funds, ensure better value of money and to improve the quality of service delivery, particularly, delivery of social services like health care, primary education, provision of quality transportation facilities in the form of roads, railroads, ports and airports and safe drinking water and sanitation.

(vii) In accordance to the recommendations of a High Powered Committee for improving administrative efficiency by using IT, all the Central Ministries/ Departments have to make a provision of 2-3 % of their Plan/Non-Plan for programmes/schemes relating to IT application, and to incur the expenditure exceeding 2-3 % of their budget (from plan and non-plan) for initiatives relating to furthering the use of Information Technology.

Major Challenges of the 11th Plan

The 11th Plan mainly focused on the following Challenges

(i) Agricultural Crisis: Regaining Agricultural Dynamism

(ii) Changing Employment Patterns

(iii) Providing Essential Public Service to the Poor.

(iv) Increasing Manufacturing Competitiveness

(v) Developing Human Resources

(vi) Protecting the Environment

(vii) Improving Rehabilitation and Resettlement Practices.

(viii) Improving Governance

Thrust Areas of Eleventh Five Year Plan

The Sector-wise thrust areas identified for Eleventh Plan are given below:

(i) *Education:* Quality upgradation in Primary Education, Expansion of Secondary Education, major emphasis on upgradation of Higher Education including Technical Education, ICT throughout education system.

(ii). *Health, Nutrition, Drinking Water & Sanitation:* Major upgradation of rural Health infrastructure, Medical

Education, Nutritional support to children and Pregnant & Lactating Women through ICDS, Health Insurance Base Urban Health, Health care for elderly; Achieving sustainability, improvement in service levels and moving towards universal access of safe and clean drinking water.

(iii) *Agriculture & Irrigation:* Ensuring Food Security, Supporting State specific agriculture strategy and programmes, Better seed production, Focused agricultural research, Extension, Development of modern markets.

(iv) *Rural Development, Land Resources & Panchayati Raj :* Universalization and improvement in programme delivery of NREGP; Integrated Watershed Management including management of underground water level.

(v) *Social Justice & Empowerment:* Special attention to the needs of SCs, STs and Minorities and other excluded groups through Pre-& Post metric scholarship, Hostel for Boys/girls, income and employment generation opportunities, multi-sectoral Development programmes for minority in Minority concentration Districts.

(vi) *Physical Infrastructure:* Emphasis on the Public Private Partnership in investment, Initiate policies to ensure time bound creation of world-class infrastructure, especially in remote and inaccessible rural areas and NE, Hinterland connectivity through improved rail & road infrastructure.

(vii) *Energy:* Electrification of all villages & extending free household connections to all 2.3 crore BPL households through RGGVY; Nuclear Power Development.

(viii) *Scientific Departments:* Development of satellite launch capabilities to GSLV-Mk-III; Development of New Energy Systems viz. Advance Heavy Water Reactor and Nanotechnology.

Growth Potential

The growth potential of the economy can be judged to some extent by the performance of the economy in the past and especially the performance in recent years. Table.1 presents the growth rates achieved in each Plan period since the First Five Year Plan.

It shows that the economy grew at 6.5% per year in the Eighth Plan period (1992- 1996) and then decelerated to 5.5% in the Ninth Plan period (1997-2001) but recovered sharply to achieve a growth rate of 7.6% in the Tenth Plan. The last four years of the Tenth Plan recorded an average of about 8.5% and this momentum has continued into 2007-08 which is the first year of the Eleventh Plan and is likely to record a growth of around 8.5% or even perhaps a little higher.

Table 1
Growth Performance in the Five Year Plans

(percentage)

Plan period	*Period*	*Target*	*Realization*
First Plan	1951-55	2.1	3.5
Second Plan	1956-60	4.5	4.2
Third Plan	1960-65	5.6	2.8
Annual Plan	1966-68	-	3.9
Fourth Plan	1969-73	5.7	3.2
Fifth Plan	1974-78	4.4	4.7
Annual Plan	1979-80	-	-5.2
Sixth Plan	1980-84	5.2	5.5
Seventh Plan	1985-89	5.0	5.6
Annual Plan	1990-91	-	3.4
Eighth Plan	1992-96	5.6	6.5
Ninth Plan	1997-2001	6.5	5.5
Tenth Plan	2002-2006	7.9	7.6
Eleventh Plan	2007-2011	9.0	–

Note: The growth targets for first three plans were set with respect to National Income. In the Fourth Plan it was Net Domestic Product. The actual growth rates are in terms of GDP at factor cost. Average growth rates over a short period can be misleading because of fluctuations in agricultural output due to variable monsoon.

Source: Eleventh Five Year Plan Document (2007-2012), Planning Commission

In this background, the 9% growth target for the Eleventh Plan period 2007-2011 approved by the NDC, which involved accelerating gradually from around 8.5% in the first year of the Plan to 10% by the end of the Plan period, appears entirely feasible, provided supportive policies are put in place. China has achieved growth rates exceeding 9% for two to three decades and while circumstances in India are not identical, the Indian economy has much strength and now looks well positioned to achieve this goal. The economy has been accelerating gradually for the past fifteen years and the further acceleration needed to achieve the Eleventh Plan target is only modest. If this target is achieved, it would mean that per capita GDP would grow at around 7.6% per annum during the Eleventh Plan period. Per capita consumption would grow by about 7 percent a year which would double per capita consumption in about 10 years. Further, if further growth is sufficiently inclusive, it will certainly provide an environment conducive to bringing about a broad based improvement in living standards. Accelerated growth will also boost tax collections in both the Centre and the States, allowing the public sector to finance the special programmes needed to ensure inclusiveness.

Allocation of Public Sector Resources-Centre and States

The projected assessment of resources of the public sector for the Eleventh Plan at Rs. 36,44,718 crore at 2006-07 prices comprises of the Center's share at Rs.21,56,571 crore and States/ UTs share at Rs.14,88,147 crore. The resources for the Central Plan includes the GBS component of Rs.10, 96,860 crore and the IEBR component of Rs.10,59,711 crore at 2006-07 prices.

The Eleventh Plan resources of the States and UTs are projected at Rs. 14,88,147 crore at 2006-07 prices, out of which States' Own Resources are Rs. 11,63,296 crore and the Central Assistance to States and UTs is Rs. 3,24,851 crore at 2006-07 prices. These allocations would be finalized in consultation with States. Table-2 indicates the resources and allocation of public sector resources for the Eleventh Plan.

Table 2
Public Sector Allocation for Eleventh Plan

(Rs. Crore at 2006-07 Prices)

Center	
Sources of Funding	*Allocation*
Budgetary Support	10,96,860
IEBR	10,59,711
Total-Centre (1+2)	21, 56, 571
States& UTs	
Sources of Funding	*Allocation*
State Own Resources	11,63, 296
Central Assistance to State/UT Plan	3,24,851
Total States & UTs(4+5)	14,88,147
Total Public Sector Outlay	
Grand Total (3+6)	36,44,718

Source: Eleventh Five Year Plan Document (2007-2012), Planning Commission

A comparison of the distribution of the total GBS in the Tenth and the Eleventh Plan has been shown in Table- 3, In comparison to the Tenth Plan realization, there is an increase of 125 percent in the projected GBS for the Centre for the Eleventh Plan. The Central Assistance to State/UT Plans for State sector programmes is about 85.6 percent higher than the grant component realized during the Tenth Plan. The share of projected grant component of the Central Assistance to States/UT plan in the total GBS for Eleventh Plan has decreased slightly from what has been realized in the Tenth Plan (from 26.4% to 22.8%) primarily because a much higher allocation has been made to the Centrally Sponsored Schemes. The allocation to Centrally Sponsored Schemes has increased from 1.40 % of GDP for the Tenth Plan to 2.35% of GDP in the Eleventh Plan.

The projection of GBS allocation to different sectors, Ministries/Departments and the support to State/UT Plan has been made in tune with the approach adopted for the Eleventh Plan for "faster, more broad-based and inclusive growth". The Eleventh Plan aims at putting the economy on a sustainable growth trajectory with a growth rate of 10% by the end of the Plan period by targeting robust growth in

Table 3
GBS Allocation in 10th and 11th Plan

(Rs. Crore at 2006-07 Prices)

	Tenth Plan Realization		*Eleventh Plan Projections*		
	Amount	*% Shares Total GBS*	*Amount*	*% Shares Total GBS*	*% increase over 10th Plan*
Central Sector	4,86,798	73.6	10,96,860	77.2	125.3
Support to State Plan*	1,75,021	26.4	3,24,851	22.8	85.6
Total	6,61,819	100	14,21,711	100	114.8

* Grant Component Only
Source: Eleventh Five Year Plan Document (2007-2012), Planning Commission

agriculture at 4% per year and by creating productive employment at a faster pace than before. The Eleventh Plan focuses on poverty reduction, ensuring access to basic physical infrastructure, health and education facilities to all while giving importance to bridging the regional /social/gender disparities and attending to the marginalized and the weaker Social Groups. Accordingly, a major structural shift across sectors has been proposed by allocating more resources to the priority areas identified for ensuring inclusiveness. A broad picture of the structural change in terms of sectoral allocation of resources has been shown in the Table 4.

Table 4
Sectoral Allocaion: 10th Plan and 11th Plan

(Rs. Crore at 2006-07 prices)

	Tenth Five Year Plan		*Eleventh Five Year Plan*	
Sectors	*BE#*	*% to Total*	*Projected Allocation*	*% to Total*
Education	62,461	7.68	2,74,228	19.29
RD, LR & PR	87,041	10.70	1,90,330	13.39
Health, FW & Ayush	45,771	5.62	1,23,900	8.71
Agriculture and irrigation	50,639	4.47	90,273	6.35
Social Justice	36,381	4.47	90,273	6.35
Physical Infrastructure	89,021	10.94	1,28,160	9.01
Scientific Development	29,823	3.66	66,580	4.68
Energy	47,226*	5.81	57,409	4.04
Total Priority Sector	4,48,403	55.10	1,052,436	74.03
Others	3,65,375	44.90	3,69,275	25.97
Total	8,13,778	100.00	14,21,711	100.00

X Plan BE represents the actual allocation during the five years and not the original X Plan Projections

* Includes APDRP grant component only

About 74 percent of the total central allocation for the Eleventh plan has been put aside for the priority sectors listed in Table-4, whereas, their share was only 55 percent in the Tenth Plan. It may be noted that the share of Infrastructure and Energy in the GBS allocation has fallen despite their being in the priority list. This is not a reflection of lack of priority but a reflection of a conscious policy to shift from public sector funding in these sectors to a strategy of increased IEBR and Public Private Partnership.

Budget Estimates for Various Schemes during 2008-09

The Eleventh Five year Plan has started on a robust growth. Significantly, the plan started with a first year (2007-08) growth rate of 8.7 per cent. The government believes second year of the plan (2008-09) as extremely critical to the success of the plan. As a result the budget allocations, 2008-09 have been made keeping in view the objectives and strategies outlined in the Approach Paper to the Eleventh Five Year Plan for faster and more inclusive growth. Accordingly, special attention has been paid to Agriculture, Education, Health, Women & Child Development, SC/ST/Minorities, Urban Development, Infrastructure (Irrigation, Road and Power), Science & Technology. In determining the allocations for the Central Sector, Planning Commission has also been guided by the needs of the ongoing Flagship programmes including Bharat Nirman. Emphasis on physical infrastructure, higher education and Science & Technology will expand the production base of the economy and enhance growth there by providing employment and generating resources. Emphasis on primary education, health and other basic essential services will ensure that the benefit of growth are evenly spread and will mitigate the perception of the masses of being excluded from the growth process. The eleventh plan is also focusing on rural employment Programmes like NREGP, SGRY with a special package for the second year of the plan. As a part of the realizeD vision of inclusive growth which was instigated in the Approach Paper of the Eleventh Five Year Plan, the government has allocated financial resources in the budget for the Annual Plan 2008-09, for the implantation of the various programmes and schemes. The allocation proposed for the ongoing flagship programmes for the Annual Plan 2008-09 in comparison to 2007-08 BE is given in the following Tables 5 & Table 6.

Education Sector

Education is the greatest equalizer as it enables the masses to participate in the growth process. Accordingly, the GBS for the Department of School Education & literacy has been raised

Table 5

Budgetary Estimates (BE) for 2007-08 and BE proposed for 2008-09 for Flagship Programmes

(Rs. Crore)

Name of the Scheme	*BE 2007-08*	*Allocation for 2008-09*	*% Increase over BE 2007-08*
Sarva Shiksha Abhiyan (SSA)	10671.00	13100.00	18.54
Mid Day Meal Scheme (MDM)	7324.00	8000.00	8.45
National Rural Employment Guarantee Programme (NREGP)	12000.00	16000.00	25.00
National Rural Health Mission (NRHM)	11010.00	12050.00	8.63
Total Sanitation Campaign (TSC)	1060.00	1200.00	11.67
Integrated Child Development Services (ICDS)	5293.00	6300.00	15.98
Jawaharlal Nehru National Urban Renewal Mission (JNNURM)	5500.00	6866.00	19.90
Bharat Nirman			
Rural Roads (PMGSY)	6500.00	7530.00	13.68
Rural Telecom Connectivity (USO Fund)	–	–	–
Rural Housing (IAY)	4040.00	5400.00	25.19
Rural Drinking Water (ARWSP)	6500.00	7300.00	10.96
Rural Electrification (RGGVY)	3983.00	5500.00	27.58
Irrigation (AIBP)	3580.00	5550.00	35.50

Source: Union Budget -2008-09

Table 6

(Rs. Crore)

Ministry/Department	*BE 2007-08*	*BE 2008-09*	*% increase*
Department of Atomic Energy (R&D Sector)	1215.00	5920.00	79.48
Department of Science and Technology	1526.00	1530.00	0.26
Department of Biotechnology	675.00	900.00	25.00
Department of Space	3420.00	3600.00	5.00
Department of Scientific and Industrial Research	1070.00	1200.00	10.83
Ministry of Earth Sciences	690.00	750.00	8.00
Department of Information Technology	1500.00	1952.00	23.16

Source: Union Budget -2008-09

by 22% to Rs.26,800 crore primarily to meet the requirements of Flagship programmes namely, Sarva Shiksha Abhiyan (SSA) & Mid Day Meal (MDM). Besides, the focus will be on bringing drastic reduction in dropouts and improving the quality of elementary education. The Approach Paper to the 11th Plan pays special attention to the needs and requirements of the SCs, STs and minorities and other excluded groups to bring them at par with the rest of society. Accordingly, the GBS for the Ministry of Social Justice & Empowerment, Ministry of Tribal Affairs and Ministry of Minority Affairs has been raised to Rs. 2,400 crore, Rs. 805 crore and Rs. 1,000 crore, respectively. Scholarships: Pre and post-matric scholarship programme announced in previous budget for SC, ST, OBC and Minorities. Scheduled Castes Rs. 804 crore, Scheduled Tribes Rs. 195 crore, OBCs Rs. 164 crore and Minorities 100 crore (post-matric) allocated for the year 2008-09.. Rajiv Gandhi National Fellowship Programme supporting SC, ST students pursuing M.Phil, Ph.D courses allocated Rs. 75 crore in 2008-09. The Ministry of Finance has provided Rs. 3, 966 crore for schemes benefiting SCs and STs exclusively and Rs. 18, 983 crore for schemes where at least 20 per cent of the benefits are earmarked for SCs and STs.

National Means-cum-Merit Scholarships: Rs. 750 crore allocated to build up a corpus of Rs. 3. 000 crore in four years. 1,00,000 scholarships to be awarded in the beginning of 2008-09.

Sarva Siksha Abhiyan provided 13,100 with the focus to shift from access and infrastructure at the primary level to enhancing retention and improving quality of learning. Mid day Meal Scheme has been provided 8000 crore; Rs. 4, 554 crore for secondary education.

Jawahar Navodaya Vidyalaya has provided an allocation of Rs. 130 crore in 2008-09 to establish Navodaya Vidydlaya in 20 districts having large concentration of SC ans STs.

Kasturiba Gandhi Balika Vidyalaya: As a part of SSA, funds provided for additional 410 Vidyalayas in educationally backward areas. Rs. 80 crore allocated to set up new or upgrade existing hostels attached to Balika Vidyalayas.

The Knowledge Services sector has emerged as a major growth engine in our economy. However, the severe skill constraints will limit our ability to gain and maintain competitive advantage in this area. Hence, Approach Paper to the 11th Plan has stressed upon the need to revamp our existing educational system focusing on "expansion, inclusion and excellence". Accordingly, the Plan outlay for the Department of Higher Education has been provided Rs. 7,600 crore.

The Oversight Committee on Reservation for OBCs (Moily Committee), based on the principle of "expansion, inclusion and excellence" has proposed 54% expansion in Central Universities, IIMs, IIT/NIT's and engineering / medical / agricultural institutions for providing 27% reservations to OBCs. Accordingly, the Ministry of Human Resource Development, Ministry of Health and Family Welfare, Department of Science & Technology and Department of Agricultural Research & Education have been provided Rs. 34, 400 crore, Rs. 16, 534 crore, Rs. 1, 530 crore and Rs. 1, 760 crore, respectively for implementing the recommendations of the Oversight Committee

Health Sector

The 11th Plan focusing on a comprehensive strategy for better health and ensure substantial improvement in health indicators such as maternal mortality, infant mortality, total fertility rate and anemia particularly among pregnant women. Accordingly, the plan outlay for Ministry of Health & Family Welfare has been raised by 13.4 % to Rs. 16,534 crore. It includes provision of Rs. 12,050 crore for National Rural Health Mission (NRHM). The National Rural Health Mission is the key instrument of intervention by the Central Government. The goal is to establish a full functional, community owned, decentralized health delivery system. 462, 000 Associated Social Health Activists (ASHAs) and link workers have been trained and are in place and 177, 924 Village Health and Sanitations Committes are well-designed. Accordingly, 323 district hospitals have been taken up for upgradation. NRHM is expected to address the gaps in the provision of effective health care to rural population with special focus on 18 states, which have weak public health indicators or weak infrastructure. It aims at effective integration of health concerns with determinants of health like safe drinking water, sanitation and nutrition through integrated District Plans for Health.

The plan allocation for Department of Women & Child Development has been raised by 19.5% to Rs. 7,200 crore with a view to making adequate provision for Integrated Child Development Scheme (ICDS) which is aimed at improving the nutritional and health status of the young children especially the girl child in the age group of 0-6 years and pregnant and lactating mothers. The budgetary allocation of Rs. 6, 300 crore for ICDS includes supplementary nutrition, and for training of ICDS functionaries and provision for launching of a new scheme "Rajiv Gandhi Scheme for Empowerment of Adolescent Girls" after merger of Kishori Shakti Yojana & Nutrition Programme for Adolescent Girls. For the first time a statement on child related schemes has been introduced in the budget. The total expenditure on scheme for child welfare would be of the order of Rs. 33, 434 crore. Rs. 11, 460 crore has been provided for 100 per cent women specific schemes and Rs. 16, 202 crore for schemes where at least 30 per cent is earmarked for women specific programmes.

The National AIDS Control Programme, has provided Rs. 993 crore for the year 2008-09. Studies have shown that the prevalence rate of HIV/ AIDS has come down from 0.9 per cent to 0.36 per cent which is a matter of some satisfaction. Significantly, Rashtriya Swastya Bhima Yojana scheme was instigated to provide health cover of Rs. 30,000 for every worker in the unorganized sector falling under below poverty line category and his/her family.

The National Programme for the Elderly to be started in 2008-09 with a plan outlay of Rs. 400 crore. Two National Institutes of Ageing, eight regional centers, and a department for geriatric medical care in one medical college/tertiary level hospital in each State to be established during the Eleventh Plan Period.

The main constraint in rapid growth is the inadequacy of infrastructure and its quality. Accordingly, the budgetary allocation of Rs. 5, 500 crore has been provided for Rajiv Gandhi Grameen Vidyutikaram Yojana (RGGVY). This is aimed at providing access to electricity in all un-electrified villages and connecting all BPL households. Plan outlay of RGGVY to be continued during the 11th Plan period with a capital subsidy of Rs. 28, 000 crore: Rs. 5, 500 crore allocated for 2008-09.

Central Assistance to States/UT Plans

GBS for State/UT Plan has been fixed at Rs.85, 477.87 crore which includes Rs.83, 708.28 crore for State Plans and Rs.1, 769.59 crore for UT Plans. Normal Central Assistance (NCA) has been increased from Rs.34, 135.31.10 crore in 2007-08 (BE) to Rs.63, 431.50 crore in 2008-09. The major ACA schemes, where enhancements are provided, are: Accelerated Irrigation Benefit Programme (AIBP) and other Water Resources Programme with a grant element of Rs.5, 550 crore and National Social Assistance Programme of Rs.3, 442.24 crore. Tsunami Rehabilitation Programme has been provided Rs. 876 crore which includes Rs.460 crore for State Plans.

Conclusion

It is projected that the eleventh Five Year Plan can achieve the targets of 9 per cent growth rate and the strategy for faster and inclusive growth, which was outlined in the approach paper of the Eleventh Five Year Plan presents alarming challenges and requires determined action by both the Centre and the States. Achieving these targets will not be an easy task, but it is definitely viable. The knowledge that the economy is in many ways better placed today rather than it has ever been should help us achieve such ambitious targets. It is indispensable to the centre and the state governments might strive hard for the accomplishment of 9 per cent growth rate and for the strategy of inclusive growth as well by end of the Eleventh Five Year Plan. It is said that the exclusion of human development is an impediment for the attainment of faster and inclusive growth. Although, the government has provided more resources for the development of education sector, health sector and for the welfare of the socially disadvantaged groups of SCs and STs in the first two years budget, that determination be required to carry on in the rest of the three years to realize the vision of faster and inclusive growth.

References

Planning Commission, Govt. of India, New Delhi

Approach Paper of Eleventh Five Year Plan (2007-2012), Planning Commission, Govt. of India, New Delhi, 2008

Eleventh Five Year Plan, Planning Commission. Govt. of India, New Delhi

Budget Speech of the Finance Minister (2008), Govt. of India, New Delhi, 29th Feb.

Union Budget (2008-09), Govt. of India

13

Economic Hardships and Social Denigration of Dalits of Ayodhya Lanka: A Case History

Jesurathnam Devarapalli

Introduction

The pluralistic nature of Indian society is attributed to high diversity in languages spoken, cultural patterns followed, dress and food habits, religions practices, ethnic identities, caste compartments / caskets and a lot many others. Though each one of these factors meticulously contributes to the group identities, but flexible enough so that, at will, one can opt for a change excepting caste. With regard to caste, its dividing spirit is altogether everlasting such that the individuals are segregated into closed compartments at the time of birth and are supposed to continue in it till death inspite of the life long effort to come out of it. More over caste extends its tentacles into every sphere of social life such that the other dividing forces like religion, ideology, value system etc, are not free from its impressions in India. In the efforts to understand social and economic conditions of lower castes, it is inevitable to make an inventory into the very nature of caste system.

Caste has a formidable organic structure which can be understood by analyzing its important characteristics features.

A number of anthropologists and sociologists have made attempts to underline these features in the functional roles of the caste. Risley (1915) has pointed out that endogamy and hereditary occupation as important characters of caste which are also agreed by Krober(1939), emphasizing upon the social esteem resulting in hierarchical ranking of such units. Upholding the above mentioned features, Bougle (1958) specified that repulsion or opposition between different castes is another inherent quality. Further more the social intercourse between upper and lower castes is restricted (Ghurye1969) though the services of the latter are much dearer to the former. By analogy caste can be viewed as a unit and as a system. As a unit it is a closed status group with restricted field of conjugal relations, occupational reservation, and social interaction. As a system it focuses on interrelated statuses, restrictions on change of membership, occupation, and commensal relations. The caste system fosters for economic interdependence and cooperation excluding the element of competition (Leach, 1960) bolstering the economic growth of the lower castes as they are outside the ambit of competition to uphold caste ideology and *varna dharma*. This indicate that the caste system provides for various functions necessary for social life ranging from education to menial kind and makes this provision under the religious dharma of *karma* (Hutton ,1963). And growth can never be expected without competition. The observation made by Dumont (1988), that caste status is ritually legitimized and the ritual norms encompass the norms of power and wealth whereby a few advanced in education and position among the lower castes still carry the caste stigma.

In this context a case study of Ayodhya lanka is presented which is inhabited by both the upper and the downtrodden castes along with the middle rung castes. It is found that the Dalits of the island suffer high degree of poverty, social denigration, and economic vulnerability. An ethno-historical approach is applied and followed while applying anthropological methods in this study so to document the state of socio-economic conditions of Dalits ever since their habitation on the island and the impact of upper caste dominated political decisions at the regional and state level. Here an attempt is made to document the kind of resources found on the island and the accessibility of various caste groups to them and impact of intervening caste stigma in the process.

Caste wise Population Distribution

Ayodhya lanka is a relatively large river island village with an area of 4.625sq.km having a population of 2768 persons with almost equal representation of males and females. The 556 households of the island are distributed over ten settlements. Kapu, Settibalija, Marakallu and Mala in the same hierarchical order, are the four major caste groups of the island and together constitute 98.20 per cent of the population (Table.1). Of the remaining population belonging to 13 households, seven of the households are of Mala Dasu and 3 are of Madiga. These two castes along with Mala are a part of untouchable castes in the traditional caste hierarchy commonly referred to as Panchamulu. The remaining three households are one each of Brahmin, Vysya and Rajulu caste, who are all immigrants. For all these people Telugu is the mother tongue which is the state language.

Table 1
Showing the Caste Wise Distribution of Population

Name of the Caste	*No. of Households*	*% of Household*	*Male*	*Female*	*Total*	*Percentage*
Kapu	157	28.24	383	375	758	27.39
Settibalija	135	24.28	319	350	669	24.17
Marakallu	110	19.78	290	278	568	20.52
Mala	141	25.36	363	360	723	26.12
Mala Dasu	7	1.26	11	14	25	0.90
Madiga	3	0.54	6	6	12	0.43
Vysya	1	0.18	4	2	6	0.22
Brahmin	1	0.18	4	0.18		
Rajulu	1	0.18	1	2	0.07	
Total	556	100.00	1381	1387	2768	100.00

In all, there are ten settlements distributed over the island under study. Of these even of the settlements viz.

Manikondavaripet, Pallipalem, Baddeveripet, Mattaparthi Musalaiah Pet, Gudalavaripalem, Pithalavari Pet and Agnikula Kshatriyula colony are clustered in the north eastern part of the island popularly referred to as Marrimula. These seven settlements and the remaining three viz., - Yatamvari kapu palem, Muppinavaripet and Merakapalem in the southern part of the island are interconnected by a *kaccha* road locally called as '*puntha*' with coconut groves and bushes on either side.

All the Kapu of the island stay in Kapupalem settlement which is the single largest settlement on the island and is the centre that controls the affairs of the panchayat and is the hub of village politics. The kapu settlement is fairly planned with rows of houses on either side of lanes. The houses of Kapu are built with spacious courtyards extending from 5 to 10 cents. The Settibalija, however, are distributed over six settlements among wherein three settlements viz., Marakaplaem, Gudalavaripalem and Mattaparthi Musalaiah pet they are the single largest group. In other three settlements they are in minority. The Marakallu reside in two settlements–Agnikula Kshatriyula colony and Pallepalem.. These two settlements are well planned with parallel streets. Earlier these fishermen used to live in two congested settlements. As these fishermen have no land ownership on the island, the government has purchased jiraithi land of an absentee landlord of rajulu caste and allotted a house plot of 5 cents to each nuclear family. The remaining four settlements are occupied by the Mala–Manikondavaripet mostly by Manikonda lineage. Baddevaripet and Pithalavaripet are the two other settlements situated on the western edge of the island in between Merakapalem and Kapupalem (Table. 2). Except in the kapu and marakallu settlements, the other settlements are crowded with overlapping houses for want of space.

Social Scenario

Of the nine castes inhabiting the island the top ranking caste in the local hierarchy is kapu by reason of its numerical strength, economic development, and political power. Though the Mala are also close to kapu in numbers economically and

Table 2
Showing the Population Distribution in Different Settlements

Name of the Settlement	*Kapu*	*Settibalija*	*Marakallu*	*Mala*	*Mala Dasu*	*Madiga*	*Vysya*	*Brahmin*	*Rajulu*	*Total*
Merakapalem	-	185	-	-	-	-	-	-	-	185
Muppinavari peta	-	-	-	180	-	-	-	-	-	180
Kapupalem	733	92	-	-	-	-	-	5	-	830
Agnikula Kshatriyulacolony	-	60	143	-	-	-	-	-	-	203
Peethalavari pet	-	21	-	66	-	-	-	-	-	87
Gudalavari palem	-	157	-	27	-	-	-	-	-	184
M.Musalayya pet	-	122	5	-	-	-	-	-	-	127
Beddevari peta	-	-	-	211	25	12	-	-	-	248
Palli palem	-	-	420	6	-	-	-	-	-	432
Manikodavari pet	-	-	-	203	-	-	-	-	-	203
Scattered in coconutGrove	25	32	-	30	-	-	-	-	2	89
Total	758	669	568	723	25	12	6	5	2	2768

politically they are lacking behind. In that sense sattibalija dominated the Mala with respect to local ranking following by Marakallu who claim a higher status than Mala and Maladasu. The lone vysya and Rajulu families though insignificant in the local affairs due to their recent entry, they enjoy the traditional respect among all the castes. But the lone Brahman, though not perform the sacredotal functions he commands respect and reputation from all section of the island population by reason of his medical services and automatically due to his ritual status. The Madiga who are numerically insignificant and economically poor are under counted by Mala, though Madiga, Mala and Mala Dasu together termed Panchamulu (Dalits) are lowly placed in the eyes of all other castes. The unity among the three Panchama castes is not to be seen at any level. The food taboos prevail among these three castes as it is common among any of the two castes on the island.

The island community has passed through undulating economic situations as far as the memory of the islanders goes in the recollection of ethno-history. Due to the non-availability of irrigation facilities and modern technology till 25 years back all the agriculture dependents had a tough time to eke daily bread and it is much worse with regard to the Dalits as they have no lands of their own. They have to go to mainland for wage labour as the island farmers could not engage all the landless. The labour was cheaply valued and the payments were delayed as to the convenience of the farmers. As such the plight of the Dalits was unimaginative. This led to the dislocation of many families of Dalits to mainland and never had they turned back. Till the field labour cooperative society movement (discussed in later section) came to the island the Dalits suffered hunger, ill health, humiliation, untouchability and illiteracy. Only after much struggle and confrontation the Dalits could get small fragments (even less than 0.5acre) of land which are not economically significant as it is not sufficient to support a nuclear family. Due to the over all changes taking place there is slight improvement, such as, there is not severe food shortage and younger generation is motivated towards education among Dalits. But the caste stigma still persists. At this juncture, be recalled an incident when the ferry man suddenly hurling abuses at a woman who at unawares touched him while boarding boat. On enquiry it was revealed that, that woman is a Dalit and by her touch the Marakadu ferry man got polluted.

The political power is exercised by the kapu whether or not Sarpanch is from their caste. Even the Mala Sarparnch works as per the tune of kapu leadership. Though no strict jajmani system prevails the Panchama still have clientele relationship of kapu. This tendency actually leads to the social denigration of the Panchama, that a kapu boy can address an old Panchama man or woman by name or even by derogatory terms.

Hinduism prevails on the island. The temples originally located in kapu settlement and all the major festivals are organized under the leadership kapu and even sattibalija cannot be active participants. This led to development of two other temples one in a sattibalija settlement and another in the lanka land of Settibalija. The beleaguered Panchama can find any respectable place in these religious activities and as such many of the Mala sought asylum under Christianity.

Resource Base and Economic Activities

In the words of White (1959:51) "some habitats are suitable for agriculture, a pastoral economy, or fishing, manufacturing etc. and others are not". Agriculture and fishing are the two major occupations on the island which are effectively supported by the two major resources of the island, viz, land and water. Agriculture is practiced by all caste groups on the island except Marakallu who subsist upon fishing alone. Literally kapu means 'Kayuvadu' (Who takes care of land) or farmer in other words. Most of the kapu basically subsist upon agriculture. They are the largest land holding group as 82.80 per cent of them own lands. Their individual acreage is also higher than other caste men. Then remaining 17.20 per cent of landless kapu work as agriculture labour or carry out jaggery and coconut business and a few look after coconut gardens of non-resident Rajulu (Kshatriya caste) for monthly salary with other fringe benefits. The onus of agriculture activities is solely carried out by kapu men as their women are tabooed to move out of their houses for work.

An old kapu man said "the kapu woman rather starve a week for food but would not go out for work". Inspite of this seclusion, the kapu women participate in secondary income generating activities at home. Except a few new daughters-in-law, almost every kapu women meticulously meddles with her needle and thread from day break till the sunset, making beautiful lace work which has great value in international markets. The lace traders from Palakollu visit the island supply the raw material–the thread and collect back the finished product. A few of the poor kapu women and girls make *'eenala chipurlu'* (brooms) out of the midribs of the coconut leaflets, which are purchased by the Daddipatla businessmen. They also make dung cakes which are used as fuel for cooking and, the excess are sold. Thus the kapu women though not involved in agriculture endeavour's, still generates income by undertaking various profit making activities at home.

Among the Settibalija 77 per cent of the households possess land. Among these, a great majority own land ranging from 0.5 acres to 4 acres. Only one Settibalija joint family own over 10 acres. Both men and women unlike kapu equally take part in agriculture activities. The landless Settibalija works as agriculture labour under the kapu, their own caste men or even under Mala during critical periods of agriculture operations. A few of the sattibalija boys work as *palerlu* (annual farm servants) under kapu. But kapu do not work as labourers under Settibalija and Mala.

Only eight of the sattibalija families follow their traditional occupation of toddy trapping which is only seasonal i.e. during flowering season of palmyra. The toddy trapper has a special type of equipment called *balla*, to climb stalk strips which encompasses shoulder and waist a sitting pad and a sickle case and hooks to hang the pots. He also carries a stout wooden pole on his shoulder called *'banda'* from which hangs the pot. This *'banda'* is coated with sand at one end to sharpen sickle. He also carries with him a narrow ladder of about 7 feet long to climb the palm to some height. The toddy trapper's wife accompanies him with a big earthen pot or an aluminum vessel and collects the toddy. She sells it at the palm itself or at home in the evening hours. In the ripe season a healthy palm can give about four tumblers (1 tumbler of about 100 ml capacity) of toddy.

Table 3
Showing the Land Holding Particulars of Different Caste Groups

	Landless Households		*Land owning Households*	
Caste	*Number*	*Percentage*	*Number*	*Percentage*
Kapu	27	17.20	130	82.80
Settibalija	31	22.97	104	77.03
Mala	53	37.59	88	62.41
Marakallu	106	96.36	4	3.64
Mala Dasu	7	100.00	-	-
Madiga	3	100.00	-	-
Vysya	1	100.00	-	-
Brahmin	1	100.00	-	-
Rajulu	1	100.00	-	-

During the rainy season the toddy tapers resort to agriculture since the palms either male or female doesn't bear inflorescence. But some toddy tapers spares for rainy season one or two female palms called *pandu thadi* which generally gives high yield of sap. Such trees gives toddy palms are owned by the kapu or the non resident Rajulu, planted to mark the boundaries of their fields. The toddy taper has to pay Rs.25/- per palm per year to the owner of the palm for giving usufruct rights. At the same time he has to pay Rs.15/- per palm to the government as manual tax. The president of the toddy tapers association collects the tax from the individual lessees and pay, it to the government. Evasion of this tax is a serious offence.

Among the males 37.58 per cent (i.e. 53 out of 141 households) do not own land. Among, the land owing households 28 possess less than half acre of land. The highest land holdings among malas are 3.5 acres owned by two households. The rest of the households possess land between 0.5 acres to 3 acres. This description shows how meager amount of land is in possession of each Mala family. As the out put on this amount of land is not sufficient to maintain the family through the year, all the Mala families irrespective of land owing and non land owing work as agriculture labourers under any caste group within the island and on the mainland. Many of the adolescent boys and even married men work as '*palerlu*' in the island under kapu and sattibalija. Broom making is common among sattibalija and Mala women and girls. Both Settibalija and Mala women work in fields as daily wage labourers. They take part in many agriculture activities like '*thavvu*' (turning soil upside down by spade before sowing), sowing, weeding, spraying fertilizers and pesticides, and harvesting except ploughing. Mala Dasu are the traditional priests to Mala who use to perform life crisis ceremonies for Mala. But now-a-days their services are not utilized and they have not acquired lands and as such eke their livelihood through daily wage. The three families of Madiga are the landless labour on the island, while two of the Madiga youth work as *palerlu* for a non-resident landlord. The lone Brahmin, Vysya and Rajulu are the recent emigrants to the island and all are landless. The Brahmin man is the unqualified medical man while the Vysya carry out their traditional occupation business (provisions shop). The Rajulu family guards the coconut grove of one the absentee landlord.

Though the island Marakallu live among with the farming communities they have developed neither skills nor interest in agriculture, like their caste men in the adjacent mainland villages. They solely subsist upon fishing round the year, except for four families who live by ferrying. When profitable catches are not possible around the island, a few of the fishermen migrate for short duration to Narasapurm or Antarvedi where the waters are deep providing plenty of fish. The Marakallu women sell the fish on island or in the shandy. There is a taboo on the participation of unmarried girls in fish marketing. The undisposed fish are dried and preserved which are again sold either on the island or in the nearby shandies. Thus optimum utilization of fish resources could be observed. None of the fishermen work as agriculture labourers, except a few of their women harvesting, when higher wages are paid.

Field Labour Cooperative Society Movement [FLCS]

The field Labour cooperative society movement which originated on the mainland has significant impact on the island community. This movement, though started under the British regime has suffered many twists at the hands of the upper caste dominated politics in free India and ultimately proved not to be an exclusive favour for Dalits. Our interest here is to examine how the changing land ownership rights influenced the socio-economic conditions of the island and especially the Dalits. In 1921 the Indian National Congress held a conference at Kakinada where historic decision was taken to broaden the base of the independence struggle for making it a mass movement by extending the activities to rural areas also. Sensing trouble the British Government wanted to counteract it. The discontentment brewing up among the downtrodden, especially the Harijans against the socio-economic humiliation suffered by them at the hands of the upper caste Hindus was seized upon by the then British Government. In the then existing conditions, majority of the lower caste groups, especially the Harijans did not own land or house without title deeds sites, inadequately paid for their services, enjoyed little freedom, occupied low status and often humiliated. The ranking of the individuals as superior and inferior on the basis of caste, categorization of castes on the basis of occupation were the social evils plaguing the Hindu society, often leading to social tensions and conflicts. The situation proved to be a fertile ground for the British to encash.

In its efforts to win the favour of Harijans and weaning them away from the independence struggle the British

Government initiated some important measures. Apart from enacting certain reformist legislations, it also extended certain measures which have visible, immediate material gains for the downtrodden. In the region of Konaseema comprising of Kothapet, Amalapuram and Razole taluks also called as Godavari central delta, house sites were allocated in almost all the villages. The most important measure is establishment of field labour cooperative societies for Harijans by allocating government waste lands both on the mainland and the islands, to improve their socio-economic status, indirectly inculcating cooperation and solidarity among them.

The first Harijan Field Labour Cooperative Society [HFLCS] was established during 1921-1922 at Kesavadasupalem-main and village in Razole taluk, which is about 20 km. away from Ayodhyalanka. The government allocated six hundred acres of land-part of it was lanka land near Kesavadasupalem and remaining on the sea coast. As a related measure the Madras Christian Cooperative Central Bank was established in 1923 to extend financial assistance to the Harijans under the aegis of HFLCS.

Just around that time the Communist Party of India entered the scene and extended its activities among the Harijans agricultural labourers in this region, fighting for their cause. A number of HFLCS came under their influence and control. By mid 1940s it had an impressive following among the landless groups. In the 1946 provincial elections its candidate narrowly lost to the rival congress party candidate. The rivalry between the congress and communist parties had their impact on HFLCS also. The banning of the Communist Party of India in 1949 in the region hardened the attitude of the congress party in power towards HFLCS, since they were dominated by communists. Some of these societies which were strong holds of the party were deprived of fresh leases on the banjara lands and the already existing leases were cancelled on one pretext or the other. In the year 1950 lease agreements of many of these societies were cancelled on the plea that they were not clearing their dues in time. Only a few could survive.

Simultaneously, at many places All Castes Field Labour Cooperative Societies [ACFLCS] were formed in the place of liquidated HFLCS and they also applied for land lease. Though the nomenclature indicates the heterogeneous nature that the field labourers from all castes could be members of these societies, majority of the members were non-Harijans. The party in power saw to it that a significant proportion of the land earlier held by HFLCS was now allotted to these new societies and also it was the best of the lands. Besides, some more blocks of lands which were not earlier leased out to the HFLCS but were auctioned to big landlords and others, were also now given to these rival societies [ACFLCS]. In subtle ways the HFLCS, were harassed and discriminated while ACFLCS, were showered with favours. Not only best of the lands were allocated to ACFLCS but also for long leases, unto 10 years. The inferior land was given to the few existing HFLCS that too for shorter durations of one year or two. It was also gathered that ACFCS, were given affiliation to the central cooperative bank which gave them financial assistance for cultivation while similar facilities were denied to the HFLCS, though they were also eligible for assistance. As much injustice was done to HFLCS, a Harijan politician interfered into the affair and pressurized the Government for a suitable action which could give greater security for the HFLCS. As a result the then existing HFLCS were converted into Joint Cooperative Forming Societies [JCFS] in 1963. These newly formed cooperative farming societies were headed by a special assistant commissioner and deputy registrar with other subordinate staff members for an effective functioning of the cooperatives. Similarly a reorganization of the 59 all caste FLCS into 60 collective cooperative farming societies [CCFS] took place in 1966 under the same administrative frame work of JCFS [Parthasarathy and Ramana 1975]. In course of time the JCFS and CCFS were termed as FLCS as they both were brought under the same administrative structure.

The ongoing agitation of the downtrodden communities in the adjacent mainland for socio-economic equality, the actions and counter actions of the National Congress and the then British Government, the rivalries between the congress government and the communist party of India, antagonisms and caste based favourtism among political leaders of the area had their echo on the lives of the islanders under study. The course of these events have disturbed the social environment and economic position of the islanders from time to time as could be understood from the following account.

Three Harijan field labour cooperative societies viz,. Nakkidilanka HFLCS, Baddevari HFLCS, and Nethalavari HFLCS had come into shape on Ayodhaya lanka also in mid 1920s. These three societies consisted of Malas of the island and also from nearby Puchallanka and Nakkidilanka. The lanka lands on the island viz., Subbadu lanka, and Baddevari lanka and on the east bank i.e. Raai lanka were assigned to these three HFLCS, respectively. The lands in the former in majority were waste non-arable lands with huge deposits of sand, uneven surface and wild vegetation, whereas the lands of Raai lanka were already under cultivation, leased out by the government to the Arimilli landlords. Due to the limited irrigation facilities, lack of capital investment, poor management, these HFLCS, especially the former two could not flourish. Along with those on the mainland, the three HFLCS of the island were also cancelled by 1948 (?) on the pretext of the long pending dues. The local Mala leaders connived with the kapu munsif and misappropriated the tax collections made from the cooperative societies, leading to their liquidation. The lanka lands held by these three HFLCS were then auctioned for lease and the Kapu were the successful bidders.

By that time the all caste FLCS movement had already gained momentum on the adjacent mainland under the aegis of the upper caste dominated congress party. This encouraged the Kapu on the island to come into a group and sought registration of their ACFLCS with the blessings of a prominent kapu congress leader of west Godavari district. Thus came into existence the Ayodhaya lanka ACFLCS dominated by Kapus. To justify the 'ALL CASTE' nomenclature two mala and one marakadu were drafted as members with the rest 97 being Kapu. Simultaneously the Settibalija of the island and the neighbouring hamlets came together and formed Puchallanka ACFLCS. The Puchallanka ACFLCS initially registered with 60 members of whom six were kapu, four Mala and the remaining Settibalija. This led to discontentment among rest of the Settibalija and quickly another 80 members were included with a total strength of 140. Finally, among the 130 Settibalija members of this ACFLCS, 110 are from Ayodhyalanka and 20 are from Puchallnaka.

The lanka lands of the three erstwhile HFLCS of the island, in between held by individual kapu through auction are now passed on to Ayodhyalanka ACFLCS and Puchallanka ACFLCS dominated by kapu and Settibalija respectively. Thus the Raai lanka and a portion of Baddevari lanka lands came to the share of kapu and part of the Subbadulanka and and the rest of Baddevari lanka into the hands of Settibalija initially. But in due course of time the hitherto vacant waste lands on the island and on the east bank were added to these two societies. Thus the Ayodhyalanka ACFLCS had 200 acres in all viz., Raai lanka -120 acres, Baddevarilamka -8 acres, Maddilamka -25 acres, Thummalanka -70 acres, Kamayya-garilanka -6 acres, Jillellagaruvu -12 acres, Buduthodulanka - 8 acres, Narapbadava -6 acres, Rajulanka/Dasu lanka- 8 acres. The 153 acres of Raailanka,Baddevarilanka /Rama Rao lanka and Maddilanka put together is distributed equally among the initial 100 members of Ayodhyalanka ACFLCS. Another 70 members who later joined this society were allotted 47 acres of land in the remaining 6 lankas.

Simultaneously the Puchallanka ACFLCS had lanka lands in eleven lankas viz., Subbadulanka- 90 acres, Baddevarilanka -12 acres, Suryaraolanka -10 acres, Thippalanka -8 acres, Jaggabbagadda -12 acres, Gangulabadava -20 acres, Bhrahmaiah lanka -3 acres, Burragadda-8 acres, Veerannalanka and Bulliswamilanka together-4 acres, and Gandralanka-12 acres. As the lands of Subbadulanka and Gandralanka are of good quality, there was intense competition among the members for a share on these lankas. As a result Subbadulanka is divided into bits of 70 cents each and so is the case with Gandralanka.

The Mala, in the process were deprived of land during the period between the cancellation of erstwhile HFLCS and the establishment of the restructured Marrimula and Nakkidilanka FLCS around 1995 with the active participation of the local Mala youth who mobilized their caste men........ All the members of these two FLCS are only Mala. Due to the late formation of these two societies, the best of the lands were already passed on to the other groups as described above. Only small patches of new land formation like Thippalanka, Garuvulanka and others came to their share. The Marrimula FLCS of 124 members got 22 acres, of Subbadu lanka and 23 acres, of Thippa/Kotha lanka. The Mala suffered misery during this interim period. Poverty and unemployment forced some of them to leave the island permanently.

During early 1970s when the government decided to give individual land Pattas to members of the FLCS the hopes of better future arose among the Mala. Though Mala resigned to the loss of prime lands to kapu and Settibalija originally held by them (through three HFLCS), the new policy announcement by the government fueled their dormant frustration over the loss of those lands into open and conflicts ensued. Armed clashes broke between the Mala and the kapu and between Mala and Settibalija over the issue of Raai lanka, Baddevarilanka and Subbadulanka during this period. The fight between Mala and kapu was suppressed with the intervention of the state using force and the issue was settled permanently in favour of the kapu under the influence of the kapu congress leader of the area. The clash between Mala and Settibalija was pacified by offering 22 acres of Subbadulanka to Mala. After the award of individual land pattas the FLCS lost their relevance. Thus the FLCS movement along with the changes in land ownership rights had brought important changes in the land use patter in Ayodhyalanka and social harmony.

Conclusion

Inspite of many changes taking place in Indian social system, including caste system, the scars left by the caste order are very reflective in perpetuating the socio-economic inequalities especially towards Dalit castes. Restriction on change of occupation has been weakened and occupational mobility has become feasible after industrialization of the country, particularly after the world wars (Ahuja1993). Even then the Dalits remain to be agriculture labour or found in low ranking and marginal income callings to a large extent. The FLCS movement clearly shows that how the lands assigned to HFLCS by the British were abolished by liquidating those cooperative societies with some pretext or other. The upper caste dominated state and local politics played a vital role in carving out ACFLCS which are having a nominal representation of the Dalits and passing on the cultivable lands to locally dominant upper caste kapu. When it came to the catering of the lands the Dalits dominated ACFLCS were assigned unproductive waste lands. As in the words of Mencher (1993)-" it is quite clear that the superior economic and political power of the upper castes have kept the lower castes suppressed......the system functioned to keep the people separated from one another in a situation in which they are not allowed to own land". The mere ownership of land could not solve the problem as the quality and quantum of land and availability of technology and investment are also equally important to raise the economic levels. The traditional caste dynamics of ritual purity, and occupational denigration, not by reason of profession carried but owing to the birth into a particular caste are still active to fix one's social status and thus historical caste stigma is visible

Reference

Ahuja, R.. 1993 *Indian social system*. Rawat Publication: New Delhi.

Bougle, C.1958. "The essence and reality of the caste system", *Contributions to Indian sociology. No.2.*

Dumont,L .1988 *Homo hierarchicus :The caste system and its implications*. Oxford University Press: Delhi.

Ghurye,G.S. 1969 *Caste and race in India*. Popular Prakashan: Bomby

Hutton, J.H. 1963 *Caste in India: Its nature, function, and origins*. Oxford University Press: Delhi.

Kroeber,A.L. 1939 'Caste' *in Encyclopaedia of social sciences.* London.Vol.3, pp 254-257.

Leach,E.R. 1960 *Aspects of caste in South India, Ceylon and North - West Pakistan.* Cambridge University Press: Cambridge

Mencher,J.P. 1993 The caste system upside down.. (excerpted from his article in *Current Anthropology* ,Vol.15 No. 4,1974) *in Social Stratification* .Edited by Dipankar Gupta, Oxford University Press: Delhi.

Parthasarathy,G and K.V.Ramana.1975 *Peasant organization in Razole: A case study in Andhra Pradesh, India.* Waltair: Andhra University Press.

Risley,R.R .1915. *The People of India.* W.Thacker & co: London.

White,L. 1959 *The evolution of culture* .New York, London: Mc Graw-Hill Book co .Inc.

14

Sustainable Development Through Innovative Strategies of Political Economy

S.V. Lakshmana Rao

Introduction:

Political economy is the name given to an important division of the science of government. The object of government is, or ought to be, the happiness of men, united in society; it seeks the means of securing to them the highest degree of felicity compatible with their nature, and at the same time of allowing the greatest possible number of individuals to partake in that felicity. But man is a complex being; he experiences moral and physical wants; therefore his happiness consists in his moral and physical condition.

The division of the world into a small group of rich nations and a large group of poor nations has been apparent to careful observers for a long time. The division of the poor nations between a very small group of affluent persons and the vast majority of very poor persons living continually on the brink of disaster is also apparent. *Russell Roberts*'s points out one of the major barriers to development, the richest people in the poorest countries live as well as the richest people in the richest countries. The real problem is that in most so-called poor countries, the powerful people, the government and their friends, live at the expense of the rest of society. This is related to an argument that *Andrew Janos* has made. Historically, underdeveloped countries were stuck in a vicious cycle that kept them underdeveloped. The author wants to explain the pressures on administrators, ethical framework, need for accountability and responsibility and innovative strategies of political economy for corruption free sustainable development.

Pressures on Public Administration System

All governments in the industrialized as well as developing world have undergone pressures to reform their public administration system to adequately respond to the needs and requirements of increasing democratization, globalization, liberalization and market economy. These are not the only pressures, other factors like changing public perceptions regarding the role and performance of their public institutions and public services, changing socio-demographic profile, increasing pressures from business groups and industry to provide a more conducive environment for domestic and foreign investment propelled governments throughout the world to innovate and reform.

In addition, prevalence of an all pervasive phenomenon of political and bureaucratic corruption has been compelling the governments world over to evolve new strategies for combating the evil and to cleansing the administration system and realistically affecting transparency in the process of governance.

Although many of the traditional value sets have been eroded and replaced with the borrowed administrative norms, such traditions still continue to influence administrative decisions and processes in these developing regions. The globalization and its attendant interdependence between developing and developed nations are posing external pressures for enhanced governmental performance and stability, the growth of stable and adequate economy and protection of human rights.

An apparent decline in public confidence in government constitutes an important political challenge for both developed and developing countries. Today, public administrators face new and different objectives and sometime conflicting goals due to reforms in the public sector, such as devolution of responsibility and greater managerial discretion, the changing relationship between public and private sectors, and increased reliance on market mechanisms. Governments are faced with challenges of limited resources leading to downsizing, restructuring and private trends. Ethics of public service requires that public agencies as fair, accountable, flexible and competent to carry out their mission.

Present Position of AP

In our state 1,30,00,000 people are under BPL category. Poverty decreased from 15.5% to 11%. The statistics of 2001 tells that our state has low literacy rate. About 40% are illiterates only. Illiteracy rate of SCs is 46.5%, and STs is 62.9%. 32.8% houses have no current, 67% houses have no toilets, 51.9% houses have no taps and 50% of the people are not getting healthy food. Unemployment is a major problem. There are 36,168 beds, 7,415 Dotors and 349 General hospitals in our state. According to State HRD report these are not enough for the sake of about eight crore people in the state.

Corruption as a Major Barrier for Development

In this paper, is noted periodic rural protest against the Government's mismanagement, marketing and corruption, show how discourses surrounding corruption are politicized along the lines of caste and class, and conclude by relating empirical material to debates on local state society relations in India, and stress on the need to understand corruption with reference to local political economy and the broader distribution of social and economic opportunities in rural society and point to future avenues for geographic research on corruption in the Indian landscape.

Recent researches on Development have tended to examine corruption with reference to the state and the macro-economic implications of public officials' abuse of office, examine the role of corruption in social differentiation and how rural agents construct corruption in discourse, focusing on low level corruption, relatively routine forms of malfeasance involving low ranking officials who act as patrons or brokers in the disbursement of state resources. A vibrant public culture appears to have emerged in rural areas of India.

Local government bodies are partly responsible for the disbursement of development resources in rural India. Most of the eminent personalities shouted that dominant classes in rural India, who control the land ownership and usually belong to an upper or middle ranking caste, have been able to convert their economic strength into power over local body decisions and administration. Dominant classes are shown to be fairly (but not often wholly) successful in manipulating the local police force and judiciary through bribery, influence and pressure. Dominant classes are able to obtain privileged access to government contracts, employment and grants. These dominant classes are then able to act as brokers between poorer sections of the rural population and the state (*Lieten* 1996; *A.Gupta* 1998; *Liete* and *Srivastava* 1999).

The economic, political and geographic implications of this analysis require further consideration. How far can institutional reform of local level state institutions reduce corruption in the absence of a more profound redistribution of economic and social resources in rural areas of India? Political economic accounts of corruption provide a solid basis for understanding how corrupt practices are implicated in social reproduction and resistance to this reproduction.

What is an Innovation Strategy?

An innovative strategy aims to mobilize the performers involved in a particular area of activity, whether an Economic or Social sector, in order to review the situation in the domain or sector of activity in the region and compare it to that in other competing regions; establish objectives and sectoral priorities, justifying these choices; identify and allocate financing available for each sector or area of activity.

Innovation is a process in perpetual evolution. It is important for regions and Member States to continue to test new ideas and approaches in order to identify those which, once generalized, can contribute to innovation and regional competitiveness in development. So the Commission should recommend the operational programmers to include a section describing the approach to be adopted for experimentation, indicating management arrangements and the implementation method (which may be different from that for other operations of the operational programme: e.g., specific calls for proposals, shorter duration of projects, close analysis of the results, etc.)

Innovative Strategies of Political Economy:

Traditionally local government economic development policy has focused on attracting new business through incentives and subsidies. However, recognition that these economic development strategies often did not benefit low income residents or neighborhoods, led to development of new community economic development strategies during the 1970s and 1980s to target investment and control to local neighborhoods. Often initiated by non-profit community development corporations, these innovative approaches have come to scale and now attract support from the majority of local governments according to a recent survey.

New strategies for local economic development involve planning to identify key characteristics of the local economy and to design strategic interventions which will enhance local competitiveness and support a cluster of local firms. These initiatives are characterized by public-private partnerships focused on strategic planning to identify and develop industrial policy for the local economy. Job training and marketing are addressed in addition to issues of finance and infrastructure. The focus is on the role of government and private institutions in providing information, technical supports and economic development infrastructure needed to support a range of local firms. These approaches may emphasize new technology related sectors, existing firms in the local economy, or economic development for low-income communities.

Ethical Framework

Ethical behaviors by public agencies involve promoting values of democracy, responsiveness to citizens, equality, justice, commitment to the public service and responsible stewardship of public resources including physical, financial and environmental resources and shaping of public policies with long term benefit of the people in mind.

Ethical dilemmas most often occur when two or more values, defined by law, custom or social standards are in conflict i.e., there is no single path by which all ethical decisions can be reached in a particular situation. When a setting is new and ambiguous and no standard gives a clear, definitive guide for action, it can lead to a moral gridlock characterized by an inability to act decisively. Inaction is not a choice for public administrators; they must be able to act in the public interest and be decisive in difficult contexts of action.

Innovative strategies, reforms and improving ethical climate of public bureaucracies continue to be a major item on the agendas of many governments in developing democracies. Reforms are typically aimed at improving perceived problems of organizational performance, building confidence in public institutions, and enhance accountability and responsibility on the part of public officials. Corruption is commonly defined as the abuse of public office for private gains.

Community Economic Development

Community Economic development strategies attempt to increase private capital investment in low-income neighborhoods through economic development zones and promotion of job training. They also use community development corporations and community development loan funds to make financing and technical assistance available to local residents and businesses.

Not surprisingly, local government support is highest for economic development zones that use a familiar tool, tax incentives, targeted to promote investment in neighborhoods with high poverty or high unemployment. Job training is also quite common. Again, this is a common tool (often part of a business attraction package) so expanding the focus to meet the training needs of a wider set of local workers and businesses is a natural extension. While less common, over half of all responding governments support community development loan funds and community development corporations. Programs specifically focused on welfare to work were also reported by almost half of all governments. Micro-enterprise programs were the least common, supported by only a quarter of all governments, but this compares favorably to those governments supporting small business programs more generally.

Importance of Partnerships with Local Government

These community economic development programs reflect an important set of partnerships between government and the non-profit sector. Local governments use non-profits to support community development corporations and micro-enterprise programs more than 50% of the time, and over a quarter of governments use non-profits to provide job training, welfare to work programs and community development loan funds. Non-profits combine social support, training, community organizing and economic development expertise. These collaborative public-private partnerships increase the scale and impact over what local government or non-profits could provide alone.

A challenge for the community economic development movement is to increase involvement of the for-profit sector. Many for-profit institutions perceive limited profit potential from investment in low-income communities and are reluctant to make investments unless large subsidies or tax breaks are provided. However, community economic development programs will demonstrate that profitable economic development can be fostered in low-income neighborhoods. Community economic development programs, which promote neighborhood revitalization and workforce development, are beneficial to private sector competitiveness over the long term. While local governments have built important partnerships with the non-profit sector, they need to encourage more direct investment by the for-profit sector in community economic development programs.

In order to target public action effectively, testing new approaches aimed at improving local innovation systems should be based on an analysis of regional needs, and also of the socioeconomic and competitive situation of the region.

Promoting Innovative Policies: For Sustainable Development

Better perception of what should be done to promote innovation policies to adopt, participation in partnership actions are

- Better cooperation among performers and better circulation and sharing of knowledge
- Comparison of the innovation policies followed in the region with those of other regions
- Development of strategies which lead to an action plan of concrete measures to be carried out on specific issues
- Development of an iterative process: identification of the priority sectors and the actions to be implemented, testing of the identified actions, evaluation of their effects, generalization of the best
- Increase in public budgets for the promotion of innovation
- Development of a culture of innovation based on the ownership of the new approaches by the actors

Communication: An Essential Element of the Strategy

As with evaluation, communication is often the poor relation of regional strategies. It should contribute to strengthen the strategy in a number of ways. It should:

- make citizens aware of the issues;
- identify and mobilize relevant actors, for example informing them about calls for project

- proposals launched within the framework of the strategy;
- associate them with the results of the strategy; and
- Promote the region with a view to attracting capital and talent.

Continuous Evaluation: The Key to Success

Ongoing evaluation of strategies is often confused with technical and financial monitoring and can be perceived by those responsible for the actions as a tool for control of sound management of the funds. It plays a different role, however, since it should make it possible to modify actions underway or even to redirect the strategy in order to maximize its regional impact.

The quality of evaluation depends on the choice of indicators, which should facilitate the measurement of achievements compared to objectives, as well as on the establishment of a monitoring system which provides data and analysis. Evaluation should not lose sight of the fact that the success of a strategy is not measured only in terms of immediate results (job creation, etc.) but also in terms of processes: achieving the expected results, identification of the side effects for the region.

Conclusion

Economic reforms require the government to be more caring and responsive both to the needs of a growing economy and to the unserved sections. Bureaucracy should try to develop more citizen based governments especially at the local level. Trust between the administrators and citizens can only emerge from the process of building authentic relationships, interweaving the two wills in the larger whole. As *Bill Gates* expressed delay in procedures and lack of speed in decision-making are breeding grounds of corruption, thus if IT is used, process can be rapid and corruption can be reduced, steps should be made for better record keeping, movement of files.

If the political parties are really working for the welfare of the people then not only to declare the schemes but also to implement perfectly through innovative strategies. Government has to decide the prime factors and urgent needs while planning for the constant development of the state. If the budget allotted to one field is more, then automatically some other field will get low budget allocation. So while allocating budget the government should be careful and should be allotted only after a keen observation of the problems throughout. At present *Bharat Nirman* (2005-06) and *NREGA* (National Rural Employment Guarantee Act) (Feb. 2006) are acting as a fuel for Economic Development so government should take care for proper implementation. Controlling corruption will lead to the sustainable development of the nation.

References

Caste, Class, and Clientelism (2002), A Political Economy of Everyday Corruption in Rural North India Craig Jeffrey *Economic* Geography, Vol. 78, No. 1 (Jan.), pp. 21-41 Published by: Clark University.

Community and Economic Development: Mildred Warner, Department of City and Regional Planning, Cornell University.

Eenadu Daily, 30. Sep. (2008), Article of P.S.M. Rao "*Problems are Here.. Where are the Solutions?*"

Innovative Strategies and Actions (2006), *European Union Regional Policy*, October.

R.B. Jain (2004), "*Corruption–Free Sustainable Development, Challenges and Strategies for Good Governance*" Mittal Publications, New Delhi.

15

Agrarian Crisis and Agrarian Struggles—A Global Scenario

M. Ramesh, B. Addai

A Crisis has broken out in the field of Indian agriculture. The crisis is most glaringly manifested in the growing incidence of starvation deaths and farmers' suicides. The largest number of starvation deaths are still routinely reported for the backward regions of the country especially Orissa and now increasing from Rajasthan. The trend of suicides generally prompted by heavy indebtedness, crop failure or inability to find a market for the produce. The same trend has happened even among well-to-do farmers in the agriculturally developed areas of Punjab, Maharashtra, Karnataka and Andhra Pradesh. The crisis has also led to a new phase of agrarian unrest. Peasants and farmers have strongly opposed the WTO, growing penetration of giant agribusiness firms and attempts to corporatise agriculture. The corporate agriculture is started at Kuppam area of Chittoor District in Andhra Pradesh. Once again powerful farmers' movement are being witnessed in the areas of green revolution, Punjab and Haryana in particular. However, the original exponent of farmers' movement in the country, Mr. Sharad Joshi, now stands on the other side of the fence. The erstwhile World Bank official-turned-farmer leader today advises the union government on matters of agricultural policy while the armors are braving lathes and bullets on the streets.

Apart from attempts to suppress the farmer's agitation the ruling government is trying hard to divide and divert the movement. The Cavery water crisis that recently rocked Karnataka and Tamil Nadu, the Almatti water crises between Karnataka and Andhra Pradesh. Instead of coming up with any solution to save the crops the central government made it into an issue of inter-state wrangling while bourgeois politicians in both the states addressed the issue in the narrow framework of regional interests and whipped up sectarian passions. While the WTO agreements, especially the removal of quantitative restrictions (QRS) on imports, and as a result, the thoroughly unequal competition with heavily subsidized big corporate farmers from the western countries have aggravated the present crisis situation, at the root of it lies the accumulated anomalies of the underlying landlord path of capitalist development in Indian agriculture. The landlord path pursued in India under the slogan of the green revolution had typically been based on the betting-on-the-strong strategy with little benefits really percolating to the lower rungs of the agricultural population. The macro-level results were of course quite impressive with food grains production recording major increases and thus enabling a gradual transition from extreme food scarcity and dependence on external aid to semblance of food security and self-reliance. However, the green revolution is spread to relatively backward areas was constrained form the beginning by serious infrastructural problems. With declining public investment in agriculture and rising prices of all key inputs, the green revolution soon reached a point of saturation even in its initial strongholds. The farmers' movement in the 1980s with its loud demand for remunerative prices and cheaper inputs reflected this brewing crisis.

Against this backdrop, bourgeois ideologues within the farmers' movement started demanding liberalization of agricultural trade and reversal of land reforms Sections of big farmers started dreaming about exporting to the world market and securing super-remunerative prices. This was quite akin to the corporate clamour for freedom from 'license-permit-quota raj' However, whether for the would-be 'Indian' MNCs or the Indian farmers eyeing their shares in the world agriculture market, it did not take long for the dream to turn sour. Then just as the corporate sector started demanding level-playing field even as it began urging closer ties of collaboration with the MNCs, big farmers came up with the demand for insulation from the WTO. Yet, behind this demand they too are developing a close nexus with agribusiness corporations. Just as the working class has to see through the corporate clamour for level-playing field, agricultural labourers, poor peasants and their small farmer allies must not be misled by the rich farmers apparent crusade against the WTO but intensify their independent mobilization against WTO.

The official explanation of the present crisis veers around the hypothesis of overproduction. Instead of expanding the system of public procurement and distribution, the government wants to privatize the foodgrains trade and run a truncated distribution system in the name of better targeting. Farmers unable to sell their crops at minimum support prices announced by the government are therefore being advised to go in for crop diversification and switch over to cash crops. This indiscriminate diversification is bound to pose a serious threat to food security. Figures of per capita availability of food grains already show a stagnating and even declining trend.

The agrarian programme attaches a lot of importance to the issues and demands of the middle peasants. This line calls for a resolute alliance with middle peasants while winning over the capitalist farmers. Given the intensity of caste-class divide in many parts of rural India, especially in states like Bihar and UP, and the rise of bhooswami or rich landlords or Jothydars or kulak-based regional parties. It has been difficult for the party of the proletariat with its strong identification with the rural proletariat to make inroads among the middle peasantry. The present crisis marks a major opportunity to boldly address the issues of the middle peasantry without diluting primary commitment of the rural proletariat. Against this backdrop, we have reviewed the ongoing agrarian struggles. This has witnessed a surge in Orissa, West Bengal, Jharkhand, Chhattisgarh and Punjab. Land tenancy, wages and employment remain the basic and most common issues of agrarian struggles. Many powerful initiatives on issues like electricity rates, debt relief, procurement of food grains and various aspects of rural development and functioning of the panchayat system.

In Bihar, West Champaran district bordering Nepal and Uttar Pradesh has emerged as the latest storm centre of land struggles. This district still has a very high incidence of well-entrenched landlordism. Estates controlling thousands of acres of land are still quite common. Electoral politics in the district is directly dominated by these estates and apart from their own-armed henchmen. They also enjoy the loyalty of the local police. The Khet Mazdoor Sabha (agricultural labourers' association) in the district has successfully redistributed 400 acres of land in Gaunaha block among 600 agricultural laborers. In Mainatand block, landless poor peasants have secured control over 300 acres of land illegally controlled by one absentee landlord. The district administration is trying to suppress these struggles by unleashing barbaric police repression, but the masses are offering a determined resistance.

In the key central Bihar districts of Bhojpur, Patna and Jehanabad, where agrarian struggles had temporarily been relegated to the background by the reactionary violence unleashed by the Ranvir Sena, land and wage struggles are again gathering momentum. In Baruthi, village of Sahar block in Bhojpur district, control has been wtested over 10 acres of ceiling-surplus land. This land had originally been captured in 1992 but the Ranvir Sena had managed to snatch it back. In July 2001, landless and poor peasants reestablished their control defying the police-administration –Ranvir Sena nexus. The next month, hundreds of agricultural labourers and poor peasants occupied 46 acres of math land in Andhari village.

The Ranvir Sena hitherto controlled the land. In Raipura village of Charpolhri block an absentee landlord was gradually selling off land that earlier used to be leased out. The agricultural labour organization intervened and rescued 38 acres of land. In Baga math of Sandesh block, 55 acres of calling surplus land had been lying fallow. When the Mahanth tried to get the land cultivated with the backing of the Ranvir Sena and the police, hundreds of people from neighboring villages chased away the Ranvir Sena goons, seized the land, and resumed cultivation in a part of it. In recent times, Jehanabad district has witnessed a series of wage struggles. During June-July 2001, Daidi village of Ghosi block became the centre of a determined strike that began around the issue of payment of compensation to an injured agricultural laborers. When the employer refused and all employers were united around a henchman of the local MLA and Jehanabad strongman Jagadish Sharma and threw up a challenge to the labourers, the latter took up the cudgel and the strike now raised the demand for minimum wages. Eventually the administration intervened and a sum of Rs.15, 000 was awarded as compensation. The wage settlement however came later after another round of struggle. When the employers tried to violate the settlement by taking away the customary facilities enjoyed by the labourers, denying equal wages to women workers, the labourers again resorted to strike, and eventually the employers had to concede the demands. Protracted wage struggle is also going on in Rostampur village of Ghosi block where the local PWG leader has sided with the employers who, in turn, are backed by the Chairman of the District Council, while most of the PWG supporters have joined the struggle. Even in the face of police repression, the morale of the striking workers continues to be quite high.

In Koil village of Kaler block of the newly carved out Arwal district, the Khet Mazdoor Sabha won an important victory this year. This is the village of the health minister of the RJD government. Initially, in June this year when the noval labourers struck work demanding wage increase and reduction of working hours, the pro-Ranvir Sena employers tried to crush the struggle with the help of the police and started hiring labourers form outside. The labourers fought back with a show of great unity and determination and forced the labourers from outside to stop work. A dharna was staged in Patna exposing the role of the minister and the Ranvir Sena-police nexus. Eventually the district administration was forced to intervene and concede most of the demands including increase in wages form 2.5 kg to 3.5 Kg, reduction of working hours from 12 to 8, transfer of the guilty police constable and withdrawal of all cases foisted on the striking workers. We can also see a revival of land struggle against Math's and absentee landlords in Kako. The struggle for Konikuti Math land in Kaler block has seen a landlord from the same caste unite poor peasants belonging to Yadav caste against the illegal occupation of the Math land.

In Patna, following our impressive victors in the panchayat election in Dulhinbazar block, struggle was intensified to establish peasant control over the 28 acres of land lying with the Khapuri Math. The BPKS had seized this land in the early 1980s, but of late landlords backed by the Ranvir Sena as well as the local RJD MLA and the administration, have been trying hard to evict the peasants and stop all agricultural operation. On 16 August 2001, hundreds of peasants and agricultural labourers braved police lathis and firing by the Ranvir Sena to complete the work of paddy transplantation. A leading member of the Party District Committee and mukhia were arrested and several people injured by the police. In Bara village of Naubatpur block, landlords belonging to the erstwhile Bhumi Sena and regrouping currently under the banner of the PWG unleashed severe terror and evicted 125 families from the village. The Khet Mazdoor Sabha launched a determined struggle on this issue and on 6 July 2002, a march was organized from Naubatpur to Bara. Armed men of the Ranvir Sena and PWG fired on the march but were bravely resisted by the people. An indefinite gherao of the block office followed and after two weeks the evicted families returned to the village following an agreement with the administration.

In Jharkhand, beyond our old pockets of peasant struggle in the Palamau-Garwah Lather belt, the Dumaka-Jamtara belt of Santhal Pargana has emerged as a centre of intense agrarian struggles in recent times. In 1998, agrarian labourers/poor peasants of 13 pachayats in Kundahit PS of Dumka Distict waged a fortnight-long strike on the demand of minimum wages and better sharecropping terms. In 1999, this movement spread over another ten panchayats. Similar struggles broke out in Raneswar block as well. Because of this movement sharecroppers are now getting half of what they produce. In Kundahit a land seizure movement has also been successful. In this zone our work has now spread over 35 panchayats and around 3000-4000 people now get mobilized at the Party's call.

In Uttar Pradesh, land struggle has acquired fresh momentum in the Lakhimpur Pilibhit belt of Terai region. More that 100 displaced families of Sharda project area have been successfully rehabilitated in 300 acres of fallow land lying with the forest department. Defending the new settlement, known as Kranti Nagar, against constant attacks by the local land mafia-police-criminal nexus remains of major challenge. So far, the rehabilited families have been successful in retaining their control and beating back the enemy nexus. In Guthna Buzurg village of the district, struggle is on against attempts to evict allottees form 104 acres of land. Recently when the local land mafia, which enjoys political patronage of the BSP, tried to forcibly harvest the standing crop of the land, women agricultural labourers offered heroic resistance. Several of the injured and hospitalized, but the women remained firm. Other local women also joined in and burned effigies of Chief Minister Mayawati. Powerful protests were organized in the district headquarter and eventually the district administration had to intervene and uphold the legal rights of the threatened tenants and stop the land mafia from harvesting the crop. In Puranpur Tehshil of Pilibhit district, our comrades have successfully frustrated attempts to evict the people settled in Rahul Nagar and 9 adjoining villages.

In East Godavari district of Andhra Pradesh, fierce land struggle is on centering on more than 80 acres of ceiling-surplus and bhudan land in Peddasankarlapude village located about 50km away from Kakinada. The landlords, closely aligned with different TDP MLAs in the district have hired the services of a local mafia outfit is operating under the banner of a self-styled CPI (ML) faction. In this district, outfit operating under the banner of a self-staled CPI (ML) faction. In this district more than 3,000 acres of land have been captured and distributed during the last two decades. In Rayagada district of Orissa, intense land struggle is going on in Padampur and Ramanaguda blocks. In addition to 75 acres of land captured and distributed during the last two decades. In Rayagada district of Orissa, intense land struggle is going on in Padampur and Ramanaguda blocks. In addition to 75 acres of land captured and cultivated since last year, another 60 acres of ceiling surplus land has been rescued from the illegal occupation of landlords well connected to both the Congress and BJP. On several occasions, hundreds of tribal people have gheraoed the block office, police station and even court and jail. The secretary of our Rayagada district unit has been booked under several false cases and is currently in jail. Peasant struggle is also gathering momentum in kalahandi district.

In Tamil Nadu, some initial success has been achieved in organizing agricultural laboourers. In August 2000,in about 45 villages of Thanjavur and Nagapattinam districts, women agricultural workers led by the Tamizhaga Vivasaya Thozhilar Sangam (Tamil Nadu Agricultural Labourers, Union) struck work for days together to demand the legally stipulated minimum and equal wages. Though the strike succeeded in winning only a partial victory, the message spread every where and generated tremendous enthusiasm among women agricultural workers. In North Dinajpur district of West Bengal, poor peasants and agricultural labourers belonging to various SC-ST communities' wrested 82 bighas of ceiling-surplus land in Raiganj block from illegal control of local CPI (M) BEGWIGS. Hundreds of peasants by our party and the peasant association had successfully repulsed the CPI (M),s initial attacks to regain control over the land. Several activists, including a member of the Part's West Bengal State Committee, were arrested in connection with this struggle.

In Sonitpur district of Assam, work is going on among agricultural labourers. The agricultural labourers association has succeeded in compelling the block panchayats to pay wages at the officially stipulated rate. In most other states, our work among the rural poor has still not acquired stable and organized character. In Uttaranchal, some primary efforts have been initiated in Almora region to highlight the need for land reforms suited to the specific conditions of the state. The sixth party congress had emphasized the task of organizing agricultural labourers as an independent class force. Even though agricultural labourers and landless peasants have always formed the mainstay of the peasant movement organized by the party, in is only recently that we have started organizing agricultural labourers separately under the banner of agricultural labourers association. This was taken up as a special point of emphasis during the strengthen-the-party campaign conducted between April and October 2000. More than 3,00,000 members were recruiteD in Bihar during this campaign. State level organizations have since been built in Bihar, Uttar Pradesh and west Bengal while district and regional level organizations are functioning in Andhara Predesh , Tamil Nadu and Chhattisgarh.

Apart from leading the spontaneous and localized struggles of agricultural labourers breaking out during busy seasons to clinch a wage hike or secure job guarantees in the face of increased mechanization, the agricultural laborers associations have started launching campaigns on a larger scale to popularize the class demands and strengthen the class identity of the rural proletariat. State - level strike actions have been organized so far in Bihar and West Bengal. In Bihar, the agricultural labourers strike held in July this year was implementeD in nearly 2000 villages and demonstrations were held in 134 blocks. Some 70,000 agricultural labourers joined this class action all over the state to demand implementation of the minimum wages act, enactment of welfare legislation at central and state levels, CBI inquiry into the PDS (public distribution system) scam in Bihar and mandatory inclusion of all families with an annual income of less than Rs.20, 000 in the BPL (below poverty line) list.

World agriculture has undergone drastic changes during the last few decades. Agricultural production has increased. Similarly world food supply is also increased 18 percent. The per capita food supplies in developing countries have increased to 27 percent. While there, populations grew from 2.1 billion to nearly 4.0 billion (FAO, 1995b: 427). Yet, while the sector on average has kept up with population growth and demand for agricultural produce, many countries and population groups have been bypassed. Progress in some countries has been negligible and in sub-Saharan Africa, nutritional levels have actually fallen. World wide, about 800 million people are still chronically undernourished. Furthermore, the rate of growth in agricultural production has not contributed to the alleviation of poverty, on the contrary, in the 1980s average income declined in46 of the 82 developing countries reviewed by FAO. On a regional basis, both Africa and Latin America were especially affected. Here the percentage of poor people increased during the 1980 s from 41 to 47 percent (FAO,1994:5).

There are many reasons for this situation, ranging from agro-climatic conditions to changes in international commodity prices to government policies. Misguided government policies and priorities have not recognized the importance of the agricultural sector in the overall development process. In many developing countries, this sector has been neglected or outright taxed. Proceeds from agricultural taxation were used to finance the development of other sectors, mainly industry and manufacturing, while only a small share was returned to agriculture.

Yet, experiences in south and southeast Asia reveal the importance of agriculture-based development strategies in which the transfer of resources to the non-agricultural sector has been the result of surplus generation in agriculture as opposed to surplus extraction; from Japan to Indonesia, governments followed a strategy, which gave early priority to agriculture, especially to raising the productivity of rice farmers to ensure food security, investments were made to improve the efficiency of the domestic marketing systems in rural areas. In contrast, many African countries have undervalued the agricultural sector and rural infrastructure and have attempted to displace markets rather than invest in improving their efficiency. Since 1960, the rice - based economies of Southeast Asia have outpaced the coarse grain and root crop-based economies of sub-Saharan Africa. A large part of Africa's failure and Southeast Asia's success can be attainted to the differential treatment of the agricultural sector (Timmer, 1997: 13).

In the early 1980s , terms of trade collapsed as oil prices soared and prices of other commodities fell, increasing the difficult debt burden of many developing countries, between 1982 and 1991 , the total foreign debt of sub- Saharan African countries grew from US$ 57 billion to US$ 144 billion. The total foreign debt of Latin American countries grew from US$ 354 billion to US$ 470 billion. In order to overcome these financial difficulties and to enable countries to repay their international debts, the World Bank introduced structural adjustment and stabilization programmes in the 1980s that required changes in economic policy and management as well as institutional reforms. They implied the reduction of the role of the state, support to the private sector, dismantling of parasitical agencies such as marketing boards, abolition of subsidies, and devaluation of overvalued exchange rates, because of the need for immediate economic gains; many countries favoured the establishment of large-scale farming enterprises which produce mono crop export crops and neglected the sector of small farmers whose situation deteriorated, leading to increased poverty, indebtedness and growing landlessness.

The landless and near landless rural population constitute the largest single group of those affected by poverty. Some 30 million rural people in developing countries are landless.

138 million are near landless, and numbers in this category are growing throughout the developing world, especially in South Asia. Resources to accommodate the poor and the landless are shrinking with the expansion of arable land growing more slowly than that of the rural population. In search for employment and income, as many as 70 million people, mostly from developing countries, are working, legally or illegally, in other countries. Each year, more than one million people migrate permanently, in addition, because of adverse political and ethnic conditions, the number of refugees has increased continuously. It rose from 2.8 million in 1976 to 17.3. million in 1990 (FAO, 1994: 5).

For most developing country particularly in Africa and Latin America, the 1980s were a 'lost decade '. Policies and strategies, which attempted to alleviate poverty through a few isolated projects, even if there where successful, did not bring about the expected results, since they were carried out within a political and economic framework that was not conducive to rural development. On the other hand, many indicators of social performances, such as literacy rates, disease eradication or at least suppression, longevity, secondary school attendance, infant and childhood mortality, and population growth rates continued to improve for the developing countries as a whole. For some, however, especially in sub-Saharan Africa, they deteriorated. In Central and Eastern Europe and the Soviet Union of the 1980s, the twin objectives of military strength and socio-economic progress proved increasingly difficult to achieve simultaneously. The resulting strains on centrally planned economic systems precipitated the major transformations that began in the late 1980s. A major reason for the poor performance of the agricultural sector was a heavily centrally planned economy chat operated through large production units and did not provide incentives for private initiative. Yet, while the productivity of the socialist farming enterprises was low, they guaranteed employment, income and a modest, but rather balanced, living standard for the majority of the rural population.

Recent Political and Economic Changes

The breakdown of the control economies of Central and Eastern Europe and the former USSR marked the beginning of a difficult and painful process of transition toward more open market-oriented economies. The early stages of this process interrupted traditional trading patterns, drastically reduced real per capita incomes, reduced demand, and disrupted production processing and distribution. As part of the transition process, even the most basic legal and economic institutions had to be adjusted to allow and encourage the private sector to operate as part of a functioning market economy.

Political and economic changes were not restricted to the former socialist countries of Europe. They also occurred in many developing countries. In order to overcome their debt burden many developing countries continued their policy reforms and structural adjustment programmes, reduced government spending and intervention in agricultural input markets, phased out subsidies and privatized the former prostates. These reforms were intended to reduce state interference in productive activities through a gradual transfer to the private or cooperative sector of such areas as distribution of input supplies, agricultural credit, marketing of products and utilization of agricultural infrastructure. Therefore the state is becoming less involved in the management of rural development projects. Its activities will increasingly be restricted to the provision of favourable policy and structural conditions for rural development to take place under the aegis of other institutions.

In the late 1980s, when the negative impact of structural adjustment programmes on the social situation became evident, renewed emphasis was placed on the human dimension of development. This orientation has a number of important implications. First, it was recognized that adjustment had to a be carried out with a human face, i.e. in such a way that it would attenuate its excessive effects and alleviate acute disparities and social hardship. Second, the importance of people's knowledge, skills and aptitudes, together with the appropriate institutions that would enable them to participate in the development process was recognized. Third, the need to enhance food security and nutrition policies became apparent with the recognition that food access often depends more on income than on supply. And forth, attention was focused on the need to promote the sustainability of agriculture and rural development.

Many governments also started to reduce their support of state-run cooperatives and encouraged farmers to create new cooperatives, based on voluntary membership and administered and financed by their members. Several countries, such as Fiji, Kenya, Myanmar, Namibia, Nepal, Swaziland, Tanzania and Uganda, have enacted new cooperative laws that foresee the transformation of the former state-controlled cooperatives into voluntary organizations. In Ethiopia, India, Laos, Vietnam and Zambia such laws are under preparation. The rise of democracy and the widespread decentralization of government allowed the rural poor to make new claims on their political representatives. Several rural development schemes, particularly in Latin America are being managed by NGOs using resources transferred by central or local governments. The role of NGOs and the private sector in rural development will be further enhanced in the face of shrinking government budgets and services.

Growing environmental concerns arising from massive deforestation in the humid tropics, deforestation and soil erosion in the watersheds and depletion of underground water tables, has increased interest in rural development strategies, which internalize some of the externalities created by poverty. The debt crisis has further increased the cost of these externalities, e.g. the need to import food and oil because water reservoirs are rapidly silted by soil erosion in the watersheds. The possibility of using rural development to promote environmental protection transferring resources by taxing those who would benefit from reducing the externalities of poverty has opened new approaches. (De Janvry and Sadoulet, in the field of land tenure, there is a growing recognition among researchers and policy-markers, particularly in Africa, of the importance of customary rights and the participation of local communities in the management of natural resource use. While in the past, customary land tenure systems and institution were perceived as inhibiting agricultural development, several countries are now giving due consideration to traditional forms of access to land. The Rural Code Ordinance of Niger of 1993, for example, aims at elevating customary land rights to written rights and thus contributes to developing from an informal market to a more formal market that will allow secure land transactions.

These new approaches to rural development are only beginning to emerge, but some of their main traits can be discerned. They will rely largely on a new partnership between government and grassroots organizations. They will be based less on the transfer of resources, e.g. subsidized credit, than on the promotion of new institutions able to mobilize local resources, e.g. the Grameen Bank. They will have a strong non-agricultural component to capture the linkage effects of agricultural development. These activities will be located as far as possible in the rural areas to provide complimentary sources of income for peasant households and reduce the external costs of rapid urban migration. And they will have strong environmental purpose, involving the transfer of resources as payment for the reduction of increasingly costly national and international externalities of poverty (Ibid: 144)

In addition, in many countries the state's capacity, authority and autonomy are being eroded by rapid advances of the activities of transnational corporations (TNCs) in the fields of finance, trade, transport, communications, production and consumption i.e. by globalization (UNRISD, 1985). Many national institutions have gone into decline and governments have been unable to protect their people from disturbing trends in the international economic environment. Among the most powerful of these external forces are TNCs, many of which are financially more powerful than national economies. Their main objective is the maximization of profits and this objective is frequently achieved without concern for the economic, social and environmental conditions of the developing countries in which they operate.

Impact

As a result of market-oriented economic reforms, some developing countries have been successful in stabilizing their economies, shown by widespread reductions of inflation rates and political and social stability in some countries and areas formerly affected by civil strife and armed conformation. China, which started its economic reform as early as 1978 with the introduction of the Household Responsibility System, has achieved an unprecedented increase of its economy and its agricultural sector. In 1993, China's economy grew by 13.4 percent and in 1994 by 11.8 percent. Despite unfavorable weather conditions, agricultural growth has been 3.5 percent in recent years (FAO, 1995A: 105).

In Central and Eastern Europe, however, the agricultural sector has faced dramatic shocks. With the breakdown of the command economy, production structures and regional trade, all countries of the region have experienced sharp drops in agricultural production and declines in per capita food consumption. Large population groups have faced malnutrition because of declining incomes. In some cases, changes have been so great and abrupt that they seriously disrupted national food balances and endangered the functioning of national, regional and local food supply and trade systems. Although there are some encouraging signs in selected countries that agricultural production has increased slightly in the last two years, output has not yet reached pre-reform levels. In Africa, some countries benefited significantly from the new opportunities provided by recent developments in agricultural commodity markets. The gains from improved terms of trade are estimated to benefit 13 sub-Saharan countries by an average of four percent of GDP (FAO, 1995A:95). While the devaluation of the CFA in early 1994 has had a positive impact on the export sectors and overall economies of the 14 CFA zone member countries. It also has resulted in sharp increases in the prices of imported goods, including food staples which caused a wave of strikes and demonstrations in several countries. Negative social effects continue to be felt. The living standard in urban areas has fallen and access to health care and resources for schools have been seriously affected (FAO, 1995A: 78).

In India, the substantial nominal devaluation of the rupee in June 1991 made exports of many of its agricultural commodities more competitive. Exports of rice, wheat, cotton, fruit and vegetables, fish and fish products, and meat received a tremendous boost. Yet, here again, the resulting increases in local food-grain prices have had a negative impact on food security for the poor. Poverty has increased during the last three years. In Mexico, the peso devaluation significantly altered the price relationships between domestic and imported products. Higher prices for imported grain resulted in competitive gains for domestic and imported products. Higher prices for imported grain resulted in competitive gains for domestic producers. More direct purchases from local producers by the milling and livestock industries. In Venezuela, too, the strong devaluation of the Bolivar resulted in lower food imports. At the same time, farmers suffered from drastic cuts on subsidized credit and price support measure (FAO. 1995a: 132).

The effects of trade liberalization also negatively affect the Near East. The region is heavily dependent on food imports, so the reduction of subsidies on European agricultural goods (which accounts for more that 75 percent of the cost of production) is expected to cause greater budgetary outlays on imported food. The effects of policy reforms on the poor vary considerably among different population groups. The extent of benefit or loss will depend on their income, resources, education and their access to productive resources, such as land. Reductions in expenditures for social safety nets, including cuts in the public payroll and in welfare programmes for the poor, as well as the increase of prices for imported items, including basic goods such as food, medicines and fuel, due to devaluation have had detrimental effects on the weakest segments of the population.

It is expected that higher prices for agricultural products will have a positive effect on the agricultural sector in general. The distribution of gains and losses among rural people depends on whether they are net food sellers or buyers; Or they are producers of export or subsistence crops. Or they have access to land, labour, credit, input and product markets. Structural adjustment programmes have had the positive effect or facilitating the decentralization of authority and responsibility to local and regional governments and to locally base "popular organizations." The 1980s saw a massive rise of grass-root organizations in part as a response to the suppression of traditional social organizations by socialist and military governments. These new organizations have taken the form of community groups, neighborhood associations, producers associations, etc. they provide new channels for the transfer of resources and for the management of rural development schemes. A new trend toward more democracy has emerged gradually, providing more opportunities for the rural population to participate through organizations of their own choice in the process of decision- making.

The reduction of the influence of the state has also had its impact on the flow of information, since censorship has been alleviated in many countries, together with the rapid advances in communications and information technology, the international circulation of news and of development models has had important consequences for the cultures of developing countries. On the one hand, it has opened windows on the outside world in closed societies, regarding, for example, the exercise of democratic freedom, and enriched life through contact with other cultures and societies. On the other hand , the demonstration of violence in the relations between people , the confusing of human with economic values, and the widespread glorification of western lifestyles inaccessible to the masses in the developing countries work powerfully against the establishment of development policies based on solidarity, self-confidence and long-term effort(UNESCO, 1995:32).

In the field of land tenure changes, very few countries have followed the examples of east Asia. Japan, the Republic of Korea and Taiwan implemented sweeping land reforms in the 1940s and1950s which helped to stimulate production and equity. In some countries of Asia and the near east, land reform measures introduced in the late 1950s and early 1960s have generated worthwhile results. Efforts in Latin America suffered from the lack of supporting services, which put the reform beneficiaries into difficult situations and created the impression that other, less drastic measures could be a substitute for reform. Currently only a few countries, such as the Philippines, are implementing land redistribution programmes. The main reasons for the lack of progressing land reform in its traditional form are political considerations and stakes. Yet, there are many countries, where land reform has a role to play. A country, which is in urgent need of an agrarian reform, is South Africa. In south Africa, the average size of a farm in 'white areas' is 1300 ha, and 1 ha in 'black areas'. A land reform law, which aims at overcoming this discrepancy, is currently under preparation.

In Algeria, the transformation of state-owned farms to private farms is changing the historical structure of production in the agricultural sector and improving the efficiency and competitiveness of farm activities. In central and eastern Europe and the former soviet union, such transformations take place with varying speed and intensity. While some countries have made considerable progress in the privatization of landed property, other is reluctant to abolish the previous production structure and aim at changing the pattern of management. In this proceed; however, a strong polarization between the former administrators of the cooperative and ordinary cooperative members is noticeable, whereby the former frequently acquire cooperative assets under false pretenses and at the expense of the latter.

As the 1990s unfolded, a new pattern of international relations began to emerge. The end of the cold war reduced political tensions among the superpowers and resulted in some cutting of military expenditures by the developed and the former centrally planned economies. Yet, the "peace dividend" resources have not yet been utilized to assist developing countries. The transition from centrally planned to market-driven economic systems has been accompanied by problems (assumed to be short run) of economic depression and unemployment. therefore, some economic assistance has been diverted from developing countries to countries in central and eastern Europe and central Asia, which are in the process of transition. In the field of agriculture and rural development, the new economic environment poses a number of advantages for some. It is expected that the ongoing changes towards liberalization will raise the price for agricultural produce. It has to be recognized, however, that this development will benefit only those commercial producers and peasants who have clear access to land and that the rural poor and others who are net buyers of farm produce will lose in this process. As it is most unlikely that the traditional type of government - initiated land reform is going to take place in the course of liberalization, it is necessary to explore new approaches to land reform.

In South Africa, for instance, the government wants to follow market-oriented reforms, rather than a state-controlled reform, which in Zimbabwe and other parts of the world has proven to be costly and difficult to implement. The government intends to reduce its support to the large commercial farms in the hope that this may aid the land reform process and result in land sales by those large-scale farms, which would be unable to survive in an unprotected environment. Furthermore, funding would be provided to employees in large commercial farms so that they can acquire equity and associated ownership and decision - making powers in such enterprises. Experiences in agrarian reform in Latin America and elsewhere seem to indicate that allowing the market to determine the future course of agriculture based on a viable land market and market prices is a right step into this direction. Such an approach allows for maximum individual incentives, is more efficient and avoids bureaucratization (Thiesenhusen, 1993" 17).

As the imposition of large-scale farming in the former centrally-planned economies did not bring about the results expected from the alleged economies of scale, many new governments have adopted a new land policy which favors the movement away from group or collective farming and toward ' land to tiller " (Thiesenhusen, 1993" 13). Yet, this policy was not accepted by many of the former members of the cooperative. As they had become specialized agricultural workers on these farms, they do not possess the skill, experience nor the physical prerequisites to manage a farm on their own. Therefore, many cooperative members in central and eastern Europe preferred to stay on the farm unit even after it changed its form of organization and operation. What is needed, however, to make these enterprises suitable to the new economic conditions is a flexible type of management, which is able to respond to the needs of the market and allows participation in decision-making.

The ultimate objective of agrarian reform and rural development is the alleviation of rural poverty. As governments are gradually deducing their leading role and their staff, new actors, such as cooperatives and NGOs have to fill this gap. Because of their knowledge of local conditions, NGOs are frequently in a better position to address rural development problems than government officials living in urban centers. Yet, a word of caution is needed. While many NGOs have been successful in promoting rural development, they have had les success in translating project success achieved at the micro level in development that is significant at the macro level. "the literature tends to assume or hope that micro level experiences are generalizable, but rarely it explores the mechanisms through which project- oriented NGOs can transcend the spatial and temporal limitations of the project approach" (Vivian, 1994 " 168).

Conclusion

The recent economic and political changes, which have taken place in many developing countries and in countries in transition, provide new possibilities and challenges for rural development and rural poverty alleviation. But much remains to be done to define and implement a new approach to rural development adapted to the situation of market liberalization, state contraction, newly-recovered democratic rights and a burgeoning of grass-roots organizations, new social actors and new social movements (de Jeanery and sedulity, 1993: 144).

While parts of structural adjustment programmers, such as the withdrawal of input subsidies and the establishment of remunerative prices for out put, will improve the efficiency of agriculture, the acceleration of agricultural growth alone will not alleviate poverty; agricultural growth take not long to trickle down to the rural poor. The right delineation between public and private participation in development is difficult to define, yet there is more and more general agreement that development depends to a large extent on organization, good governance, institutions, people's participation in decision-making and political consensus.

The need for community participation in development has been increasingly recognized. National government is recommended to consider decentralized approaches to their social and development programmers. Such decentralization would increase the efficiency of government spending and be more cost effective, since projects would be more selectively suited to local needs. Local employment would increase and , since the local community will in a sense be spending its own money and residents will feel more included in the process, there would be an added incentive to lower cost and increase performance.

Development failures in the past were largely due to attempts by governments and donor agencies to do too much for too many groups, circumventing market activities. Recent experience indicates that, in order to improve this situation, government should play a role in correcting the conditions that cause markets to fail, such as information deficiencies, lack of clear property rights and lack of a stable legal framework. Within a market framework, governments also have other important regulation responsibilities such as to establish and enforce property rights, provide public goods, carry out specific interventions to alleviate poverty and improve food security and nutrition.

While the state gradually withdraws from productive and commercial activities and focuses its role on orienting and regulating rural development activities, there is an urgent need to protect produces and consumers, safeguard national resources, and give preferential assistance to the needy segments of the population. Governments have to play an important role in this process in order to prevent market forces from leading to the exploitation of the weaker sections of society by the stronger ones.

In the past, policy orientation was in favor of large farms, although it was known that small-holders agriculture is often more sufficient in terms of the ratio of energy inputs to product yields, helps to preserve biodiversity and provides a stable base of employment. Small-holder agriculture also provides a supportive base for rural communities because it has a strong multiplier effect. This in turn contributes to the development of stronger institutions for sustainable development. A new concept of rural development should include a shift away from preoccupation with large- scale farmers as symbols of growth and toward recognition of small producers as both investments worthy and capable of producing added value (Mafeje, 1993: 22). Yet, small producers have serious problems. The lack of irrigation and the inability to purchase chemical fertilizers and other inputs means that small farmer are unable to benefit fully from new high yielding varieties. Small farmers are unable to influence agricultural prices, which are often kept low by the government's deliberate attempt to keep fopperies inexpensive for urban consumers. In order to overcome the difficulties of the small enterprise, agricultural producers have no choice other than to organize themselves, engage in self–help activities, pool their resources and cooperate with each other.

Land reform could significantly relieve pressure on marginal and ecologically fragile lands, because in many developing countries land distribution is highly skewed with most agricultural land being concentrated in small percentage of holdings. Land reform is, however, most difficult to implement because land ownership and land distribution reflect the power structure within a country. One possibility to improve the land tenure situation without drastic reform is the introduction of a progressive land tax. This would induce intensive use to land and discourage the holding of land for speculative purposes. Attractiveness of land to the rich may also be reduced by the withdrawal of input subsides.

As little progress can be expected in the field of land redistribution programmers in a market economy, land tenure questions have to be tackled in an indirect manner, i.e. through the reduction of subsidies, increase of land tax, provision as credit, and support to the smooth functioning of a land market. The recognition of traditional land rights and the enforcement of those rights can provide the assurances needed by the poor to lengthen their time horizons and thus broadened their options for resource management. This recognition needs to include traditional land tenure arrangements, such as common property regimes, which are important for the sustainable use of natural resources. Common property regimes, as opposed to open access, also can provide an institutional framework for internalizing externalities by resources. A common property framework can facilitate the collective action that is needed for integrated approaches to sustainable development through the pooling of knowledge and resources. Experience have shown that centralized political systems and a policy which does not give due attention to the agricultural sector are not conducive to the alleviation of rural poverty.

The success of rural development requires the creation of an enabling policy environment, since isolated projects and efforts will not be able to operate under adverse political and economic conditions. Governments should locate their limited resources to activities, which are necessary for the efficient functioning of the economy and society. Even under a market economy, governments have the responsibility to assist the poor to increase their productivity and thereby try to close the gap between the rich and the poor.

References

De janvry, A. and Sadoulet, E. (1993), Adjustment Policies, Agriculture and Rural Development in Latin America.

Singh A. and Tabatabei, H. (1995a), *Economic Crisis and Third World Agriculture,* p.118-146, Cambridge University Press, FAO.

The State of Food and Agriculture (1995), Rome. FAO (1995b)

World Agriculture: Towards 2010, edited by N. Alexandratos, John Wiley, Chichester, FAO (1995c).

Strategies for Sustainable Agriculture and Rural Development, New Direction for Agriculture, Forestry and Fisheries, Rome.

Mafeje, A.B.M. (1993), "Where the Theory Does Not Fit", *Ceres, No.* 139: 18-23.

Melicxek, H. (1995), "If Poverty is the Problem, Land Reform must be Part of the Answer", *Cares No.* 152: 21-25.

Timmer, C.P. (1994), "Food Prices and Agricultural Development: The Relevance of Asian Experience to Africa", *Agriculture And Rural Development, Vol.* 1, No. 1: 13-19.

World Bank (1993), *Agricultural Sector Review,* Washington, D.C.

16

Cooperative Societies and Weaker Sections

C.S.N. Raju, B. Sudheer

The Primary Agricultural Credit Society provides foundations to the cooperation on which cooperative edifice is built. The credit cooperative, assertive part of rural credit in India celebrated its centenary in March 2004. The rural cooperative systems are mainly credit cooperatives, whose structure is very unique when compared to any other credit institution in the world. They are very close to the rural people's problems and their conditions. They are capable of developing as a single delivery system at the doorsteps of the poor peasants. They also have the ability to contribute to consequential financial requirements at different stages of agricultural production.

The Primary Societies deal with the individuals, but the emphasis is usually changing from the tangible assets to production requirements, and from the credit-worthiness of the person to the credit-worthiness of purpose. At the same time, they do not strictly follow the norms of a bank. Yet, they perform the objectives of bank i.e. sanctioning loan and accepting deposits. Hence, they are regarded as tiny banks for villages, who are the ultimate borrowers working in villages. Since they perform the objectives of banks to extend cooperation, they are popularly known as cooperative banks.

Thrift and savings constitute fulcrum of the working of cooperative banks. Cooperative lending is the means to promote the thrift and savings and service, and the profit is not the motto. They teach the rural farmers to borrow at the right time and in the right amounts and for appropriate use and to repay on the in times, and they alone can teach them to save, so that they may not have to borrow at all . It serves around 120 million rural house-holds residing in about 7 lakh villages through its 5.03 lakh primary societies and disbursing around 46 per cent of total agricultural credit.

Agricultural Credit Cooperatives can be divided into the period of credit and purpose i.e., (a) Short term and Medium term and b) Long term.

Short term loans : Short term loans are for a maximum duration of 18 months (1 ½ year) and are given to farmers for the purchase of production inputs (seeds, fertilisers and pesticides) and to competent them to meet the cost of cultivation, including labour charges for agricultural operations, irrigation and power charges. These loans are commonly known as "Production loans" or "Crop loans".

The crop loan needs of agriculturists depend on the over type of cultivated land, the nature of the crops grown, the level of cultivation, when other method of cultivation have been adopted etc., since the credit needs for crop production vary from region to region, farmer to farmer and crop to crop.

Medium term loans : Medium term loans, which are for a maximum period upto 5 years and, in the case of small farmers 7 years, are sanctioned for development purpose. These loans are commonly known as "investment loans".

The loans for the following purposes may be classified as medium term loans, but their period does not exceed 5 years.

- Minor irrigation development
- Purchase of bullock-carts, build up of farm houses, purchase of tractors, sprayers, threshers and agriculturing machinery, for land improvement schemes, to build godowns, setting us other allied activities.

Long term loans : Where a scheme has a long gestation period and repayment is spread over a period of 10 to 15 years (with the necessary temporary ban) the loans for it are known as long-term loans. Long term loans are issued for the following purposes:

- Development of plantation crops.
- Development of horticulture
- Development of integrated schemes

Objectives and Methodology

The present paper is concentrated to study and examine the socio-economic conditions of the weaker sections in the selected Tenneru society. The total farmers are 764 (23.1 per cent out of total population 3,580). For investigation,hundred samples have been selected on Proportionate Purposive Random Sampling Method. In this technique equal and proportionate representation is given to the sub-strata.Among 764 total farmers, 70.7 per cent, i.e., 540 are marginal farmers. As the number of marginal farmers is larger, their sample is taken in higher size, i.e., 70 (12.9 per cent out of 540) and the number of small farmers 224, i.e., 29.3 per cent is lesser and so their sample is taken in small size, i.e., 30 (13.3 per cent out of 224). These samples are chosen with the purpose, as they possess all common characteristics of the parent population and equal chance has been given to all items to adopt random sampling.

Need for the Study

The need for agricultural credit is extensively widening, where farmers are weary of withered resources. Credible and rational terms and conditions are needed to be framed to nourish the weaker sections financially to process their agricultural operations and enable them to adopt better system of credit disbursement and utilize the cooperation to achieve sustainable development.

Cooperative Societies and Weaker Sections

Credit societies are formed long back, to uplift the weaker sections economically and socially by providing financial assistance in agricultural activities. They contribute credible coordination to compensate the feeble financial status of weaker sections, accounting for two-thirds of country's population, who depend upon rural economy. In addition, 55 per cent of them eke out their livelihood from agriculture sector. Their prosperity and stable economic status depend upon the progressive development of agriculture, consequently enhances nation's economy, provided that the weaker sections are catered with credit at cheaper interest rates by the cooperative credit societies. In a recent study it is observed that majority of the weaker sections haven't got benefited with credit facilities from Primary Agricultural Credit Society (PACS). Surprisingly, their membership is not in proportion to their population. Besides, their participation in relation to the activities of PACS is inadequate.

Among one hundred sample respondents marginal farmers constitute 70 per cent and small farmers constitute 30 per cent. Male respondents dominate with 78 per cent and 22 per cent female are respondents. Respondents belonging to O.C. community are with greater percentage, i.e., 42 per cent, than that of the percentage of S.Cs and S.Ts. who are with 30 per cent and 1.0 per cent respectively, where as B.Cs are less than S.Cs with 27 per cent. Among the 100 sample respondents, the illiterates nearly equivalent with 49 per cent to the literate percentage, i.e. 51 per cent. 65 per cent of the sample respondents have large size of families consisting of 3 to 6 members in each family. Cent-per cent of the marginal farmers get less than Rs 50,00/- of annual income and cent-percent of the small farmers get an income between Rs. 50,000/- and Rs. 75,000/- per annum.

The amounts of loan borrowed by the 100 sample respondents are indicated in the above table. Among 100 sample respondents 61 per cent (61) of them have borrowed below Rs.15,000/- from PACS. Out of these 61 farmers, 80.3 per cent i.e., 49 of them, constituting 70 per cent of the total

Socio-Economic Profile of the Respondent Borrowers

			Possession of land holdings of the borrowers (in acres		
			Marginal Farmers below 2.50 acres	*Small Farmers 2.50–5.00 acres*	Total
Sex-wise Division of the Respondent					
	Male	Count	55	23	78
		Row%	70.5%	29.5%	100%
		Col %	78.6%	76.7%	78%
		Table%	50.0%	23.0%	78%
	Female	Count	15	7	22
		Row%	68.2%	31.8%	100.0%
		Col %	21.4%	23.3%	22.0%
		Table%	15.0%	7.0%	22.0%
Community -wise Division of the Respondent					
	OC	Count	23	19	42
		Row%	54.8%	45.2%	100.0%
		Col%	32.9%	63.3%	42.0%
		Table %	23.0%	19.0%	42.0%
	BC	Count	20	7	27
		Row%	74.1%	25.9%	100.0%
		Col%	28.6%	23.3%	27.0%
		Table %	20%	7%	27.0%
	SC	Count	26	4	30
		Row%	86.7%	13.3%	100.0%
		Col%	37.1%	13.3%	30.0%
		Table%	26.0%	4.0%	

Contd.

	ST	Count	1		1
		Row %	100.0%		100.0%
		Col %	1.4%		1.4%
		Table %	1.0%		1.0%
Literacy Status of the respondents					
	Primary	Count	17	5	22
		Row%	77.3%	22.7%	100.0%
		Col%	24.3%	16.7%	22.0%
		Table %	17.0%	5.0%	22.0%
	Secondary	Count	16	8	24
		Row%	66.7%	33.3%	100.0%
		Col %	22.9%	26.7%	24.0%
		Table%	16.0%	8.0%	24.0%
	Degree	Count	3	1	4
		Row%	75.0%	25.0%	100.0%
		Col%	4.3%	3.3%	4.0%
		Table %	3.0%	1.0%	4.0%
	And above	Count	1		1
		Row%	100.0%	-	100.0%
		Col%	1.4%	-	1.0%
		Table %	1.0%	-	1.0%
	Illiterate	Count	33	16	49
		Row%	67.37%	32.7%	100.0%
		Col%	47.1%	53.3%	49.0%
		Table %	33.0%	16.0%	49.0%
Family size					
	Below-3	Count	16	11	27
		Row%	59.3%	40.7%	100.0%
		Col%	22.9%	36.7%	27.0%

Contd.

		Table %	16.0%	11.0%	27.0%
	3-6	Count	50	15	65
		Row%	76.9%	23.1%	100.0%
		Col%	71.4%	50.0%	65.0%
		Table %	50.0%	15.0%	65.0%
	6- above	Count	4	4	8
		Row%	50.0%	50.0%	100.0%
		Col%	5.7%	13.3%	8.0%
		Table %	4.0%	4.0%	8.0%
Annual income of the barrowers					
	Below 50,000	Count	70	-	70
		Row%	100.0%	-	100.0%
		Col%	100.0%	-	100.0%
		Table %	70.0%	-	70.0%
	50000- 75000	Count	30		30
		Row%	-	100.0%	100.0%
		Col%	-	100.0%	30.0%
		Table %	-	30.0%	30.0%
How much amount have you borrowed?					
	Bellow Rs.15,000/-	Count	49	12	61
		Row %	80.3%	19.7%	100.0%
		Col %	70.0%	40.0%	61.0%
		Table %	49.0%	12.0%	61.0%
	Between Rs.15,000/- to Rs 30,000/-	Count	21	18	39
		Row %	53.8%	46.2%	100.0%
		Col %	30.0%	60.0%	39.0%
		Table %	21.0%	18.0%	39.0%

Contd.

When did you borrow the credit?					
	2002-2004	Count	22	11	33
		Row %	66.7%	33.3%	100.0%
		Col %	31.4%	36.7%	33.0%
		Table %	22.0%	11.0%	33.0%
	2004-2006	Count	10	8	18
		Row %	55.6%	44.4%	100.0%
		Col %	14.3%	26.7%	18.0%
		Table %	10.0%	8.0%	18.0%
	2006-2008	Count	38	11	49
		Row %	77.6%	22.4%	100.0%
		Col %	54.3%	36.7%	49.0%
		Table %	38.0%	11.0%	49.0%
What type of loan you have availed from the society?					
	ST	Count	51	20	71
		Row %	71.8%	28.2%	100.0%
		Col %	72.9%	66.7%	71.0%
		Table %	51.0%	20.0%	71.0%
	LT	Count	19	10	29
		Row %	65.5%	34.5%	100.0%
		Col %	27.1%	33.3%	29.0%
		Table %	19.0%	10.0%	29.0%

Source: Completed from the collected data

marginal farmers and 49 per cent of the total sample respondents, are marginal farmers. Out these 61 farmers, who borrowed less than Rs.15,000/-, 19.7 per cent, i.e., 12 respondents farmers, constitute 40 per cent of the total small farmers and 12 per cent of the total sample respondent farmers, are small farmers. Among 100 sample respondent farmers 39 per cent, i.e., 39 of them have borrowed an amount between Rs. 15,000/- to Rs. 30,000/-. Out of these 39 respondents 53.8 per cent, i.e., 21 of them are marginal farmers. They constitute 30 per cent of the total marginal farmers and 21 per cent of the total sample respondents. Out of 39 farmers 46.2 per cent, i.e., 18 of them, constituting 60 per cent of the total small farmers and 18 per cent of the total sample respondents, are small farmers.

The respondents selected as samples have obtained loans during 3 different periods of years. 33 farmers out of the total 100 sample respondents obtained loans during the years 1998-2000. Among these 33 farmers, 66.7 per cent, i.e., 22 respondents are marginal farmers. They constitute 31.4 per cent of the total marginal farmers and 22 per cent of the total sample respondents. And 33.3 per cent i.e., 11 out of 33 are small farmers. They constitute 36.7 per cent of the total small farmers and 11 per cent of the total sample respondents.

During 2001-2004, 18 per cent, that is, 18 out of 100 sample respondents obtained loans from PACS. Among these 18 farmers 55.6 per cent i.e., 10 are marginal farmers, who constitute 10 per cent of the total sample respondents and 14.3 per cent of the total marginal farmers. Similarly 8 farmers out of the 18, who obtained loans during the same period are small farmers. They constitute 44.4 per cent of the total respondents and 26.7 per cent of the total small farmers and 8 per cent of the total sample respondents.

During 2004-2006, 49 farmers out of one hundred sample respondents obtained loans from PACS. Out of these 49 farmers, 77.6 per cent, i.e., 38 respondent farmers are marginal farmers. They constitute 54.3 per cent of the total marginal farmers and 38 per cent of the total sample respondents. And 22.4 per cent, i.e., 11 respondents. Out of these 49 farmers are small farmers. They constitute 36.7 per cent of the total small farmers and 11 per cent of the total sample respondents.

As per the period of repayment loans are categorized as two types, i.e., 1) Short term loan and 2) Long term loan. When the respondents are posed a question regarding the type of loan they obtained, 71 out of 100 sample respondents have stated that they have obtained short term loans and 29 of them have obtained long term loans. Among 71 barrowers of short term loans, 71.8 per cent, i.e., 51 of total short term, are marginal farmers. They constitute 72.9 per cent of the total marginal farmers and 51 per cent of the total sample respondents. 20 farmers constituting 28.2 per cent out of 71 total short term loan borrowers are small farmers. They constitute 66.7 per cent of the total small farmers and 20 per cent of the total sample respondents. Remaining 29 per cent of the total sample respondent farmers have obtained long term loans. Among these 29, long term loan borrowers. But 19 farmers constituting 65.5 per cent are marginal farmers, who constitute 27.1 per cent of the total marginal farmers and 19 per cent of the total sample respondents. And 10 farmers constituting, 34.5 per cent are the small farmers, who constitute 33.3 per cent of the total small farmers and 10 per cent of the total sample respondents.

Observations

- In Tenneru PACS marginal farmers 70 per cent while 30 per cent are small farmers.
- Forward community members dominate with 42 per cent, followed by 30 per cent of Schedule Castes, are 27 per cent of Backward Castes and only 1 per cent of STs in the society.
- Literates and illiterates are nearly in equal proportion, whereas 15 per cent have technical qualifications.
- Majority of the respondents have large size families.
- Cent per cent of them are marginal farmers, who have an income of Rs.50,000/- per annum.

- Majority of the respondents have been the members in Tennuru PACS for 10 years and have obtained less than Rs.15,000/- as short term loans and all most all the members have utilized the loan for agricultural purpose.

Suggestions

- As the marginal farmers constitute larger percentage, they should be provided required facilities so that they may attain prosperity.
- Motivation should be provided to the S.C., S.T. categories to improve their membership and to uplift them socially and economically.
- Society should provide certain facilities to the artisans also belonging to the weaker sections, besides providing literacy programmes to the illiterates, so that they could acquire awareness of the society and its utility.
- As majority of the respondent borrowers have Rs.50,000/- and less as their annual income, the society should provide provisions to improve their income standards besides educating them of thrift and savings. It should extend support to uplift these weaker sections, who have meager income.
- As most of the borrowers stated they should be provided adequate and sufficient amount of loans to meet and fulfill their agricultural needs.

Conclusion

The Primary Agricultural Credit Society is the foundation of co-operative banking in rural areas catering to the credit requirements of small and marginal farmers. Co-operation contributes credible contribution to compensate the weaker sections to achieve socio-economic development.

References

Sharada. V. (1986), *The Theory of Cooperation*, p. 104, Himalaya Publishing House, Bombay.

Satya Sundaram . I., (2002), *Rural Development*, 2nd Revised Edition 2007, p. 65, Himalaya Publishing House, Bombay.

Ibid. p. 385.

Tripathy. K.K. (2004), "Cooperative Credit and Rural India", *Yojana*, Vol. No. XI, No. 42, April-2004, p.23.

Satya Sundaram . I. (2002), *Rural Development*, 2nd Revised Edition, 2007, p. 365, Himalaya Publishing House, Bombay.

Hajela. T.N. (1987), *Principles, Problems and Practices of Cooperation*, p. 259, Shivalal Agarwala and Company Publishers and Book Sellers, Agra-3.

Satya Sundaram . I. (2002), *Rural Development*, 2nd Revised Edition 2007, p.365, Himalaya Publishing House, Bombay.

Sharada. V. (1986), *The Theory of Cooperation*, p. 195, Himalaya Publishing House, Bombay.

Ibid. p. 196.

Tenth Five Year Plan (2002-07), *Sector Policies and Progresses*, Planning Commission, Government of India, Vol. II, P. 513, New Delhi.

Sharada. V. (1986), *The Theory of Cooperation*, p. 195, Himalaya Publishing House, Bombay.

Hajela. T.N. (1987), *Principles, Problems and Practices of Cooperation*, p.281, Shivalal Agarwala and Company Publishers and Book Sellers, Agra-3.

17

New Generation Financial Institutions and Poverty Alleviation in India

T. Geetha Madhuri, P. Shoba Rani

Poverty as a global phenomenon has varied genesis, dimensions, and definitions. The definition of poverty is to be derived from a holistic approach to understand the multidimensional problem. While human poverty is generally interpreted based on motivation levels, income poverty is defined on the basis of minimum income levels required to meet basic consumption needs and amenities. The definition of poverty needs to go beyond these conventional interpretations and cover the deprivation of human dignity caused by vulnerability to social and cultural shocks resulting in a low quality of life. The eradication of poverty has been an integral component of the strategy for economic development in India. 'Poverty line' the basic indicator of poverty according to the Planning Commission is defined as "total consumption expenditure at which one can expect a person to be adequately nourished in the specific society under consideration". The underlying assumption is that people at the poverty line have just enough money to provide themselves with food that translates into 2200 calories per person. Large sample surveys are conducted by the National

Sample Survey Organization (NSSO) to obtain the consumption expenditure of various groups of the population at an interval of approximately five years. Based on this the incidence of poverty is estimated at national and state levels. It has indeed declined from 54.9% in 1973-74 to an all-time low of 26.1 % in recent groups.

In recent public debates microfinance has been mentioned as an important instrument to combat poverty. Therefore, microfinance has received a lot of attention, both from policy-makers as well as in academic circles. Especially during the past 10 years, microfinance programmes have been introduced in many developing economies. Well known examples are the Grameen Bank in Bangladesh. To support the view that microfinance can be an important instrument to fight poverty, the UN declared 2005 to be the international Year of Micro credit. Recently, the attention for microfinance and its role in reducing poverty was further increased when Muhammad Yunus received the Nobel Peace prize. According to the Nobel Committee, microfinance can help people to break out of poverty, which in turn is seen as an important prerequisite to establish long lasting peace [Nobel Committee 2006].This has led to an almost euphoric attitude among policy-makers and aid organizations about potential poverty reducing effects of micro credit.

Perspectives of Povertyalleviation in India

Empowerment of the poor encompasses three basic dimensions-reduction of poverty, creation of employment and erasing inequality. Since the magnitude of poverty challenges the very basis of State as an independent economic and political unit, it has been realized by the policy planners that development, needs to be people centered and participation oriented across various interfaces. Poverty Alleviation has thus assumed a new thinking and new practices have emerged through integrated community participation of the poor. The basis of the concept of micro finance is self-organization of the poor at the community level driven by a desire and an inherent capacity to improve their living conditions by themselves. Inspired by the success of the Bangladesh Grameen experiment, the self-help group approach in India has taken strong roots as an effective and viable channel to take the poor to a new domain of economic empowerment and social upliftment. Micro finance, which synergies the thrift and credit habits of the poor in a participatory and informal setting, is now widely acknowledged as a strategic tool to dent poverty in all poverty alleviation programmes. With the fast expanding Self Help Groups movement covering nearly 2.89 million SHGs across the country on march 31st 2007, India is poised to provide pragmatic solutions by demonstrating the 'success of micro finance for eliminating total poverty in the coming decade. In view of the larger distribution of poor geographically as well as the magnitude of the population below poverty line, the central government has taken a pro-active stand in dealing with the problem. Policy planners have explored the following approaches in designing different poverty alleviation programmes.

Area development to decrease regional disparities and to take care of vulnerable regions affected by natural calamities.

- Sectoral approach to assist the poor in their livelihood activities with major emphasis on farming.
- Targeted approach for a section of people by creating employment generation through development programmes.
- Empowering approach through financial incentives and credit support for self- employment enterprises in farm and non-farm sector.
- Multipronged approach with integrated spatial and social development

Conclusion

The impact of microfinance on poverty alleviation is a keenly debated issue, however, when implemented and managed carefully and when services are designed to meet the needs of clients, microfinance has had positive impacts, not just on clients, but on their families and on the wider Community.

References

Daley-Harris, S. (2006), *State of the Micro Credit Summit Campaign Report 2006*, Micro Credit Summit Campaign, Washington DC.

Norwegian Nobel Committee (2006), *'The Nobel Peace Prize 2006'*, Press Release, Oslo, October, http://nobelprize.org/nobel_prizes/peace/laureates/2006/press.html

Dun ford, C. (2006), *Evidence of Microfinance's Contribution to Achieving the Millennium Development Goals: Freedom from Hunger*, http://microfinancegateway.org/files/35795_file_Evidence_on_MDGs_Dunford.pdf

Karlan, D. (2001), 'Microfinance Impact Assessments: The Perils of Using New Members as a Control Group', *Journal of Microfinance*, Vol 3, No 2, pp. 75-85.

Armendáriz De Aghion, B and J Morduch (2000), 'Microfinance beyond Group Lending', *Economics of Transition*, Vol 8, No 2, pp. 401-20.

(2005), *The Economics of Microfinance*, MIT Press, and Cambridge, MA.

18

Indira Prabha: An Evaluation Study of Land Distribution Scheme- A Case Study of Visakhapatnam District

B. Lakshmi Bhavani, S. Appala Naidu, N. Bhaskara Reddy

Introduction

The weakest aspect of our economic reforms so far has been scanty attention paid to the social sectors and poverty alleviation progammes. It is true that considerably large amounts of resources have been allocated to rural development, for economic upliftment through provisions of universal primary education, primary health services, housing and other minimum needs including agricultural development programmes aimed at marginal and small farmers in general and agricultural labourers in particular. In fact, social development and poverty alleviation programes are not merely matters of financial allocations but are of social engineering with a strong political commitment. Otherwise, relative poverty and inequality among ruralites remain either constant or will tend to increase.

Failure of land reforms in the country indicates the living conditions of rural poor particularly agricultural labourers. Agriculture is not only to provide gainful employment and incomes to a vast population, but also it is a safety net available for those agricultural labourers who do not have any other employable skills to be absorbed elsewhere. Thus, there is a strong correlation between rural poverty on one hand and a number of major economic and social development programs on the other.

One of the important measures adopted by the Government of A.P to improve the welfare of the weaker sections in recent years is implementation of novel schemes like Rural Housing Programme and Land Distribution Scheme. These social and economic support programmes are not new to the State. Since the formation of the State in 1956, every successive five year plans have attached prominent importance to it and accordingly funds were allocated.

The previous governments ruled by different political parties, and leaders could not effectively implement these programmes for some reasons. However, they partially succeeded in allocating house sites, distribution of waste lands, and surplus lands to weaker sections etc. But, the growing population in rural areas is highly dependent on agriculture which has increased the pressure on land both for house sites and for cultivation purposes.

The Visakhapatnam Case:

Since the State's formation, the land distribution and housing programmes were undertaken in the District to benefit the rural poor. During 1977-78 a massive programme of distribution of waste and surplus lands and development of surplus to S.C., S.T. and B.C. communities in the District was launched by congress-led Govt. At that time, the District

Administration worked with dedication and scrupulously implemented the housing schemes' with other economic support programmes like allotting land to house holds, distribution of milch cattle, plough cattle, bullock carts etc. Thus, a comprehensive benefit programme to the rural poor by identifying the deserved beneficiaries was launched. But, latter these programmes (land distribution and housing) were given a low profile.

Again the present Government which is also a Congress led one, after 28 years has been trying to implement the land distribution programme in the District, as well as in the State. In the District, about Ac 4,504 cultivable waste was distributed among 3467 beneficiaries in the first and the second phases put together covering 26 mandals in the District.

Objectives of the Evaluation Study:

1. To examine whether the lands assigned to the beneficiaries are fit for cultivation.
2. To find out whether the land development activities like levelling and soil conservation were undertaken for the assigned lands and
3. To examine the change, if any, in incomes and work status of the beneficiaries after possessing the assigned land.

Methodology

The Study was conducted during 2003, 2004 and 2005 (reference period) and to study the above objectives a pilot study was conducted in Visakhapatnam District in four villages purposively selected for the Study. Two villages from two mandlas of Chodavaram and Sabbavaram were purposively chosen. From these villages all the beneficiaries (130 households) were taken as the census population. Primary data, with the help of a detailed questionnaire were elicited. In addition, secondary data relating to the village economy and also data relating to land distribution and total number of beneficiaries under Phase-I and II in the District were also collected.

It will be worthwhile to point out at this stage, that it is too early to evaluate the real benefit of the programmes as only one year has elapsed since 2005 the date of its implementation, actual possession of these pieces of land took place at a much latter date.

However, it could be quite useful to analyse the attitude of the beneficiaries regarding the effectiveness of this Programme on their well being. The real success of this

Programme largely depends upon then socio-economic conditions of the beneficiaries.

The significance of owning a pieace of land among rural communities is a strength for any social and economic activity. Sound property rights on agricultural land in rural India create more empowerment to rural poor to face any uncertainly and risk from globalization policy. The growth of population, illiteracy, rural unemployment, absence of skilled labour are some of the reasons for more pressure on land.

Analysis

The real success of any programme largely depends on the socio economic background of the beneficiary households, and enables one to suggest appropriate policy measures for strengthening any such programme and for its proper implementation.

Method of Evaluation of Land Distribution Programme

Two villages each in Chodavaram and Subbavaram Mandals in the Visakhapatnam District under Phase I and Phase II were selected as noted earlier. The total number of beneficiaries from these villages was 130 covering SC, ST and BC communities. Out of 130 households (Table-1) STs constitute 48 percent, followed by BCs (31 percent) and SCs households (22 percent) .All these were landless agricultural labourers. Now they got the cultivator status after possessing the land under 'D' Farm Patta.

Table 1
No. of Beneficiary House-holds by Caste

Caste	*No. of beneficiary households*	*Percent (%)*
SC	28	21.53
ST	62	47.70
BC	40	30.77
Total	130	100.00

Demographic Characteristics of Sample Beneficiaries

The demographic characteristics of the beneficiary households are presented in Table–2. The family members of the beneficiary households are classified into three groups based on age. It is revealed from the Table that out of the 495 members, about 47 percent are below 20 years of age and about 46 percent are in 21 to 51 age group. Only 7 percent of them are in the age group of 51 to 70. This reveals that a majority of members in the beneficiary households are either in potential working group or pursuing education. It is distressing to note that only 20 percent of households are adopting family planning.

Table 2
Demographic Characteristics of the Household Members by Age

Age Group	*No. of Persons*
0-20	233(47.10)
21-50	227(45.90)
51-70	35(7.00)
Total	495(100.00)
Household adopting family planning either of the couple	97(19.60)

Occupational Status

The data relating to the work status are presented in Table-3. About 58 percent of household members are engaged in agricultural operations and a negligible percent of them are in non-agricultural works. About 15 percent of cultivators have leased in land as tenants. The proportion of school going children are about 19, while other (aged and physically handicapped persons) are 7. Thus, a majority of family members are potential workers and are engaged either in agricultural operations or cultivating their leasedin lands. It is further revealed that a major of heads of households, 56 percent, are cultivators and tenants and agriculture laboures without any pieces of owned land.

Table 3
Occupational Status of Household Members

Occupation	*Household Members*	*Head of the Household*
Cultivators	73(14.75)	73(56.20)
Agl. Labour	285(57.58)	57(43.80)
Non-Agl. Labour	7(1.42)	Nil
Studying in Schools &Collages	95(19.16)	Nil
Others staying at houses (disabled and children)	35(7.09)	Nil
Total	495(100.00)	130(100.00)

Note: figures in parenthesis are % to total

Literacy Levels of the Households

The positive role of literacy in eradicating rural poverty and unemployment needs no elaboration. Higher the education, with some skills or professional skills, the better is the chance of managing the farm job in modern agriculture. Education also helps rational use of farm inputs and adopt the new technology. Educational status of the sample household members is presented in Table-4.

Table 4
Literacy Status of Household Members

Literacy status	*Household Numbers*	*Head of the Household*
Illiterate	259(52.22)	108(83.00)
Primary & Secondary	210(42.34)	20(15.38)
Higher education	27(5.44)	2(1.62)
Total	496 (100.00)	130(100.00)

Note: figures in parenthesis are % to total

It is revealed from the Table that, about 50 percent of the members of the households are illiterate and 44 percent had primary and secondary educational status. There are about 5 percent of members with higher education status. The literacy status of family head of the house holds was also enlisted in Table -2. Out of 130 respondents (Head of the household) about 84 percent are illiterate and 15 percent had primary or secondary education. Thus, the household members as well as head of the households have had poor educational status.

Dwelling Conditions

The dwelling conditions of the beneficiary households are presented in Table -5. Out of the 130 households, 79 are living in kutcha houses of their own, while only 5 percent of them are living in pucca or semi pucca houses. Drinking water facility, though hand pump, is available to 49 households. The remaining are dependent the nearby tanks or wells. But, the sources are not dependable in summer. With regard cooking fuel, all households use firewood as the main cooking fuel.

Table 5
Dwelling Conditions of the Householders

Dwelling Conditions	*No. of Households*
Kutcha house	79(17.56)
Pucca and semi pucca house	51(11.33)
Drinking water hand pump	49(10.89)
Other sources	81(18.00)
Lavatory facility near to house	60(13.33)
Cooking fuel(fire wood)	130(28.89)
Total	450(100.00)

Changes in levels of Income

Information on the total annual income of the households was collected for three years 2003, 2004, and 2005 and it is presented in Table -6. Based on income from all sources i.e. casual labour, leased in land, non-agricultural labour and other miscellaneous sources, the households are broadly classified under different income groups. It is revealed from the Table that the proportion of households, which earn income below Rs. 5,000/-per year declined from 17 to 14. Similarly, those earrings an income of to Rs 10,000/- increased from 75 to 78 for the same period. There is no change with regard to the households with income range of Rs 10,000 /-and above during the period.

Table 6
Changes in Levels of Income of the Beneficiaries Between 2003 and 2005

Income Range	*Year 2003No.*	*Year 2004No.*	*Year 2005No.*
0 to 5000	22(16.92)	18(13.84)	18(13.84)
5000 to 10000	97(74.62)	102(78.46)	101(77.70)
10000 and above	11(8.46)	10(7.70)	11(8.46)
Total	130(100.00)	130(100.00)	130(100.00)

Households with Durable Assets and Agricultural Implements

These details are presented in Table- 7. Information relating to some household assets and agricultural implements was collected from the beneficiary households. It is revealed that except, one household all of them owned a dwelling house. Majority of households (54 Percent) possessed bycles and consumer durables like Radio, T.V are possessed by less than 35 percent. The income and employment generating wealth like milch cattle, and agricultural implements are possessed by 59 percent and 100 percent respectively. But, 25 percent of households only owned plough cattle. A majority of households needs help in getting milch cattle and plough cattle and a cart. Out of the 130 households, as many as, 100 households have active participation either in social activities like, self help groups, voluntary organizations or as panchayat members or as political party workers in the villages.

Information on land distribution scheme was made known to a majority of these households, by government officials (90 percent) and only 10 percent by the local panchayat office. It is distressing to, note that out of the 130 households as many as 77 households have incurred unnecessary expenditure to middlemen in the allotment process. Irrigated pieces of land were distributed only to 13 households in Chodavaram Mandal. A majority of households expressed that land distribution was not done fairly. Moreover the land was not distributed to the really needy in the village.

Table 7
Possession of Household Durables and Ag. Implements

Item	*Possed*	*Not possed*
House	129(99.23)	1(0.77)
Bicycle	70(53.84)	60(46.16)
Radio	42	88(87.69)
Television	32(24.61)	98(75.38)
Fan	34(26.15)	96(73.85)
Milchi cattle	77(59.23)	53(40.77)
Plough cattle	33(25.38)	97(74.62)
Ag. Implements	130(100.00)	Nill

Study of the Findings:

During the field investigation in the selected sample villages the beneficiaries expressed many practical problems to cultivate the assigned land. The major one being that the land was not plain and was full of bushes and stones or located at the foot steps of hills, on hill stopes. It is interesting to note that the government allotted land bifurcating it into small plots horizontally to the hill. But the beneficiaries desired vertical bifurcation of the hill stopes. All of them expressed that the land assigned was not ready for cultivation.

The second important issue was that eventhough the "Patta Dar Pass Books" were issued mentioning the extent of land, but the beneficiary was not able to identify the allotted land in the total assigned land.

The beneficiaries expressed that they are unable to work in their lands to clear bushes and stones because they would not get any income from that land with in year. More over, they expressed that they may lose their daily wages which provides for their livelihood. Thus, the beneficiaries expressed that they are not willing to lose work opportunities in agriculture lands and in neighbouring towns like Anakapalle, Sabbavaram and Chodavaram.

Thus, the beneficiaries wanted some financial and technical help to make their assigned lands fit for cultivation. Finally they expressed that the allotted land is useful only to grow cashewnut, and mango plantation which may provide them return only after 5 to 7 years. In their view the allotted land made them as land owners, owing Ac 1.00 to Ac 1.50 which is not technically an economic holding, to get fair returns.

Another important situation is that when nonagricultural work opportunities are available, a majority of the beneficiaries are not interested to work in their assigned land.

Moreover, too many of poverty alleviation programmes, mostly in duplication, gave more confusion to rural labour to possess them. Successive governments always changed the nomenclature name of the programmes but have the same objective and interested to cover more households but put the beneficiaries in a confusing state to enjoy the programmes without complications.

The political parties should aim at poverty alleviation programmes for social upliftment in rural areas in a stabilized manner keeping in view of their financial and revenue sources; otherwise the very objective of the program may fail.

Had the planners, and then political parties, at the time of independence, had implemented strictly family planning programmes, land reforms, and compulsory primary and secondary education programs to the poorer sections of the people in the rural areas, it would not have been a problem of social exclusion and relative poverty among rural poor.

References

Land Reform and Agrarian Change, R. Thomas Rosin (1987), Professor of Anthropology, Sonama State University, Rohnert Park, California, USA, Rawat Publications, Jaipur.

Land Reforms in India (1989), *Achievements, Problems and Prospects*, M.L. Sharma, R.K. Puri, Ajanta Publications (India).

19

Impact of DWCRA on Income and Employment Generation (A Study in Chittoor District)

M. Rukmani, M. Raghava Reddy, S. Rathna Kumari

Introduction

Empowerment of women has become a subject of growing importance around the world in contemporary times. The concern is seen at different levels and circles which include governments, bureaucracy, non-governmental organizations, researchers, women's groups and all those interested in women's empowerment.[1] There has also been a shift in the demands of women from equality in 1970s to development in the 1980s, to empowerment-social, political and economic since the 1990s. Since the term 'empowerment' came to be used from 1980s, the notion of empowerment has become central in/notion discussions on women's development and women's equality. Economic empowerment is a very important component of women's empowerment. As rightly decided at the global conference on women's empowerment during 1988, empowerment is the surest way of making women as partners in development. The Food and Agricultural Organization (FAO) also has emphasized on the empowerment of women at the grass-roots as the most recent approach to women development.In most of the Third World Countries, poverty accentuates the problems faced by women. In these countries, gender relations are influenced by traditional hierarchies based on patriarchy, caste and ethnicity and compounded by inequalities of wealth and power. Women in the lower strata are not only exploited economically but are also socially oppressed.

The excess burden of poverty has been borne by women because the responsibility of the survival of the house-hold rests on the shoulders of the woman. That the families fed, clothed and cared for is the women's concern since it ties up with her share of work as per the gender based division of labour. Under these conditions, woman has to work for longer hours-paid as well as unpaid, and cut down her own consumption. Further, excess burden of poverty on women is the result of existing patriarchal intra-household gender specific disparities in distributive rules with respect to income, resources, consumption and time.

Formulation and implementation of relevant strategies are needed to face the challenge of feminization of poverty. This can be attained through (i) the boosting of productivity in women's paid and unpaid work (ii) the expansion of women's employment opportunities (iii) the raising of income levels in women's job and (iv) the mobilization of women into participatory groups. To attain this, public action is needed. The policies of our government are always towards the achievement of gender equality. Further, the policies towards women have been shifted from women's welfare to women's development and at present, the emphasis is on women's empowerment. The efforts of government and its different agencies are ably supplemented by non-governmental organizations that are playing an equally important role in facilitating women empowerment. Despite concerted efforts of government and NGOs, there are certain gaps. Of course, we have come a long way in empowering women, yet the future journey is difficult and demanding.

Need for Specific Anti-Poverty Programmes for Women

Despite the positive policies and action programmes of the government to uplift women, their problems have been accentuated by land alienation, environmental degradation, increasing agricultural poverty, concentration of resources in few hands, increasing polarization of the rich and the poor and polarization between urban and rural areas. The Sixth Five Year Plan document also recognizes that inspite of the development measures and the constitutional legal guarantees; women have lagged behind in almost all sectors. Majority of labouring women were found in the self-employed and informal sector. They do arduous work as wage earners, piece-rate workers, casual labour and paid and unpaid family labour; still their economic and social conditions are dismal.

The labour market is also not gender-neutral. It favours men against women. Gender inequalities exist in almost all sectors. Unskilled, nerve and back- breaking and low paid work will usually be done by women. In addition, feminization of jobs can also be seen where the operations that fetch higher wages are male preserves and work of arduous nature bringing in lower wages is done by women. Gender inequality also manifests in acquiring educational and vocational skills. Inspite of the impressive increase in total number of literate women, the male–female gaps remain large and a slow rate of progress of women's education is noted with a virtual stagnation in the area of technical education.

Women, who are working in the informal sector of economy, operate in a vicious circle of subsistence, deprivation and survival. They are largely assetless and do not own any productive assets in relation to their work. Even when some of these assets are held by the family, women's own access to and control over these assets have been marginal. Therefore, provision of productive assets in the hands of women, working in the informal sector will result in the qualitative improvement in their lives over a period of time, given other inputs such as knowledge, skill, organization and confidence. Thus, there is a need for the formulation and implementation of programmes that specifically benefit women. While recognizing this need, the Government of India has launched Development of Women and Children in Rural Areas (DWCRA) in September, 1982 as a sub-scheme of IRDP. The objectives of the programme are:

- Improving the status and quality of life of Women and Children living in rural areas
- Enabling women to take up income generating activities
- Providing credit facilities to the rural poor women living below the poverty line to undertake economic activity and
- Involving the community in planning and implementation of the programme.

The economic activities under the above scheme are mainly cottage and house-hold industrial activities in nature, with less technical skill and small investment. The identified women are given training for six months by paying Rs.200 as stipend per month. After this, a group of organizers is selected for each group of 10-15 women. Once the training is completed, each beneficiary would be given a loan ranging from Rs.4000 to Rs.6000, depending upon the nature of the activity, to start their own business as self-employment ventures. Regarding the organizational structure of the scheme, it is managed and supervised by an Assistant Project Officer (A.P.O), preferably a woman, who must spend adequate time in educating the target group of women. The purpose of the programme is to organize women into socio-economic activity groups with the duel objective of providing self-employment opportunities and social strength to them.

Objectives

The major objectives of the study are:

1. To assess the progress of DWCRA programme in the state of Andhra Pradesh in general and Chittoor district in particular.

2. To examine the impact of DWCRA on the generation of income, employment and analyse its impact on expenditure and savings
3. To evaluate the impact of DWCRA on the role of women in decision- making process and
4. To identify the problems faced by women in implementing the DWCRA schemes and suggest suitable measures for effective implementation.

Sample Design

The study is conducted in Chittoor district of Andhra Pradesh. The sample respondents were selected on the basis of multi-stage stratified random sampling. Revenue Division is the first stage unit of sampling, income generating activity is the second stage unit of sampling and respondent is the last stage unit of sampling. Chittoor district is broadly divided into three revenue divisions viz., Tirupati, Chittoor and Madanapalli. Two activities were selected from each division based on the number of DWCRA groups in each activity. The number of DWCRA groups under each selected income-generating activity was broadly divided into SC/ST and non SC/ST groups. Three groups under each category under each income- generating activity was selected on simple random sampling basis. Totally, 36 SHGs were taken up for the study comprising 360 beneficiaries. To evaluate the real impact of the DWCRA on sample beneficiaries, there is need to compare them with non-beneficiaries because some changes in income, employment and assets are likely to take place even without the influence of the scheme. To assess these, a group of non-beneficiaries who belonged to the same village, caste, occupation and income classes as the beneficiaries prior to the coverage under the scheme were selected as a control group for the study. The non-beneficiaries too were post-stratified into occupational and social groups. A total of 144 non-beneficiary house-holds were drawn on random basis (40 per cent of beneficiaries). Thus, the study covers 504 sample women house-holds, 360 representing DWCRA members and the remaining 144 representing non-DWCRA members.

Impact of DWCRA on Income Generation

Development of Women and Children in Rural Areas (DWCRA) aims at improving the socio-economic status of the poor women in the rural areas through creation of group of women for income-generating activities on a self-sustaining basis. The main strategy adopted under the programme was to facilitate access for poor women to employment, skill up-gradation, training, credit and other support services so that the DWCRA women as a group could take up income-generating activities for supplementing their incomes.

Income Generation: Scheme-Wise Analysis

The data with respect to net house-hold income by various activities for 'pre' and 'post' periods are depicted in Table 1

It is evident from the Table 1 that the average house-hold income increased in the post-DWCRA period in case of beneficiaries of all activities. The average house-hold income in the case of Kalamkari has tremendously increased from Rs. 41,100 to Rs. 62,080 registering 51.05 per cent rise in the

Table 1
Scheme-wise Average House-hold Income in the Pre-Post DWCRA Periods in Chittoor District

(in Rupees)

Particulars	*Pre-DWCRA*	*Post-DWCRA*	*Incremental Income*	*Percentage Increase*	*Paired 't' value*
Beads making	59585	75383	15798	26.51	5.295**
Vegetable cultivation	28150	38132	9982	35.46	8.841**
Milch animals	43035	58245	15210	35.34	9.936**
Kalamkari	41100	62080	20980	51.05	8.062**
Tailoring & Embroidery	30805	40860	10055	32.64	8.720**
Non-timber Forest Products	18540	23295	4755	25.65	3.863**
Total Beneficiaries	36869.17	49665.92	12796.75	34.70	11.569**
Non-Beneficiaries	35035.42	36560.42	1525	4.35	2.739*

Source: Field Survey data.

Note:

**: Significant at 1 per cent level.

*: Significant at 5 per cent level.

post-DWCRA period, followed by Vegetable cultivation and milch animals, whereas, the percentage increase in income was the least in the case of non-timber forest products where the average house-hold income was Rs. 23,295 during post-DWCRA period. However, the increase in income was found to be significant as indicated by computed paired't' values were significant at 1 per cent level in all activities. While the incremental income was observed to be marginal in the case of non-beneficiaries.

Income Generation: Caste-Wise Analysis

The generation of income from DWCRA scheme might not be identical among different caste groups. In order to find out the differences, if any, in generation of income from DWCRA assistance, the data were further analysed across the distinct caste group's viz., SC/STs and non-SC/STs. The particulars of average house-hold income from DWCRA schemes among different caste groups are presented in Tables 2.

Table 2 indicates the average household income figures of SC/ST and non SC/ST groups of beneficiaries during pre and post DWCRA periods. Of the total beneficiaries, the incremental income was relatively high for SC/STs (62.54 per cent) in comparison with non SC/STs (43.21 per cent). Among the various income-generating activities, there were striking variations in this regard. In case of Beads Making, the average house-hold income of SC/ST beneficiaries increased by 69.44 per cent, whereas it was 28.83 per cent for non-SC/ST beneficiaries. The same trend is noticed in almost all the categories except Veg.Cultivation and Milch Animals in which the non-SC/ST communities benefited a lot in comparison with SC/STs. In the case of Veg.Cultivation, the percentage of incremental income was 61.02 per cent in non-SC/ST categories as against 52.71 per cent in the case of SC/ST beneficiaries. The same trend is noticed in the case of Milch Animals also. It is concluded from the table that SC/ST beneficiaries benefited more under DWCRA than non-SC/ST beneficiaries. The calculated 't' values between pre DWCRA

Table 2

Caste-wise Average Household Income in the Pre-post DWCRA Periods in Chittoor District

(in Rupees)

Particulars	Pre-DWCRA	Post-DWCRA	Incremental Income	Percentage Increase	Paired 't' value
Beads Making:					
a. SC/ST	17050	28890	11840	69.44	6.472**
b. Non-SC/ST	24800	31950	7150	28.83	5.014**
Veg.Cultivation					
a. SC/ST	25100	38330	13230	52.71	7.564**
b. Non-SC/ST	26350	42430	16080	61.02	4.285**
Milch Animals					
a. SC/ST	14000	19610	5610	40.07	4.463**
b. Non-SC/ST	19247	28535	9288	48.25	7.971**
Kalamkari					
a. SC/ST	17050	27310	10260	60.17	5.233**
b. Non-SC/ST	24800	31850	7050	28.43	5.251**
Tailoring					
a. SC/ST	10500	17540	7040	67.05	10.386**
b. Non-SC/ST	19650	28600	8950	45.55	7.979**
NTFP					
a. SC/ST	10500	21435	10935	104.14	5.806**
b. Non-SC/ST	18000	26895	8895	49.42	5.214**
Total Beneficiaries					
a. SC/ST	15700.00	25519.17	9819.17	62.54	13.578**
b. Non-SC/ST	22141.17	31710.00	9568.83	43.21	11.028**
Non-beneficiaries					
a. SC/ST	12375.00	13562.50	1187	9.59	2.730*
b. Non-SC/ST	20135.83	20735.83	600	2..89	1.963NS

Source: Field Survey data.

Note:

**: Significant at 1 per cent level.

*: Significant at 5 per cent level

NS: Not significant

incomes and post DWCRA incomes of beneficiaries belonging to both caste groups were found to be significant.

Income Generation Occupation-Wise Analysis:

To find out the differential impact, if any, among the various occupational categories, the total beneficiaries were broadly classified into four groups viz., (1) cultivators (2) agricultural labourers (3) rural artisans and (4) others category. The 'pre' and 'post' DWCRA incomes among different occupational groups are indicated in Table.3

A bird's eye view of the Table 3 reveals that the percentage increase in the income in post-DWCRA period was 36.68 per cent in the case of cultivators, followed by rural artisans (18.23 per cent) and agricultural labourers (16.71 per cent). With regard to non-beneficiaries, there was no remarkable improvement in their income level even in post-DWCRA period. Further, it is observed from the table that the percentage increase of income was just 14.18 per cent in the case of cultivators and 7.46 per cent in the case of rural artisans. A very slight change was noticed with regard to others category. Obviously, the income level of the respondents of all occupational groups increased remarkably, in comparison with the non-beneficiaries whose income level did not change much.

Impact of DWCRA on Employment Generation

Growth with social justice demands that the fruits of economic growth should be shared by all, rich as well as poor. An effective employment policy is the most appropriate instrument for achieving this goal within the framework of existing economic and political system. In the absence of full productive employment, the poorest people of the developing countries would not be able to meet their basic needs because of lack of purchasing power and would continue to lack an opportunity of participating in development. One of the major objectives of DWCRA is to provide substantial employment opportunities to women through income- generating activities. DWCRA creates an asset and the act of creation of an asset

Table 3

Occupation-wise Average Household Income in the Pre-post DWCRA Periods

(in Rupees)

Particulars	*Number*	*Pre-DWCRA Period*	*Post-DWCRA Period*	*Incremental Income*	*Percentage Increase*	*Paired 't' value*
			Beneficiaries			
Cultivators	26	54421.92	74387.31	19965.39	36.68	3.5728**
Agricultural Labourers	38	24672.89	28796.84	4123.95	16.71	10.108**
Rural Artisans	31	23753.23	28003.23	4330.34	18.23	10.353**
Others	25	38551.60	43938.40	5386.80	13.97	7.796**
			Non-Beneficiaries			
Cultivators	14	16921.43	19321.43	2400.00	14.18	2.808*
Agricultural Labourers	14	18414.29	19285.71	871.42	4.73	1.310 NS
Rural Artisans	9	10722.22	11522.22	800.00	7.46	1.063 NS
Others	11	26936.36	27686.36	750	2.78	1.420 NS

Source: Field Survey data.

Note:

** : Significant at 1 per cent level.

* : Significant at 5 per cent level

NS: Not significant

and subsequently the process of maintenance and operation of the asset leads to employment generation.

Employment Generation: Scheme-Wise Analysis

To find out the differential impact, if any, among various schemes, the data were further disaggregated into six activity based categories as shown in Table 4.

The data presented in Table 4 reveals that the magnitude of incremental employment varied among the selected activities in all the divisions. The percentage increase in average house-hold employment was high in beads-making (27.91 per cent), followed by vegetable cultivation (26.61 per cent) and non-timber forest products (25.95 per cent). But the percentage increase was the least in the case of kalamkari accounting for 21.90 per cent. The incremental employment was found to be highly significant at 1 per cent level in beads-making, vegetable cultivation, milch animals and tailoring and embroidery. In the case of kalamkari and non-timber forest products, the't' value is significant at 5 per cent level.

Employment Generation: Caste-wise Analysis

The average household employment of the respondents by caste groups viz., SC/STs and non SC/STs during pre and post DWCRA periods are presented in Tables 5.

It can be seen from the Table 5 that the incremental employment was relatively high for non-SC/ST beneficiaries in the case of all activities viz., vegetable cultivation, Milch Animals, kalamkari, tailoring and non-timber forest products. To test the impact of DWCRA on employment generation, 't' test was applied in which the significant increase in household employment was noticed in both SC-STs group and non-SC-ST group; but, the level of significance varied from one activity to another activity.

Employment Generation: Occupation-wise Analysis

The data with respect to occupation-wise average house-hold Employment of respondents during pre and post DWCRA periods are depicted in Table 6.

Table 4
Scheme-wise Average Household Employment in the Pre-Post DWCRA Periods in Chittoor District

(Man days)

Particulars	Pre-DWCRA	Post-DWCRA	Incremental Employment	Percentage Increase	Paired 't' Value
Beads making	509.85	652.15	142.30	27.91	16.092**
Vegetable cultivation	511.15	647.15	136.00	26.61	9.026**
Milch animals	569.40	716.15	146.75	25.77	10.784**
Kalamkari	520.50	634.50	114.00	21.90	9.757**
Tailoring & Embroidery	618.50	751.35	132.85	21.48	9.255**
Non-timber Forest Products	452.75	570.25	117.50	25.95	10.170**
Total Beneficiaries	530.35	661.92	131.57	24.80	12.164**
Non-Beneficiaries	544.85	562.35	17.50	3.21	1.320^{NS}

Source: Field Survey data.
Note: **: Significant at 1 per cent level.

Table 5

Caste-wise Average Household Employment in the Pre-Post DWCRA Periods in Chittoor District

(Man days)

Particulars	*Pre-DWCRA*	*Post-DWCRA*	*Incremental Employment*	*Percentage Increase*	*Paired 't' value*
Beads Making:SC/ST Non-SC/ST	522.90496.80	668.60635.70	145.70138.90	27.8627.95	11.322**10.913**
Veg. Cultivation:SC/STNon-SC/ST	516.00506.30	639.40654.90	123.40148.60	23.9129.35	12.787**5.157**
Milch Animals:SC/STNon-SC/ST	626.40512.40	775.90656.40	149.5144.0	23.8628.10	7.046**7.927**
Kalamkari:SC/STNon-SC/ST	552.00489.00	656.40612.60	104.4123.6	18.9125.27	12.767**6.335**
Tailoring:SC/STNon-SC/ST	629.00608.00	758.70744.00	129.70136.00	20.6222.37	5.785**7.118**
NTFP:SC/STNon-ST/ST	441.00464.50	527.70612.80	86.70148.30	19.6631.93	6.188*11.857**
Total Beneficiaries SC/STNon-SC/ST	547.88512.83	671.11652.83	123.23139.9	22.4927.28	17.693**18.400**
Non-beneficiariesSC/ST Non-SC/ST	525.79563.91	544.79578.91	19.0015.00	3.612.65	1.270^{NS}1.844^{NS}

Source: Field Survey data.

Note:

** : Significant at 1 per cent level.

* : Significant at 5 per cent level.

NS : Not significant.

Table 6

Occupation-wise Average Household Employment in the Pre-Post DWCRA Periods in Chittoor District

(Man days)

Particulars	*Number*	*Pre-DWCRA Period*	*Post-DWCRA Period*	*Incremental employment*	*Percentage Increase*	*Paired 't' value*
			Beneficiaries			
Cultivators	26	604.00	835.20	231.20	38.27	6.987**
Agricultural Labourers	38	511.15	647.15	136.00	26.61	5.170**
Rural Artisans	31	452.75	570.25	117.50	25.95	4.255**
Others	25	618.50	751.35	132.85	21.48	3.026**
			Non-Beneficiaries			
Cultivators	14	477.27	495.89	18.62	3.90	1.451[NS]
Agricultural Labourers	14	411.12	425.23	14.11	3.43	1.310[NS]
Rural Artisans	9	402.50	418.30	15.80	3.92	1.063[NS]
Others	11	441.00	459.23	18.23	4.13	1.420[NS]

Source: Field Survey data.

Note:

** : Significant at 1 per cent level.

NS : Not significant.

A bird's eye view of the Table 6 reveals that the percentage increase in employment in post-DWCRA period was 38.27 per cent in the case of cultivators, which was followed by agricultural labourers (26.61), rural artisans (25.95 per cent). With regard to non-beneficiaries, there was no remarkable improvement in their employment level. It is observed from the table that the percentage increase of employment is just 3.90 per cent in the case of cultivators and 3.92 per cent in the case of rural artisans. It is clear from the table 6 that the employment level of the beneficiaries increased remarkably in comparison with the non-beneficiaries whose employment level did not change much.

Conclusion

The primary objective of the DWCRA is to increase the income of target groups and bring them above the poverty line. The study revealed that the average household income of beneficiaries increased by 34.70 per cent and this was found to be statistically significant. Scheme-wise analysis revealed that the income-generating effects of different schemes of DWCRA were not identical. The study revealed that the increase in income is more for non-SC/STs in comparison with SC/STs. It was observed that the average house-hold employment increased by 146.75 per cent. Caste-wise analysis revealed that the incremental employment was relatively high for non- SC-ST beneficiaries. The present study revealed that DWCRA had significant impact on the expenditure of the sample beneficiaries. Among the caste groups, the improvement in the level of expenditure is observed to be more for non-SC/STs in comparison with SC/STs. The average household savings has increased during the post-DWCRA period in case of beneficiaries of all schemes. The present study revealed that DWCRA had highly significant impact on women's role in decisions making.

Suggestions

In the light of the empirical study, the following suggestions are offered for the effective role of DWCRA programme can play in the economic upliftment and improvement of the quality of life of the poor/low-income rural women.

- Governmental and non-governmental organizations should work in tandem motivating the low income rural women to form into SHGs and eventually become members of the DWCRA groups.
- Rural facilitators selected both by the governmental and non-governmental organizations should help the women members of SHGs to identify the trade/unit in accordance with specific interest and relevant skills of the rural women. Women with an attitude for specific trades/units with specific skills should be formed into homogeneous groups.
- Rural depots/kiosks may be set up to make available inputs/raw materials required by the members of DWCRA.
- Rural facilitators can identify the product specific marketing problems and help the members of DWCRA to sell their products through DWCRA bazaars. DWCRA bazaars must be set up for product marketing.
- Periodical up gradation of trade/unit/business-specific skills of the members of DWCRA will help them become technically competent and commercially competitive and socially self reliant.
- Many DWCRA groups failed to function profitably because the training imparted to the members was inadequate and unsatisfactory. Therefore, suggested that NGOs can arrange for the direct training for beneficiaries either through their own staffs or arranging for training through another institution.
- Backwardness and forward linkages by way of timely supply of required raw materials inputs and sale of the products must be ensured.

Inter-developmental co-ordination is an essential pre-requisite for the effective and successful implementation

DWCRA programme as potent instrument for the economic empowerment of rural women. Singly we fail but we succeed should be an eye-opener both to the governments departmental implementers and programme beneficiaries.

References

Vijayalakshmi K. (1999), "DWCRA Schemes as means of Empowering Women" paper presented in *Andhra Pradesh History Congress,* Proceeding of the Twenty third session, Narsapur.

Ruth Dixton- Muller and Richard Anker (1990), "*Assessing Women's Economic contributions to development*", International Labour office, Geneva, p.1.

Viswanathan, Sujatha (1997), "Grouping Women for Economic Empowerment" *Yojana,* Vol 41, No 3, March , pp. 37-38.

http:/ www.smalindustryindia.com/ssindia/census.htm

Dilip, S. Takur (1985), Poverty, *Inequality and Unemployment in Rural India, Some Conceptual and Methodological Issues in Measurement,* B.R publishing corporation, Delhi.

Amartya Sen (1999), *Inequality Re-examined,* Oxford University Press, New Delhi.

International Labour Organisation (1992), *India Employment-Poverty and Economic Policies,* New Delhi, December.

Mishra, "A.P. (1988), Rural Poverty in India: Problem in Planning and Strategy for Poverty Alleviation", Deep and Deep publications, New Delhi.

Mukul Mukharjee (1996), "Towards Gender Awareness Data Systems Indian Experience", *Economic and Political Weekly,* Vol. XXX1, No 43, pp. 63-71.

Hanumantha Rao, CH. (1992), "Integrating Poverty Alleviation Programmes with Development Strategies– Indian Experience", *Economic and Political Weekly,* Vol.27, No. 48, November 28, pp. 2603-2607.

20

HRD Practices in Small-Scale Industry (A Study with special reference to Gulbarga District in Karnataka)

Santosh Singh Bais

The real strength of the country lies in the development of the human mind and body. McGregor observed, people have got a large amount of creativity, imagination, ingenuity to solve the problems of organization. But often these potentials are not fully utilized by management through appropriate and systematic efforts. As has been were observed: "Each human being is born as some thing new, something that never exited before. Each is born with the capacity to win at life.... Each has his own unique potentials, capabilities and limitations". The HRD is multidimensional concept. Basically, HRD is three pronged focusing on: the human aspect where people are seen as having skill, having potentials and ability to grow, change and develop; the resource aspect where individuals are considered resources rather than problems; and the development aspects where there is an emphasis on the discovery and maturity of their potential. It was rightly remarked that HRD is the process of increasing knowledge, skills, capabilities and positive work attitudes and values of all people working at all levels in a business undertaking.

No nation can become strong if it ignores its most precious natural resources i.e., its people. It is clearly said by the eminent economist Adam Curie that the development of the organization as well as the nation lies in the development of their individuals[5]. India is a large country and has vast potential to become a strong and modern nation with its huge natural resources and sizeable population. It is the third largest body of scientific and technical manpower. Every human being has the ability and potentials to do remarkable things if they are provided with opportunities and congenial climate to understand, develop and utilize his or her potential· The present paper highlighted the human resources development practices in small-industry of Gulbarga district in Karnataka.

Introduction

Human Resources Development (HRD) played key role in manufacturing and non-manufacturing industry, because, the rich physical resources alone cannot help the industry to achieve the over all objectives of organization. The development of human resources facilitates to transformation of physical resources into productive resources. And the difference in the level of economic development of the industries are largely a reflection at the difference in the quality of human resources. The factors like knowledge, value, attitudes and general orientation and quality of the employee of the industry that determine the overall competitive ability of the organization. In view of this human resources are assuming increasing significance in modern small-scale industry. Obviously, majority of the problems in manufacturing industry are human and soil rather than physical, technical or economic. The failure to recognize this face cause immense loss to the industry, nation and society. Due to this reason at the enterprise level, there is urgent need for effective utilization of human resources to attain organizational objectives. This can be accomplished by understanding limitations of human resources and developing in order to face the challenges of globalization. However the Human resources development is a dynamic process, which facilitates to continue evolving out new knowledge and practices, necessitated by the exigencies of the situation challenges, fuelled by human idealism, supported by a growing knowledge base about human system and chiseled by pioneering practitioners. It is very important not only point of administration but also for corporate world. The globalization and technology charge have opened up many new opportunities and threats. In view of this human resources development is a key factor for utilizing available opportunity fully and tackling threats without fail. Rao, T. V. (1999) argues that human resources development is continuous process to ensure the development of employee's competencies, dynamism, motivation and effectiveness in a systematic and planned manner. Tiwar, T. D. (1999) they argues that the objective of human resources development is to prepare people for performing task which they may be required to perform in future as they go up in the organizational hierarchy and it also required to develop competencies, knowledge, attitudes, skill to meet the requirement of organization.

Significance of the Study

The small-scale industry sector (SSI) over the years has grown steadily and occupied an important place in the Indian economy. Contribution of the sector in terms of generation of employment, out put and export is quite significant. The sector currently account for 95% of the industrial units in the country and contributing 40% of the manufacturing sector. However at present most of the SSI not increase their core competency due to many reasons such as inadequate policy regarding human resources, inadequate training, lack of motivation, lack of sound organizational culture, lack of ethical practices towards human resources, lack of sincere effort to satisfy the needs of human resources etc. In view of the small-scale industry not able to get competitive advantages over competitors. Hence the study assumed great importance to know the plight of human resources development practices in small-industry of Gulbarga district.

Reasons Responsible for Human Resources Development

The different reasons responsible for HRD in business organization are such as need to increase the capabilities, competencies, efficiency and effectiveness of human resources, need to achieve the objectives, goals and targets of organization, need to motivate the employees in order to use their hidden talents for higher production, need to build-up good relationship between management and workers, need to increase employees moral, need to create sense of belongingness in the mind of employee's about organization, need to increase the growth and prosperity of organization, need to proper man power planning and training, need to encourage employees to take active part in decision making, need to get competitive advantages over competitors, need to sound corporate culture for individual excellence, need to optimum utilization of available resources in organization, need to reduce management turnover, need to strengthen team spirit among different teams and need to strengthen superior subordinate relationship.

Objective of the Study

1. To study the significance of human resources in small-scale industry
2. To identify the possible reasons which is responsible for HRD
3. To examine critically human resources development practices in SSI
4. To study the satisfaction level of employees towards their job.
5. To make suggestions in the light of the findings of the study to ensure effective human resources development practices in SSI.

Sample Design

In Gulbarga district the size of registered small-scale industry is very large. Since detail study of all registered small industry regarding human resources development practices is very difficult and time consuming, and in order to keep the enquiry with in manageable but reliable limits, the convenient sampling method was adopted and 150 sample small-scale units selected, for in-dept study. Hence the effective size is 150 units.

Source of Data

The study is based on both primary and secondary data. Primary data collected from the sample of small-scale entrepreneurs and employee of organization by adopting convenient sampling method through pre-tested questionnaire. The secondary data was collected through sources like, Director of Industry and Commerce, Government of Karnataka, Bangalore and DSO etc.

Scope and Limitation of the Study

The scope of the study is limited to small-scale units where the investment in plant and machinery is Rs. 1 crore. In other words the study does not cover the tiny enterprise. A tiny unit is very small and is managed by owner himself and therefore does not need maintenance of record systematically. Moreover, the owners of the tiny units do not appreciate. That is why the tiny units will be excluded from the ambit and scope of the study.

Plight of HRD Practices in SSI

Human resources Development is an emerging field in the area of personnel management, although, the human resources development practices exist since the beginning of civilization. The main aim of HRD is to prepare employees for performing the job according to need of the business organization

Human Resources Planning

Human resources planning are a key factor in any organization to ensure right number and right kind of people at the right place at the right time. The organization has no clear cut human resources planning, the organization is not able to estimate required human resources and not facilitates the organization to discharge organization functions effectively.

Table 1
Human Resource Planning

Types of Industry	*Responses* Yes	No	*Total*
Agro-bas Industry	9(26.4)	25(73.3)	34(22.6)
Electronic and Electrical	18(72)	7(28)	25(16.7)
Foundry Units	28(87.5)	4(12.5)	32(21.3)
Building Material	19(63.3)	11(36.7)	30(20)
Other Industry	22(75.8)	7(24.2)	29(19.4)
Total	96(64)	54(36)	150(100)

Sources: Field survey

Table I reveals the types of industry and human resources planning. Among 150 sample respondents 96 units have clear cut human resources planning and 54 units constituting 36 percent have no clear cut human resources planning. Further it reveals that 34 sample units selected agro base industry amounting (22.6%), 1.3% of the units belong to foundry units and 30 units belong to building material industry

Table 2
Sex of the Entrepreneur and Human Resources Planning

Sex	*Responses* Yes	No	*Total*
Male	89(68.4)	41(31.6)	130(86.7)
Female	7(35)	13(65)	20(13.3)
Total	28(87.5)	4(12.5)	32(21.3)

Sources: Field survey

Table 2 reveals the sex of the entrepreneurs and HRP. 130 sample units amounting 86.7% were male and 20 entrepreneurs constituting 13.3% were female. It shows female citizen do not find the environment favorable for them to become entrepreneurs due to many reasons such as lack of family support, male dominant society, lack of adequate education and information, low risk bearing capacity, lack of general management skill and responsibility to look after the children and other house hold activities. As the calculated value of chi-square value is 90.7. The table value of Chi-square at 5% level of significance for I degree of freedom is 3.84.

Table 3 gives information about earlier occupation of the entrepreneurs and HRP. The success of economic activities depends upon the occupation before they turned entrepreneurs and the entrepreneurial development in any Country is based on to a large extent on the trading culture of the nation.

Education is recognized as a great motivating factor and an agency of social change and it is a key factor for the prosperity of industry. However here an attempt is made to study the relationship between level of education and human resources planning.

Table 3
Earlier Occupations of the Entrepreneurs and HRP

Earlier occupation	*Responses*		*Total*
	Yes	*No*	
Business	35 (77.7)	10 (22.3)	45 (30)
Industry	20(83.3)	4(16.7)	24(16)
Unemployed	10(33.3)	20(66.7)	30(20)
Employment in Private factory	19(76)	6(24)	25(16.7)
Other Industry	12(46.1)	147(53.9)	26(17.3)
Total	96(64)	54(36)	150(100)

Sources : Field survey

Table 4
Level of Education of Entrepreneurs and HRP

Level of Education	*Responses*		*Total*
	Yes	*No*	
SSLC	10(40)	15(60)	25(16.3)
Graduate	25(62.5)	15(37.5)	40(26.7)
Post graduate	14(70)	6(30)	20(13.3)
Technical	47(72.3)	18(27.3)	65(43.3)
Total	96(64)	54(36)	150(100)

Sources: Field survey

The Table 4 reveals that the level of education and human resources planning. 25 entrepreneurs were educated them up to SSLC, out of that 60% of them have no human resources planning, 40 entrepreneurs we educated up to graduate among them, 25 entrepreneurs constituting nearly 63% have human resources planning. 65 entrepreneurs belong to technical education, out of that 47 entrepreneurs have human resources planning amounting 72.3% and 70% of post graduate entrepreneurs have clear cut human resources planning.

Recruitment and Selection

After knowing the actual requirement of manpower on the basis of job description and specification next step is to recruit right person for right job. (Edwin B Fippo). Recruitment is the process of searching for prospective employees and stimulating them to apply for jobs in the organization.

Table 5
Source of Recruitment and Selection

Sources	*No. of Respondents*	*Percentage*
From the existing Employees	95	63.3
Advertising Vacancies	49	32.6
Employment Exchange	12	8
Direct recruitment from Colleges and universities	8	5.3
Application at the Factory Gate	40	26.7
Other source	37	24.7
Total	-	-

Source: Field survey
Note: The responses more than 150 because of multiple answer and percentage calculated on 150 sample respondents.

Through this process employers are able to searching a right person for the right job for the organization by devising an appropriate application format for the job requirement. The main aim of this process is to select, develop and maintain correct size of human resources to perform organization activities in order to achieve the organization goals. Table 5 reveals that the sources of recruitment. Among different sources, prominent sources are to get manpower through existing employees amounting to more than 63.3%. 49 sample units recruit manpower through advertising the vacancies constituting nearly 33% and usually this method is used by small-scale units to recruit the skilled workers and clerical staff. Application at factory gate is third popular method, which used by the units to obtain the required manpower (26.7%). The source may be tapped to recruit causal and unskilled workers.

Table 6
Procedure Followed to Recruitment and Selection

Procedure	*No. of Respondents*	*Percentage*
Interview	120	80
Written Test	20	13.3
On the Job Test	65	43.3
No. Procedure	20	13.3
Total	-	-

Sources: Field survey
Note:
1. The response more than 150 because of multiple answer and percentage calculated on 150 sample respondents.

Table 6 reveal the information about procedure followed to recruit and selection of manpower. The small-scale units in Gulbarga district followed different procedure to get potential employees, the exact procedure depends upon nature of job. Among different method the interview method is more popular (80%). This may be because of, it facilitates to test the potential employees mental and social make-up. Above all it helps to recruitment authority to judge whether the candidate eligible to perform the job according to the need of the organization or not. 65 units followed on job test to recruit manpower, and 20 units constituting 13.3% not followed any method to recruit manpower.

Training and Development

The efficiency of an organization is purely based on training and development of personnel. The globalization exposes many opportunity and threats to business organization; therefore, the organization required to develop their employees properly to utilization of available opportunity and to tackle the threats without fail. The training is a key factor in any organization because, training brings about an improvement in quality and quantity of out put by increasing the skill of employees.

Table 7
Reveals the Training

Training Method	*No. of Respondents*	*%*
Induction Training	30	20.0
Off the job Training	4	2.7
On the Job Training	25	16.6
Supervisory Training	21	14.0
No Training	70	46.0
Total	150	100

Source: Field survey

Table 7 reveals the training method used by the SSI to increases their employee performance. 70 units not under taken any training to their employees constituting 46.7%, 30 units amounting 20% offering induction training, 25 units provide on job training and negligible percentage i.e. 2.7% offered off job training.

Factors Consider for Performance Appraisal

Table 8. gives information about factors considered for performance appraisal for measuring the performance of their employees. Among different factors, production of output is one of the prominent factor which is taken by all SSI to measure the performance of employees (100%), 120 sample units constituting 80% considered punctuality and regularity among different factors to take decision regarding employees. In addition to above factors some of the units have taken factors like loyalty to employer, acceptance of responsibility, and general co-operation and 38 units not taken performance appraisal to judge the performance of human resources.

Promotion Policy

Promotion played significant role in order to satisfy the need of the employee as well as it helps to get maximum work from the employee by the organization. Promotion concerned with advancement of the employees to a better and high position it.

Table 8
Factors Considered for Performance Appraisal

Factors	*No. of Respondents*	%
Regularity and Punctuality	120	80
Production of out Put	150	100
Loyalty to employer	106	70.6
Relation With Subordinates	35	23.3
Acceptance of responsibility	50	33.3
General co-operation	41	27.3
Not under take performance Appraisal	38	25.5
Total	-	-

Source: Field survey
Note:
1. The response more than 150 because of multiple answer and percentage calculated on 150 sample respondents.

involves higher responsibilities require a greater skill and command to perform the duty. Promotion may be horizontal or vertical. Horizontal promotion is a minor promotion with in the same classes of job such as from lower division clerk. Vertical promotion of a clerk to an office superintendent. Table 9 reveals the opinions of respondents about promotion policies. 113 units (out of 150) have promotion policies and 37 units constituting 24.7 have no promotion policies.

Table 9
Opinions of the Respondents About Promotion Policy

Response	*No. of Respondents*	%
Yes	113	75.3
No	37	24.7
Total	150	100

Source: Field survey

Incentives

Incentives are very important in any organization to motivating the employees to out their full strength towards organization to increase the quality of product, increase the capacity of employees and increase the satisfaction level of employees.

Table 10
Information Relating to Incentives

Incentives	*No. of Respondents*	*%*
Increment	150	100
Merit Certificate	29	19.3
Cash Award	27	38
Production Incentives	120	80
Bonus	111	74
Promotion	117	78
Total	-	-

Source: Field survey
Note:
1. The response more than 150 because of multiple answer and percentage calculated on 150 sample respondents.

Table 10 reveals the information relating to incentives. Among sample units, 100% provide increment to their employees, 120 units offered production incentives, 111 units provide bonus, 113 units promoted their employees from lower position to higher position and only 57 units offered cash award to their employees for motivation.

Table 11
Opinions of the Respondents Towards Working Condition

Working Condition		*No. of Respondents*	*%*
Lighting:	1. Satisfactory	125	83.3
	2. Unsatisfactory	25	16.7
Fans:	1. Adequate	106	70.7
	2. Inadequate	44	29.3
Ventilation:	1. Adequate	65	43.3
	2. Inadequate	85	56.7
Toilets:	1. Adequate	99	66.0
	2. Inadequate	51	34.0
Posture:	1. Adequate	107	71.3
	2. Inadequate	43	28.7

Sources: Field survey

Working conditions play a significant role in order to create good working environment in organization and encourages the worker to contribute their fully capacity towards organization goal. In this study to take different variable to know the working condition of sample units like lighting, fans, ventilation, toilets and posture. For achieving this objective, each unit has taken a most senior employee in organization to know the working condition of the organization. Among sample respondent 83.3% opined organization provide adequate lighting facilities, 44 respondents constituting 29.3 percent opined that the organization does not provide adequate Fan facilities, 85 respondents felt that the organization have no adequate ventilation, regarding toilet, 99 respondents stated the organization provide adequate toilet facilities and 107 respondents constituting 71.3% opined favorably about posture.

Table 12
Opinions of the Respondents Towards Wage and Salary

Response	*No. of Respondents*	*%*
Adequate	70	46.7
Inadequate	80	53.3
Total	150	100

Source: Field survey

Human resources played a significant role in any organization to transform physical resources into productive resources. And they have much expectation from the organization among different expectation one of the important expectation is adequate salary/wage for work. Table 12 reveals the opinions of respondents towards wage and salary. Among sample respondents 80 felt that the organization does not provide adequate salary for work constituting 53.3% 70 respondent amounting 46.7% express favorable opinions about wage/salary.

Conclusion

Human resources play a strong champion role and have to lead from the front. This will mean that all activities relating to employees as well as organization need to manage by human resources. This is only possible when origination available quality, knowledgeable, intelligent, satisfied human resources. So, every organization required ensuring sound human resources planning, acceptable polices regarding recruitment and suitable performance appraisal, sound motivation polices, sincere effort towards selection, proper training and development, adequate education, and fair promotion policies.

References

Rao, T.V. (1986), "*Human Resource Development in Government System*", *Management in Government,* XVIII (2), July–Sept.

Silvera, D.M. (1988), "*Human Resource Development: The Indian Experience*", New Delhi: News India.

Pattanaik, B.K. (1999), "Training Human Resource Development and Economic Development in Agricultural" *Indian Journal of Training and Development (I.J.T.D.),* April–June, Vol. XXIV, No. 2.

Nassam, W. Senior, *Industrial Efficiency and Social Economy (Ed.)* by S. Leon Levy, Vol. 1, Henry Molt and Co-University Press, Cambridge.

Rao, V.S. (1995), "Human Factor in Organization", *The Economic Times* 13th Feb.

Philip, J. (1980), "Human Resources Development in India: Experiments and Experiences", *Indian Journal of Training and Development,* No. X (1), Jan–Mar.

Reddy, R.K. (1993), "Rethinking HRD–The Context of Strategic Environment *IJTD,* July–Sept., Vol. XXIII, No. 3.

Prasanna, K. (1993), "The Emerging Role of Human Resource Development", *IJTD,* April-June, Vol. XXIII No. 2.

Chakrapani, R. (1993), "HRD as Economic Perspective" *The Hindu,* Sept. 29.

21

Impact of Green Revolution on Agricultural Development in India

D. Francis, D. Pulla Rao

Introduction

Agriculture is the largest sector of economic activity in India. The significance of agriculture in India arises also from the fact that the development in agriculture is an essential condition for the development of the national economy. It provides not only food and raw materials but also employment to a very large proportion of population. It is clear, that agriculture is the backbone of the Indian economy and prosperity of agriculture can also largely stand for the prosperity of the Indian economy. Agricultural growth has direct impact on poverty eradication. Agricultural growth is also an important factor in containing inflation, raising agricultural wages and for employment generation. But after independence our agriculture was in a hopeless and deplorable condition. Our farmers were in heavy debt to the private moneylenders. They were having small and scattered holdings. They had neither the money nor the knowledge to buy and use proper equipment, good seeds and chemical fertilizers. Most of our agriculture was dependent upon rainfall and upon the vagaries of the monsoons. Productivity of land as well as of labour had been declining and was at a very low level. In spite of the fact that nearly 70 per cent of our working population was engaged in cultivation, the country was not self-sufficient in food grains. Rapid growth of agriculture is, therefore, essential to achieve the multi-pronged objectives of the Indian planning system. These include self-reliance at the national level, food security to individual households, equitable distribution of income and wealth, rapid reduction of poverty levels, absorbing the growing labour force, facilitating export growth, achieve balance of payments equilibrium in the economy, and so on.

Trends of Food Grain Production in Agriculture

Food grain production occupies the most dominant position in India's agriculture, which covers over 65 per cent of the Gross Cropped Area (GCA). Since the beginning of the green revolution in the mid 1960s, the country has shown quite impressive growth in food grain production. Chronic food deficits and hovering Malthusian crisis were overcome and that have given way to self-sufficiency in food grains and occasional marginal surpluses by the 1980s and 1990s. However, with the population growing at nearly 2 per cent per year (nearly 18 to 20 million people being added every year) and accelerating income growth, demand for food is continuously growing in the economy. India's food grain production has also been increasing rapidly over the years.

It is estimated, that India's food grain production in the early phase of green revolution has decreased from 82,018 million tonnes in 1960-61 to 72.35 million tonnes in 1965-66 and then increased to 108.42 million tonnes in 1970-71. The food grains production further increased to 121.03 million tonnes in 1975-76 and to 150.44 million tonnes in 1985-86. However, during the early phase of economic reforms (1990-91), the food grain production was 176.39 million tonnes and ultimately it increased to 199.54 million tonnes in 2000-01. Thus, the amount of food grain production during the period 1960-2001 has grown more than two-fold. The percentage growth rate of the food grain production during first decade was 32.19; 19.52 in the second decade; 36.11 in the third decade; and 13.12 in the last decade. The percentage growth rate of food grain production was the highest in the third decade. The growth rate of food grain production was the lowest in the fourth decade. This was probably due to the erratic nature of monsoon in the country. The annual compound growth rate of the food grain production was 2.25 per cent. This suggests that economic reforms had a positive impact on green revolution for increasing the food grains production in the country. Yield of food grains per hectare of net sown area also increased substantially during our study period (except in 1965-66). Yield of food grains in 1960-61 was 710 Kg / ha and decreased to 629 kg / ha in 1965-66. The yield of food grains increased to 872 kg / ha in 1970-71 and continuously increased and ultimately it reached to 1648 kg / ha in 2000-01. Yield of food grains per hectare during the period 1960-2001 has grown more than two-fold. The percentage growth rate of the yield of food grains in the first decade of the study period (1960-61 to 1970-71) was 22.82 and second decade it was 17.32 and in third decade it was 34.90 and in the fourth decade it was 19.42. The percentage growth rate of the yield of food grains reached the highest in the third decade of our study period (i.e. 1980-81 to 1990-91). The annual compound growth rate of the yield of food grains was 2.13 per cent. There has also been a phenomenal rise in the size of the cultivable area. In 1960-61 the total amount of cultivable land was 115.58 million hectares, and it slightly decreased to 115.10 million hectares in 1965-66 and increased to 124.32 million hectares in 1970-71 and increased to 128.02 million hectares in 1985-86 and continuously decreased and ultimately stood at 121.05 million hectares in 2000-01. This was probably due to the erratic nature of monsoon and lack of proper irrigational facilities. The percentage growth rate of cultivable area in the first decade was 7.56 and second decade it was 1.89 and third decade it was only 0.92. In the fourth decade it dropped to an all time low of -5.31. This was probably due to the erratic nature of monsoon and lack of proper irrigational facilities in the county. The annual compound growth rate of the cultivable land was only 0.12 per cent. This growth rate is much less than the annual growth rates of production and yield of food grains in the study period (Please see Table-1).

Table 1
Growth of Food Grain Production in India: 1960-61 to 2000-01

Year	*Area (Million hectares)*	*Production (Million tonnes)*	*Yield (Kg / hectare)*
1960-61	155.58	82.02	710
1965-66	115.10	72.35	629
1970-71	124.32	108.42	872
1975-76	128.18	121.03	944
1980-81	126.67	129.59	1023
1985-86	128.02	150.44	1175
1990-91	127.84	176.39	1380
1995-96	121.01	180.42	1491
2000-01	121.05	199.54	1648
	Growth Rates		
1st decade(1960-61to1970-71)	7.56	32.19	22.82
2nd decade(1970-71to1980-81)	1.89	19.52	17.32
3rd decade(1980-81to1990-91)	0.92	36.11	34.90
4th decade(1990-91to2000-01)	-5.31	13.12	19.42
Annual compoundGrowth rate0.12	2.25	2.13	

Source: Indian Economic Survey.

Food Grains Production by Crop

The major achievement of the new strategy is to boost the production of major cereals like rice and wheat. Table-2 gives the production of the principal food crops during the last four decades. A close look at the table reveals the increase in rice production from 34.58 million tonnes in 1960-61 to 87.70 million tonnes in 2000-01, signifying a break through in this major crop of India. The percentage growth rate of the production of rice in the first decade was 22.09; in the second decade it was 27.02; in the third decade it was 38.52; and it was 18.05 in the last decade. The annual compound growth rate of the production of rice in the study period was 2.35 percent.

The production of wheat which stood at 11 million tonnes in 1960-61 rose to 36.31 million tonnes in 1980-81 and further rose to 69.68 million tonnes in 2000-01. The percentage growth rate of the production of wheat in the first decade was 116.64; in the second decade it was 52.37; in the third decade it was 51.86; and it was 26.37 in the fourth decade. The annual compound growth rate of the production of wheat was 4.72 per cent.

The production of coarse cereals was 23.74 million tonnes in 1960-61 rose to 29.02 million tonnes in 1980-81 and further increased to 31.08 million tonnes in 2000-01. The percentage growth rate of production of coarse cereals was 28.68 in the

Table 2
Food Grain Production by Crop in India: 1960-61 to 2000-01

(Million tonnes)

Year	*Cereals*				
	Rice	*Wheat*	*Coarse Cereals*	*Pulses*	*Total Food Grains*
1960-61	34.58	11.00	23.74	12.70	82.02
1965-66	30.59	10.40	21.42	9.94	72.35
1970-71	42.22	23.83	30.55	11.82	108.42
1975-76	48.74	28.84	30.41	13.04	121.03
1980-81	53.63	36.31	29.02	10.63	129.59
1985-86	63.83	47.05	26.20	13.36	150.44
1990-91	74.29	55.14	32.70	14.26	176.39
1995-96	76.98	62.10	29.03	12.31	180.42
2000-01	87.70	69.68	31.08	11.08	199.54
Growth Rates					
1st decade (1960-61 to 1970-71)	22.09	116.64	28.68	-6.93	32.19
2nd decade (1970-71 to 1980-81)	27.02	52.37	-5.00	-10.07	19.52
3rd decade (1980-81 to 1990-91)	38.52	51.86	12.68	34.15	36.11
4th decade (1990-91 to 2000-01)	18.05	26.37	-4.95	-22.30	13.12
Annual compound Growth rate	2.35	4.72	0.67	-0.34	2.25

Source: Indian Economic Survey.

first decade; it was -5.00 in the second decade; 12.68 in the third decade; and it was -4.95 in the last decade. The annual compound growth rate of production of the coarse cereals was only 0.67 per cent.

The production of pulses in our country is in an alarmic condition. The production of pulses was 12.70 million tonnes in 1960-61 rose to 14.26 million tonnes in 1990-91 then gradually decreased to 11.08 million tonnes in 2000-01. The percentage growth rate of pulses in the first decade of our study period was -6.93; it was -10.07 in the second decade; 34.15 in the third decade; and -22.30 in the fourth decade. Unfortunately the annual compound growth rate of pulses recorded a negative growth (-0.34 per cent).

The production of total food grains was 82.02 million tonnes in 1960-61 rose to 129.59 million tonnes in 1980-81 and then gradually increased to 199.54 million tonnes in 2000-01.The percentage growth rate of total food grains in the first decade of the study period was 32.19; it was 19.52 in the second decade; 36.11 in the third decade; and13.12 in the fourth decade. The annual compound growth rate of total food grains production was 2.25 per cent (Table-2).

Growth in the Production of Commercial Crops:

Green revolution was mainly directed to growth in the production of food grains. It did not affect initially the production of commercial crops or cash crops such as sugarcane, cotton, jute, oilseeds and tobacco; these crops did not record any significant improvement between 1960-61 and 1973-74. The production of sugarcane was recorded 110 million tonnes in 1960-61 and increased to 126.37 million tonnes in 1970-71 and then increased to 295.96 million tonnes in 2000-01. However, significant improvement in the output of sugarcane, took place after 1973-74. The percentage growth rate of sugarcane production in the first decade was 14.88; 22.06 in the second decade; 56.27 in the third decade; and 22.78 in the last decade of the study period. The annual compound growth rate of sugarcane production was 2.50 per cent.

In the case of production of cotton it was 5.60 million bales in 1960-61; 4.85 million bales in 1965-66; 12.86 million bales in 1995-96; and 9.52 million bales in 2000-01. The percentage growth rate in the production of cotton was recorded -15.00 in the first decade; 47.27 in the second decade; 40.37 in the third decade; and -3.25 in the last decade of the study period. The annual compound growth rate of cotton production was 1.33 per cent.

In the production of Jute it was 5.26 million bales in 1960-61. It has gone up to 12.65 million bales in 1985-86; but decreased to 10.56 million bales in 2000-01. The percentage growth rate of production of Jute was recorded 17.68 in first decade; 31.82 in second decade; 13.11 in the third decade; and 14.41 in the last decade of the study period. The annual compound growth rate of the Jute production was 1.76 per cent.

There was considerable improvement in the production of oilseeds but the improvement was not such as to be called a revolution. The production of oilseeds was 6.98 million tonnes in 1960-61 and increased to 10.83 million tonnes in 1985-86 and further increased and stood at 18.44 million tonnes in 2000-01. The percentage growth rate of oilseeds production was recorded 37.96 in first decade; -2.70 in the second decade; 98.61 in third decade; and -0.91 in the last decade of the study period. The annual compound growth rate of oilseeds production was 2.46 percent.

Tobacco is one of the major commercial crops in our country. The production of tobacco was not increased substantially during the period under study. The production of tobacco was 0.31 million tonnes in 1960-61; 0.48 million tonnes in 1980-81; and 0.49 million tonnes in 2000-01. The percentage growth rate of tobacco production was 16.13 in the first decade; 33.33 in the second decade; 16.67 in the third decade; and -12.50 in the last decade of the study. The annual compound growth rate of tobacco production was 1.15 percent (Table-3).

Table 3
Production of Commercial Crops in India: 1960-61to 2000-01

(Million tonnes)

	Crops				
Year	*Sugarcane*	*Cotton (1)*	*Jute (2)*	*Oilseeds (3)*	*Tobacco*
1960-61	110.00	5.60	5.26	6.98	0.31
1965-66	123.99	4.85	5.78	6.40	0.29
1970-71	126.37	4.76	6.19	9.63	0.36
1975-76	140.60	5.95	5.91	10.61	0.35
1980-81	154.25	7.01	8.16	9.37	0.48
1985-86	170.65	8.73	12.65	10.83	0.44
1990-91	241.05	9.84	9.23	18.61	0.56
1995-96	281.10	12.86	8.81	22.11	0.54
2000-01	295.96	9.52	10.56	18.44	0.49
		Growth Rates			
1st decade (1960-61 to 1970-71)	14.88	-15.00	17.68	37.96	16.13
2nd decade (1970-71to1980-81)	22.06	47.27	31.82	-2.70	33.33
3rd decade (1980-81to1990-91)	56.27	40.37	13.11	98.61	16.67
4th decade (1990-91to2000-01)	22.78	-3.25	14.41	-0.91	-12.50
Annual compound Growth rate	2.50	1.33	1.76	2.46	1.15

Note:
(1) Production in million bales of 170 kg. each.
(2) Production in million bales of 180 kg. each. (3): For nine Oilseeds out of eleven in all.
Source: Indian Economic Survey.

Growth of Inputs used in Indian Agriculture

Fertilizer, HYV, irrigation and rainfall are treated as the major components for determining the production/productivity in Indian agriculture. The trends of the above inputs have increased over the years except rainfall, which exercises large-scale regional-variation with respect to time span.

It is to be noted here that during the starting period of Green Revolution (1960-61), the amount of irrigation [measured as Net Irrigated Area (NIA) as a percentage of Net Sown Area (NSA)] and fertilizer [(measured as per hectare consumption of chemical fertilizer (NPK)] were just 18.51 per cent and 1.91 kg. However, both increased to 19.44 per cent and 9.4 kg in 1967-68; and 32.81 per cent and 63.5 kg in 1989-90. During the early phase of economic reforms (1990-91), the figures were 33.58 per cent and 67.5 kg and then increased to 39.21 per cent and 88.85 kg in 1999-2000. The percentage growth rate of the irrigation in 1999-2000 over 1960-61 was 111.83. The annual compound growth rate of the irrigation was 1.89 per cent. The percentage growth rate of the fertilizer consumption in 1999-2000 over 1960-61 was tremendously increased to 4,551.83. The annual compound growth rate of the fertilizer consumption was 10.07 per cent.

Corresponding to the figures of irrigation and fertilizer, the coverage of HYV (measured as a percentage of area under food crops) and rainfall (measured as actual rainfall as a percentage of normal rainfall) were 41 per cent and 113 per cent in1983-84. They increased to 48.3 per cent and 101 per cent in 1989-90. However, during the early phase of economic reforms, these figures were 50.9 per cent and 106 per cent, which increased to 63.5 per cent (HYV) and decreased to 96 per cent (rainfall) in 1999-2000. The coverage of HYV in 1999-2000 over 1983-84 was 54.88. The annual compound growth rate of the coverage of HYV was 2 77 per cent (Please see Table–4).

Table 4
Growth of Major Inputs Used in Food Grain Production in India 1960-61 to 1999-2000

Year	*Irrigation (a)*	*Fertilizer (b)*	*HYV (c)*	*Rainfall (d)*
1960-61	18.51	1.91	NA	-
1967-68	19.44	9.40	NA	-
1983-84	29.37	42.9	41.0	113
1989-90	32.81	63.5	48.3	101
1990-91	33.58	67.5	50.9	106
1991-92	35.21	69.8	53.1	91
1999-2000	39.21	88.85	63.5	96
% Growth rate in 1999-2000 over four decades	111.83	4,551.83	54.88	
Annual compound growth rate	1.89	10.07	2.77	

Note:
(a). Irrigation: NIA as a % of NSA;
(b). Fertilizer: Per hectare consumption ofchemical fertilizer Kg/ha;
(c). HYV: HYV area as % of area under food crops, and
(d). Rainfall: Actual rainfall as percentage of normal rainfall.
Source: Indian Economic Survey.

Conclusions and Suggestions

Agriculture is a major sector in India and continuous to be the lifeline for the Indian economy. Rapid growth of agriculture is, therefore essential to achieve the multi-pronged objectives of the Indian planning system. The government of India has taken several measures to increase agricultural production and productivity. These measures are responsible for the agricultural revolution, which is called "Green Revolution". The green revolution was mainly due to hybrid seeds, which raised agricultural yields. In addition to the High Yielding Variety Programme (HYVP) the government has taken several steps to increase agricultural production. The other aspects are short duration crops, multiple cropping, farm mechanization, extension of irrigation, price support, processing, storage and marketing facilities, improved credit facilities, institutional changes, production of supplementary food products etc. The new agricultural strategy has led to revolutionary changes in agriculture.

India's food grain production has increased from 82.02 million tonnes in 1960-61 to 199.54 million tonnes in 2000-01. Yield of food grains per hectare also increased substantially from 710 Kg/ha in 1960-61 to 1648 Kg /ha in 2000-01. But the area of cultivable land 155.58 million hectares in 1960-61 and only 121.05 million hectares in 2000-01. The area under cultivable land has not much increased as compared to production and yield during the study period. There in a much increase in the cultivable land in the first decade of the study period. But the production and yield also increased substantially in third decade of the study.

Production of rice was increased substantially in third decade, wheat and coarse cereals in first decade and pulses in the 3rd decade. Ultimately the total food grains increased much higher in the third decade than in the other decades of our study period.

In the case of commercial crops, sugarcane and oil seeds were increased much higher in the third decade; cotton, tobacco and jute were increased substantially in the second decade. The above analysis clearly suggests that the adoption of chemical fertilizer is the main factor, which determines the productivity of agriculture in the Indian economy. However, it has to be supported by other important agricultural inputs like irrigation, HYV, rainfall etc. In the face of positive impact of fertilizer on agricultural productivity, we are indeed faced with a more challenging task. This is because with a view to increase food grain production and other planning objectives, we might lean upon the use of more fertilizers and more pesticides, which would have adverse effects on ecology, environment and health conditions of both human beings and animal species on earth. Moreover, the present use of resources should not deplete the resource-base to such an extent that the development process becomes dependent and is not sustainable in the future. There are some suggestions to improve the Indian agriculture without undue dependence on chemical fertilizer:

- New agricultural strategies are almost confined to food grains. It must be extended to non food grains as well. It must be extended to other agricultural crops also.
- Irrigation facilities must be increased.
- There must be revolutionary changes in the methods of cultivation of small farmers.
- Extension of new agricultural strategies to dry farming areas must be taken up.

Nearly 70 per cent of cultivated land in India is still under dry farming because they do not have irrigational facilities. Construction of minor-irrigation projects, scientific and optimum use of available water resource in these areas, development of new methods of water utilization etc. are some of the steps to extend Green Revolution to dry areas. In other worlds, effective programme has to be launched for "green new areas".

References

Bhalla, G.S. and Singh Gurmail (2001), *Indian Agriculture-Four decades of Development*, Sage Publications, New Delhi.

Government of India (2001), "National Agricultural Policy", *Yojana,* Vol. 45, No.1, 4-11.

Handbook of Statistics on Indian Economy (2001), Reserve Bank of India, Ministry of Agriculture, Government of India, New Delhi.

Iqbal, C. (1979), "High Yielding Varieties of Seeds and their Impact on Agricultural Development", in A. Mohammad (ed.) *Dynamics of Agricultural Development in India,* Concept Publications, New Delhi, India, 71-80.

Mohammad, A. (1979), *Dynamics of Agricultural Development in India,* Concept Publications, New Delhi, India.

Rao. C.H.H. (2001), "Technological Change in Indian Agriculture: Emerging Trends and Perspectives", in K.S. Dhindsa and A.Sharma, (ed.), *Dynamics of Agricultural Development,* Concept Publications, New Delhi. Vol. 2, 31-49.

Singh, K.K. Khan, M. and Shekhawat, M.S. (2000), "Green Revolution-How Green it is?", *Yojana,* Vol. 44, No. 6, 26-28.

Tilak, J.B.G. (1993), "Education and Agricultural Productivity in Asia: A Review", *Indian Journal of Agricultural Economics,* Vol.48, No. 2, 187-200.

22

Influence of Inter Sectoral Linkages on Nature and Volatility of Growth of Major States in india

A. Vamsi Krushna

Introduction

Reforms were introduced in India since 1990. During the reform period all sectors were given importance, but at the expense of agricultural sector. This is evident from the fact that the GDP growth rate for agricultural sector during the 1980s was 3.43 per cent but it has declined to 2.97 per cent in 1990s, whereas the non-agricultural sectors GDP growth rate during the 1980s was 4.38 per cent and it has increased to 6.37 per cent in 1990s.

As development theory states that during the development process the share of Agricultural GDP in total GDP declined. This happened in Indian scenario. Share of Agriculture GDP in total GDP has come down from 32 per cent in 1991 to 20 percent in 2005-06 while during the same period Industrial Sector maintained consistent share of its GDP to total GDP as around 27 per cent and Service Sector has improved its share of GDP to total GDP from 41 per cent in 1991 to 54 per cent in 2005-06. But still India is a developing country. So, while framing development strategy the linkages between various sectors, especially the inter-linkages between agriculture and other sectors must be taken into account. So an attempt has made in this paper to examine the nature and volatility of growth of major states in India based on inter sectoral linkages in each state.

Objectives and Methodology

Objective

The objectives of this paper are to examine whether there is any relationship between nature and volatility of growth and inter sectoral linkages in each state.

Methodology

To examine the nature of relationship between the size and volatility of growth and inter-sectoral linkages 14 major states in India are selected. Andhra Pradesh, Bihar, Gujarat, Haryana, Karnataka, Kerala, Madhya Pradesh, Maharashtra, Orissa, Punjab, Rajasthan, Tamil Nadu, Uttar Pradesh and West Bengal. These 14 major states account for 93 per cent of the population and 91.5 per cent of NDP in the country and are therefore representative.

We take the inter-sectoral linkages for the above 14 states from the study of K.P. Kalirajan and U. Sankar. They considered the linkage between agriculture and manufacture and categorized the nature of linkage as uni-directional or bi-directional. Annual Growth Rates of SDP Per Capita during the period 1960-2000 and Volatility Measures of SDP Per Capita Growth during the period 1980-2000, decade wise for the above states are taken from the study of K.L. Krishna.

To examine the stability and volatility of growth rate for each state based on inter-sectoral linkages each state was classified for example AP1 for the period 1960-1970, AP2 for the period 1970-1980, AP3 for the period 1980-1990 and AP4 for the period 1990-2000, then Median Growth Rate for the total period of study for the 14 states was calculated. After that, all the states were divided as Greater than Median Growth Rate and Less than Median Growth Rate based on inter-sectoral linkages exist in each state.

Inter-linkages between Agriculture and Non-agricultural Sectors

The contribution of agriculture to the growth of the non-agricultural sector, and *vice versa,* is determined by the strength of their linkages. These linkages were defined in terms of Forward Linkages, Backward Linkages, Demand Linkages, and Employment Linkages etc. For example, contribution of agriculture to economic growth in terms of capital transfer may decline, but the sector's contribution through backward linkages, i.e. due to higher share of non-agricultural inputs in the input structure, gets progressively strengthened.

There were three forms of inter-sectoral linkages between the agricultural and non-agricultural sectors that were seen as important.

First, demand from the agricultural sector was seen as crucial to sustaining the demand for non-agricultural products and services, especially manufactured products.

Second, since agricultural commodities constituted a significant share of input costs in some industries and of the wage basket in most, increases in agricultural prices were variously analysed as affecting industrial production. In particular, if a sector was agro-based or was characterised by a tendency for money wages to rise with increases in the prices of wage goods, it would experience an increase in costs that may not be neutralised by an increase in final product prices. In the event, profits could be squeezed and manufacturing investment affected adversely.

Third, increases in agricultural prices would constrain the growth of demand in the manufacturing sector, since consumers would allocate a larger share of their incomes to food consumption and a smaller share to manufactures demand and the government may reduce public expenditure to reduce absorption and dampen price increases. This constraint on demand growth would also adversely affect the ability of firms in industries producing mass consumption goods to raise prices in order to cover higher costs.

Empirical Evidence – Indian Case

The 1982 World Development Report documented the close correspondence across countries between agricultural development and industrial growth.

The Asian Development Bank study (1977) found that the overall linkages between agricultural and non-agricultural sectors were weak in the relatively poorer countries of Asia, (e.g. India) and relatively stronger in the richer countries of the continent (e.g. South Korea).

Rangarajan (1982), using a macro economic model, showed that agriculture and industries were inter-related, but with low intensity during the period 1961-76. Using simulation analysis over the period, he found that agriculture exercises a reasonably strong influence on the growth of sectoral, with agricultural performance affecting consumer goods industries (directly) and basic and capital goods industries (through savings and investment). This one-way relationship was evident on the supply side (raw materials for sectoral) and on the demand side (consumer goods from sectoral).

A study by Ahluwalia (1985), using regression analysis, found no interrelationship between agriculture and the industrial sectors over the period 1965 to 1982.

A study by Hazell and Haggblade (1990), on agricultural growth in India found that the multiplier effect of agricultural growth is higher in the developed states, e.g. Punjab, Haryana etc. This is mainly because of well-developed infrastructure in these states, which facilitates 'spillover' effects. The implication of this finding is far reaching: as the infrastructure development takes place in other regions of the country, the linkages between agriculture and non-agriculture sectors will be further strengthened.

According to Saith (1992) India is considered to be a 'moderately good performer' but the 'industrial-primacy strategy has failed to generate employment, the relative neglect of agriculture has further reduced the labour absorptive capacity of the economy, especially when compared to the rate of expansion of the population at working age.

Study by Shand and Kalirajan (1994), using Granger's and Sims'[1] Causality tests, found neither uni-directional nor bi-directional relationships between agriculture and industries over the period 1950-89.

Kalirajan and Sankar's Study

Kalirajan and Sankar studied the intersectoral linkages between agriculture and sectoral during the period 1960-89. They framed two hypotheses.

1. Under the prevailing economic conditions in India, causal relationships exist between the two sectors and that they are likely to be bi-directional.
2. Given the differences in economic infrastructure between states, the causal relationships could vary among the states.

The Concept of Bi-direction

Concerning the bi-directional causality, the Green Revolution or the High Yielding Technology (HYT) increased the demand for agricultural inputs such as fertilizers and tractors, which led to an increase in manufacturing production in the state concerned. Increased production in manufacturing raised incomes of manufacturing workers who then increased their demand for agricultural products in the state. With improved productivity and increased agricultural incomes, farmers' demand for consumer goods increased, which influenced the growth of the manufacturing sector, thus establishing a bi-directional causality between agriculture and manufacturing in that state. When the manufacturing production did not take place in the same state, but took place in some other state, the linkage need not be bi-directional.

They performed Causality tests to obtain the results. Regarding the 1st hypothesis the results indicate that a significant link exists between agriculture and manufacturing at the All India level and that there is bi-directional causality running from agriculture to manufacturing and from manufacturing to agriculture at this level. And for 2nd hypothesis the findings indicate a strong integration and interdependency of the agriculture sector and manufacturing sector in most states. They classified 14 states based on their study as

1. Uni-directional from agriculture to manufacture-Bihar
2. Uni-directional from manufacture to agriculture-Andhra Pradesh, Haryana, Karnataka, Rajasthan, West Bengal.
3. Bi-directional-Gujarat, Kerala, Madhya Pradesh, Maharashtra, Orissa, Punjab, Tamil Nadu, Uttar Pradesh.

The prevalence and dominance of the bi-directional interdependence between agriculture and manufacturing suggests that India is well poised to attain higher growth rates because of the sectoral interdependence.

With this background we are going to analyse the pattern of nature and volatility of growth rates of above states with relation to each state's causality relationships.

Growth Rate Studies in India

Nair's study (1983) showed that inter-state disparities in per capita NSDP, as measured by the Coefficient of Variation, had declined over the period 1950-51 to 1964-65, but increased between 1964-65 and 1976-77.

Roy Choudhury (1993) reported that the C.V of per capita NSDP in current prices had increased between 1967-68 and 1977-78, but declined between 1977-78 and 1985-86. However, the C.V in terms of constant price data showed a persistent increase during the entire period 1967-68 to 1985-86.

Das and Barua (1996) examined several dimensions of regional economic disparities among 23 States/UT's during the period 1970-92. Theil's entropy measure of inequality was computed for economy wide NSDP and NSDP in different sectors for each of the years 1970-92. It was found that inter-state inequality increased in almost all sectors.

Shand and Bhide (2000) analyse the sources of economic growth in 15 major states over the period 1970-71 to 1995-96. It suggests agriculture growth has positive impacts on industrial growth and service sector growth. The study suggests that reform in the agriculture sector will yield very beneficial results as growth in this sector is found to have a positive and significant impact on overall growth.

Mathur's study (2001) reported a steep acceleration in the C.V of per capita incomes in the post-reform period of 1991-96.

Results of the Study

Nature of Growth Rates Results–Decade wise

The growth rate patterns of 14 major states was observed during the period of 1960-2000. Annual Growth Rates (%) of SDP Per Capita for 14 Major States during the study period are shown in Table-1. Based on this Table we derived Table-2 and Table-3 for obtaining our results. We analysed whether uni-directional states and bi-directional states has more than median growth rate or less than median growth rate in each decade.

In 1960's under uni-directional category two states viz., Haryana and Karnataka have greater than median growth rate and four states viz., Andhra Pradesh, Bihar, Rajasthan and West Bengal less than median growth rate. In bi-directional category six states have greater than median growth rates viz., Gujarat, Kerala, Maharashtra, Orissa, Punjab and Tamil Nadu and two states less than median growth rate viz., Madhya Pradesh and Uttar Pradesh.

In 1970's in uni-directional category of states, Andhra Pradesh, Haryana and Karnataka are the three states, witnessed greater than median growth rate and Bihar, Rajasthan and West Bengal are another three states, which witnessed less than median growth rate. In bi-directional category Gujarat, Maharashtra, Punjab and Tamil Nadu are the four states which show greater than median growth rate and another four states Kerala, Madhya Pradesh, Orissa and Uttar Pradesh show less than median growth rate.

Table 1
Annual Growth Rates (%) of SDP Per Capita for 14 Major States: 1960s, 1970s, 1980s, and 1990s

State/ All India	*1960-61 to 1969-70*	*1970-71 to 1979-80*	*1981-82 to 1989-90*	*1990-91 to 1999-2000*
(1)	*(2)*	*(3)*	*(4)*	*(5)*
Andhra Pradesh	-0.4 (4)	1.1 (8)	4.4 (13)	3.8 (8)
Bihar	-1.3 (1)	0.6 (6)	2.2 (4)	0.8 (1)
Gujarat	0.1 (8)	2.0 (11)	4.3 (12)	4.6 (9)
Haryana	2.6 (12)	2.2 (12)	3.8 (8)	2.7 (5)
Karnataka	1.2 (10)	1.8 (10)	3.6 (7)	5.2 (13)
Kerala	1.4 (11)	-0.2 (2)	2.0 (2)	4.7 (11)
Madhya Pradesh	-1.1 (2)	-1.0 (1)	1.9 (1)	3.2 (6)
Maharashtra	0.4 (9)	3.3 (14)	3.9 (10)	4.6 (10)
Orissa	7.3 (14)	0.3 (4)	3.4 (6)	1.0 (2)
Punjab	3.5 (13)	3.2 (13)	3.8 (9)	2.5 (4)
Rajasthan	-1.1 (3)	0.2 (3)	4.6 (14)	3.4 (7)
Tamil Nadu	0.1 (7)	1.6 (9)	4.0 (11)	5.4 (14)
Uttar Pradesh	-0.2 (5)	0.4 (5)	2.6 (5)	2.1 (3)
West Bengal	0.0(6)	0.7 (7)	2.0 (3)	5.0 (12)
All India	0.8	1.2	3.4	3.9

Note: Figures in the parentheses indicate rank of the state in that decade in ascending order to compute median growth rate.

Sources:

(i) Growth rates for 1960s and 1970s are trend growth rates taken from Chaudhuri (2000).

(ii) Growth rates for 1980s and 1990s are annual averages Based on SDP data in 1993-94 prices.

In 1980's three states viz., Andhra Pradesh, Haryana, Rajasthan come under greater than median growth rate states in uni-directional category and the remaining three states Bihar, Karnataka and West Bengal come under less than median growth rate states. And in the case of bi-directional category four states viz., Gujarat, Maharashtra, Punjab and Tamil Nadu come under greater than median growth rate and the remaining four states viz., Kerala, Madhya Pradesh, Orissa and Uttar Pradesh come under less than median growth rate.

In 1990's three states viz., Andhra Pradesh, Karnataka and West Bengal have greater than median growth rate in uni-directional category and another three states viz., Bihar,

Table 2

Decade Wise Analysis of Growth Rates of 14 States

	1960s MGR		*1970s MGR*		*1980s MGR*		*1990s MGR*	
Direction	>0.1	<0.1	>0.9	<0.9	>3.7	<3.7	>3.6	<3.6
Uni-directional States	H Ka	AP Bi Ra WB	AP H Ka	Bi Ra WB	AP Ha Ra	Bi Ka WB	AP Ka WB	Bi Ha Ra
Bi-directional States	Gu Ke Ma Or Pu TN	MP UP	Gu Ma Pu TN	Ke MP Or UP	Gu Ma Pu TN	Ke MP Or UP	Gu Ke Ma TN	MP Or Pu UP

Note: MGR – Median Growth Rate

AP – Andhra Pradesh, Bi – Bihar, Gu – Gujarat, Ha – Haryana, Ka – Karnataka, Ke – Kerala, MP – Madhya Pradesh, Ma – Maharashtra, Or – Orissa, Pu – Punjab, Ra – Rajasthan, TN – Tamil Nadu, UP – Uttar Pradesh, WB – West Bengal

Source: Derived from Table-1.

Haryana and Rajasthan less than median growth rate. In bi-directional category four states viz., Gujarat, Kerala, Maharashtra and Tamil Nadu have greater than median growth rate and another four states viz., Madhya Pradesh Orissa, Punjab and Uttar Pradesh less than median growth rate.

Table 3
State Wise Analysis of Growth Rates of 14 States

	Whether > or < MGR			
Direction	*1960s*	*1970s*	*1980s*	*1990s*
	Uni-directional			
Andhra Pradesh	Less than	Greater	Greater	Greater
Bihar	Less than	Less than	Less than	Less than
Haryana	Greater	Greater	Greater	Less than
Karnataka	Greater	Greater	Less than	Greater
Rajasthan	Less than	Less than	Greater	Less than
West Bengal	Less than	Less than	Less than	Greater
	Bi-directional			
Gujarat	Greater	Greater	Greater	Greater
Kerala	Greater	Less than	Less than	Greater
Madhya Pradesh	Less than	Less than	Less than	Less than
Maharashtra	Greater	Greater	Greater	Greater
Orissa	Greater	Less than	Less than	Less than
Punjab	Greater	Greater	Greater	Less than
Tamil Nadu	Greater	Greater	Greater	Greater
Uttar Pradesh	Less than	Less than	Less than	Less than

Source: Derived from Table-2.

State wise Results

We consider three types of results for each state as

1. If a state has greater than median growth rate during the reforms period then it has positive impact of reforms in that state.
2. If a state has less than median growth rate during the reforms period then it has negative impact in that state.
3. If a state has greater than or less than median growth rate during whole study period i.e., 1960-2000 then we can say that reforms have no impact in that state.

According to this type of classification of states, in uni-directional category we found positive impact in Andhra Pradesh, Karnataka and in West Bengal states. Negative impact in Haryana and Rajasthan states and we found no impact in Bihar state.

In bi-directional category states positive impact was noticed in Kerala state only and negative impact in Orissa and Punjab and no impact in majority of states, i.e., five states among eight states have sno impact. They are Gujarat, Madhya Pradesh, Maharashtra, Tamil Nadu and Uttar Pradesh.

Volatility of Growth Rates Results -Decade wise

To examine the volatility of growth rates across the 14 major states one decade of prior to reforms and one decade after reforms i.e., 1980s and 1990s are considered. The coefficient of variation of year-to-year growth rates for a state is taken as the measure of volatility. Volatility Measures of SDP Per Capita Growth for 14 Major States are shown in Table-4. Based on Table-4 we derived Table-5 and Table-6 to obtain results for our analysis. Here also we used the Median Growth Rate (MGR) to analyse whether a state in uni-directional or in bi-directional has greater than or less than the median growth rate. The results are shown below decade wise.

During 1980s in uni-directional category three states viz., Bihar, Haryana and Rajasthan have greater than median growth rate and another three states viz., Andhra Pradesh, Karnataka and West Bengal have less than median growth rates. In bi-directional category four states viz., Gujarat, Kerala, Madhya Pradesh and Orissa have greater than median growth rate and another four states viz., Maharashtra, Punjab, Tamil Nadu and Uttar Pradesh have less than median growth rate.

During 1990s in uni-directional category the results are same as in 1980s. In bi-directional category the results are nearly similar as in 1980s, but two states viz., Kerala and Uttar Pradesh have reverse results. Kerala state has greater than median growth rate during 1980s but its performance during 1990s came down and it is in less than median growth rate category. And in the case of Uttar Pradesh it is improved from less than median growth rate category to greater than median growth rate category.

State Wise Analysis

For comparing state wise analysis for the period 1980-2000 same hypotheses are used as in the case of state wise analysis in growth rates. In uni-directional category we observed that no state has neither positive impact nor negative impact of reforms. They are all constant with respect to their volatility growth rates. In bi-directional category only two states viz., Kerala and Uttar Pradesh have positive or negative impact of reforms, and the remaining states are constant in their growth volatility. Kerala state has negative impact of reforms while Uttar Pradesh state has positive impact of reforms.

Table 4
Volatility Measures of SDP Per Capita Growth for 14 Major States During 1980s and 1990s

States/All India	*1981-82to1989-90*	*1990-91to1999-2000*
Andhra Pradesh	150 (6)	113 (7)
Bihar	221 (10)	706 (13)
Gujarat	297 (14)	227 (11)
Haryana	205 (9)	134 (8)
Karnataka	100 (2)	69 (4)
Kerala	204 (8)	47 (2)
Madhya Pradesh	276 (12)	154 (10)
Maharashtra	113 (3)	99 (6)
Orissa	272 (11)	856 (14)
Punjab	64 (1)	74 (5)
Rajasthan	291 (13)	256 (12)
Tamil Nadu	126 (5)	52 (3)
Uttar Pradesh	119 (4)	141 (9)
West Bengal	167 (7)	30 (1)
All India	68	49

Note: Figures in the parentheses indicate rank of the state in that decade in ascending order to compute median growth rate.

Sources: The figures for 1980s and 1990s are based on SDP data in 1993-94 prices.

Table 5
Decade Wise Analysis of Volatility Growth Rates of 14 States

	1980s MGR		*1990s MGR*	
Direction	*>185.5*	*<185.5*	*>123.5*	*<123.5*
Uni-directional States	Bi Ha Ra	AP Ka WB	Bi Ha Ra	AP Ka WB
Bi-directional States	Gu Ke MP Or	Ma Pu TN UP	Gu MP Or UP	Ke Ma Pu TN

Note:
MGR - Median Growth Rate
AP - Andhra Pradesh, Bi - Bihar, Gu - Gujarat, Ha - Haryana,
Ka - Karnataka, Ke - Kerala, MP - Madhya Pradesh,
Ma - Maharashtra, Or - Orissa, Pu - Punjab, Ra - Rajasthan,
TN - Tamil Nadu, UP - Uttar Pradesh, WB - West Bengal
Source: Derived from Table-4.

Table 6
State Wise Analysis of Volatility Growth Rates of 14 States

	Whether > or < MGR	
Direction	*1980s*	*1990s*
	Uni-directional	
Andhra Pradesh	Less than	Less than
Bihar	Greater	Greater
Haryana	Greater	Greater
Karnataka	Less than	Less than
Rajasthan	Greater	Greater
West Bengal	Less than	Less than
	Bi-directional	
Gujarat	Greater	Greater
Kerala	Greater	Less than
Madhya Pradesh	Greater	Greater
Maharashtra	Less than	Less than
Orissa	Greater	Greater
Punjab	Less than	Less than
Tamil Nadu	Less than	Less than
Uttar Pradesh	Less than	Greater

Source: Derived from Table-4.
Note:

1. A direct test for uni-directional causality in the Granger sense can be formulated using the autoregressive equation involving both the growth rates. Based on Granger's definition of causality, given two time series x (t) and y (t) which are assumed to be co-variance stationary, 'x (t) causes y (t)' means that the past values of x can predict y more accurately than the past values of y.

References

Ahluwalia, Isher Judge (1985), *Industrial Growth in India, Stagnation since the Mid-Sixties.* Delhi: Oxford University Press.

Asian Development Bank (1977), 'Rural Asia: Challenges and Opportunities' *Report of the Second Asian Agricultural Survey,* Manila: Asian Development Bank.

Das, S.K. and A. Barua (1996), "Regional Inequalities, economic Growth and Liberalisation: A Study of the Indian economy", *Journal of Development Studies,* Vol. 32, No. 3, 364-390.

Hazell.P.b. AND Steven Haggblade (1990), 'Rural-Urban Growth Linkages in India', *Working Paper Series,* The World Bank, May.

Mathur, A. (2001), "National and Regional Growth Performance in the Indian Economy: A Sectoral Analysis", paper presented at *National Seminar on Economic Reforms and Employment in Indian Economy,* IAMR.

Nair, K.R.G. (1983), *Regional Experience in a Developing Economy,* Wiley Eastern, New Delhi.

Rakesh Mohan (2002), *Facets of the Indian Economy,* Oxford University Press (OUP), New Delhi.

Rangarajan, C. (1982), "*Agricultural Growth and Industrial Performance in India*", *Research Report* 33. Washington, DC: International Food Policy Research Institute.

Roy Choudhury, U.D. (1993), *Inter-state Variations in Economic Development and Standard of Living,* NIPFP, New Delhi.

Saith, Ashwani (1992), *The Rural Non-farm Economy: Processes and Policies.* Geneva: International Labour Office.

Shand, R. and S. Bhide (2000), "Sources of Economic Growth: Regional Dimensions of Reforms", *Economic and Political Weekly,* October 24, 3747-3757.

23

Progress of Agricultural Production during Plan Period in India

D. Pulla Rao, D. Francis

Introduction

In India, agriculture is the largest sector of economic activity. It provides not only food and raw materials but also employment to a very large proportion of the population. Besides, population has been increasing at a rapid rate, leading to increase in demand for food and other consumer goods, many of which have an agricultural base. After Independence our agriculture was in a hopeless and deplorable condition. Our farmers were in heavy debt to the private moneylenders. They were having small and scattered holdings. They had neither the money nor the knowledge to buy and use proper equipment, good seeds and chemical manures. Except in certain areas, they were dependent upon rainfall and upon the vagaries of the monsoons. Productivity of land as well as of labour had been declining and was generally the lowest in the world. In spite of the fact that nearly 70 per cent of our working population was engaged in cultivation, the country was not self-sufficient in food grains.

Objectives

The major objectives of this paper are as follows:

1. To examine the impact of green revolution on agricultural development in India.
2. To estimate the growth of agricultural production in India during the period1950-51 to 1999-2000.
3. To examine the crop wise food grain production in India during the period 1995-96 to 1999-2000, and
4. To examine the trends of major agricultural inputs used in food grain production in India during the period 1950-51 to 1999-2000.

The Data and Methodology

We have collected the required data and information from various secondary sources like Center for Monitoring Indian Economy, Handbook of Statistics on Indian Economy, and Indian Economic Survey.

In order to estimate the growth of food grain production by area, production and yield and growth of major inputs used in food grain production for irrigation, fertilizer and HIV, we have calculated the index numbers, percentage growth rate over a period of our study and also estimated annual compound growth rates for all the above variables.

New Agricultural Strategy and Green Revolution

The Government of India has taken several measures to increase agricultural production and productivity. These measures are responsible for the agricultural revolution, which is called "Green Revolution". Since the mid-1960's, the traditional agricultural practices are gradually being replaced by modern technology and farm practices in India. Initially, the new technology was tried in 1960-61 as a pilot project in seven districts and was called Intensive Agricultural District Programme (IADP). Later, the High-Yielding Varieties Programme (HYVP) was also added and the strategy was extended to cover the entire country. The basic aim of this paper is, therefore, to describe the productivity issue of agriculture, which is considered as one of the desired solutions to meet the food requirements of our nation.

High Yielding Variety Seeds

The Green Revolution was mainly due to hybrid seeds, which raised agricultural yields. In Mexico, Prof. Norman Borlaug developed new varieties of wheat, which were high yielding, disease-resistant and early maturing during 1960. These varieties were imported and planted in selected regions in India, which have adequate irrigation facilities. The yield from these Mexican varieties of wheat was more than 25 to 100 per cent compared to the old varieties. Encouraged by the results the government launched a programme of developing hybrid seeds suitable to Indian conditions. The Indian Council of Agricultural Research, Punjab Agricultural University, G.B. Pant Agricultural University etc., developed new seeds. Production of improved and high-yielding variety of seeds was also encouraged in Central and State government farms etc. As a result several high-yielding variety seeds are developed. Regarding wheat we have the Mexican varieties Lerma Rojo, Sonara-64, and hybrid varieties Kalyan, P.V.18, Sharbati sona, Pusa Lerma. In rice we have TN-1, I.R.-8, Timen-3, ADT-17, Jaya, Padma etc, for maize Vijay and for bajra H.B.-1.

Introduction of such high-yielding varieties requires adequate supply of water, fertilizes, pesticides, insecticides etc. Therefore, they have to be introduced in areas where there are adequate institutional facilities under a "Package Programme" which provides adequate supply of fertilizers, pesticides and insecticides. Areas, which are under Intensive Agricultural Area Programme (IAAP) and other areas, which are suitable are selected for introducing High yielding Varieties Programme (HYVP). In addition to the High Yielding Variety Programme (HYVP) the Government has taken several steps to increase agricultural production and remove the bottlenecks in agricultural progress. It has adopted a new agricultural strategy. The other aspects are short duration crops, multiple cropping, machinery, extension of irrigation, price support, processing, storage and marketing facilities, improved credit facilities, institutional changes, production of supplementary food products etc.

Thus, the new Agricultural strategy, which has led to revolutionary changes in agriculture, has broken agricultural stagnation in India and resulted in higher production and higher productivity. Green Revolution is a technological revolution in Indian agriculture.

Progress Achieved

Green revolution resulted in a record gain of output from 51 million tonnes in 1950-51 to 131 million tonnes in 1978-79 and thus made India as one of the biggest agricultural producers in the world. India also became an exporter of food grains around that time. Yield per unit of Net Sown Area (NSA) improved by more than 30 per cent between 1947 and 1979, when the green revolution was considered to have delivered its goods fully. The crop area under high yielding varieties grew from 7 per cent to 22 per cent of the total cultivated area during the 10 years of the green revolution. During this period, the area of HYV was covered by wheat (around 70%), rice, millet and some other crops. Crop area under HYV needed more water, fertilizers, pesticides, fungicides and certain other chemicals. This spurred the growth of the local manufacturing sector and helped the Indian economy in terms of employment generation and its contribution to the country's GDP.

Progress of Food grain Production

Food grain production occupies the most dominant position in India's a riculture, which covers over 65 per cent of the Gross Cropped Area (GCA). Since the beginning of the green revolution in the mid 1960s, the country has shown quite impressive growth in food grain production. Chronic food deficits and hovering Malthusian crisis were overcome and that have given way to self-sufficiency in food grains and occasional marginal surpluses by the 1980s and 1990s.

However, with the population growing at nearly 2 per cent per year (nearly 18 to 20 million people being added every year) and accelerating income growth, demand for food is continuously growing in the economy. India's food grain production has also been increasing rapidly over the years.

In estimation, India's food grain production has increased from a low of 50, 825 thousand tonnes in 1950-51 to 82, 018 thousand tonnes in 1960-61 and then to 95,052 thousand tonnes in the early phase of the green revolution (1967-68). The food grains production further increased to 152, 374 thousand tonnes in 1983-84 and to 171, 036 thousand tonnes in 1989-90. However, during the early phase of economic reforms (1990-91), the food grain production was 176, 390 thousand tonnes and decreased to 167, 065 thousand tonnes in 1991-92. This was probably due to the erratic nature of monsoon in the country (see rainfall index in table-3). But, despite the same erratic nature of rainfall, the amount of food grains production was increased to 208, 875 thousand tonnes in 1999-2000. The amount of food grain production during the period 1950-2000 has grown more than four-fold. The percentage growth rate of the food grain production in 1999-2000 over 1950-51 was 310.97. The annual compound growth rate of the food grain production was 2.87 per cent. This suggests that economic reforms had a positive impact on green revolution for increasing the food grains production in the country. Yield of food grains per hectare of NSA also increased substantially from a low of 522 kg/ha in 1950-51 to a high of 759 kg/ha in 1967-68 and then to 1700 kg/ha in 1999-2000. Yield of food grains per hectare during the period 1950-2000 has grown more than three-fold. The percentage growth rate of the yield of food grains in 1999-2000 over 1950-51 was 225.67. The annual compound growth rate of the yield of food grains was 2.39 per cent. There has also been a phenomenal rise in the size of the cultivable area. In 1950-51 the total amount of cultivable land was 97, 321 thousand hectares, which increased to 121, 421 thousand hectares in 1967-68 and then to 123 059 thousand hectares in 1999-2000. The percentage growth rate of the cultivable area in 1999-2000 over 1950-51 was 26.45.

The annual compound growth rate of the cultivable land was only 0.47 per cent. (Table-1).

Table 1
Progress of Food grain Production in India: 1950-51 to 1999-2000

Year	*Area (a)*	*Index*	*Production (b)*	*Index*	*Yield (c)*	*Index*
1950-51	97,321	100	50,825	100	522	100
1960-61	115,581	119	82,018	161	710	136
1967-68	121,421	125	95,052	187	759	145
1983-84	131,163	135	152,374	300	1,162	223
1989-90	126,773	130	171,036	336	1,349	258
1990-91	127,835	131	176,390	347	1,380	264
1991-92	121,605	125	167,065	329	1,374	263
1999-2000	123,059	126	208,875	411	1,700	326
% Growth rate in 1999-2000 over 1950-51	26.45		310.97		225.67	
Annual compound growth rate	0.47		2.87		2.39	

Note:
(a). Area in thousand hectares, (b). Production in thousand tonnes, and (c). Yield in Kg/ha.
Source: Indian Economic Survey.

Food grains Production by Crop

The food grain production in 1999-2000 is higher, estimated at 209.8 million tonnes compared to last year's production of 203.6 million tonnes (increase of 3.04 per cent). The sharp rise in current year's food grain output, which is the highest since 1997-98, is mainly due to the increase in Kharif Production from 102.9 million tonnes last year to 105.5 million tonnes in the current year (increase of 2.53 per cent). The Rabi food grain production is increased to 104.3 million tonnes compared to last year's 100.7 million tonnes – an increase of 3.57 percent.

Rice production in the current year is 89.7 million tonnes (86.1 million tonnes last year) and wheat production is 76.4 million tonnes (71.3 million tonnes last year). There is a small decline in production of coarse cereals to 30.3 million tonnes

(31.3 million tonnes last year). Pulses production also decreased to 13.4 million tonnes from 14.9 million tonnes last year. (Table-2).

Table 2

Crop wise Food gains production in India: 1995-96 to 1999-2000

(Million tonnes)

Crop	*1995-96*	*1996-97*	*1997-98*	*1998-99*	*1999-2000*
Rice	77.0	81.7	82.5	86.1	89.7
Wheat	62.1	69.4	66.4	71.3	76.4
Coarse Cereals	29.0	34.1	30.4	31.3	30.3
Pulses	12.3	14.2	13.0	14.9	13.4
		Food grains			
Kharif	95.1	103.9	101.6	102.9	105.5
Rabi	85.3	95.5	90.7	100.7	104.3
Total	180.4	199.4	192.3	203.6	209.8

Source: Indian Economic Survey.

Progress of Inputs used in Indian Agriculture

Fertilizer, HYV, irrigation and rainfall are treated as the major components for determining the production/productivity in Indian agriculture. The trends of the above inputs have increased over the years except rainfall, which exercises large-scale regional-variation with respect to time span.

It is to be noted here that during the early phase of planning (1950-51), the amount of irrigation [measured as Net Irrigated Area (NIA) as a percentage of Net Sown Area (NSA)] and fertilizer [(measured as per hectare consumption of chemical fertilizer (NPK)] were just 17.56 per cent and 0.48 kg. However, both increased to 19.44 per cent and 9.4 kg in 1967-68 and 32.81 per cent and 63.5 kg in 1989-90. During the early phase of economic reforms, the figures were 33.58 per cent and 67.5 kg and then increased to 39.21 per cent and 88.85 kg in 1999-2000. The percentage growth rate of the irrigation in 1999-2000 over 1950-51 was 123.29. The annual compound growth rate of the irrigation was 1.62 per cent. The percentage growth rate of the fertilizer consumption in 1999-2000 over 1950-51 was tremendously increased to 18,410.00. The annual compound growth rate of the fertilizer consumption was 11.00 per cent.

Corresponding to the figures of irrigation and fertilizer, the coverage of HYV (measured as a percentage of area under food crops) and rainfall (measured as actual rainfall as a percentage of normal rainfall) were 41 per cent and 113 per cent during the early phase of the green revolution. These increased to 48.3 per cent and 101 per cent in 1989-90. However, during the early phase of economic reforms, these figures were 50.9 per cent and 106 per cent, which increased to 63.5 per cent (HYV) and decreased to 96 per cent (rainfall) in 1999-2000. The coverage of HYV in 1999-2000 over 1983-84 was 54.88. The annual compound growth rate of the coverage of HYV was 2.61 per cent (Table–3).

Conclusions and Suggestions

The above analysis clearly envisages that the adoption of chemical fertilizer is the main factor, which determines the productivity of agriculture in the Indian economy. However, it has to be supported by other important agricultural inputs like irrigation, HYV, rainfall etc. In the face of positive impact of fertilizer on agricultural productivity, we are indeed faced with a more challenging task. This is because with a view to increase food grain production and other planning objectives, we might lean upon the use of more fertilizers and more pesticides, which would have adverse effects on ecology, environment and health conditions of both human beings and animal species on earth. Further, it is true that an increase in the critical input 'fertilizer' above optional level may amount to significant rise in production / productivity. However, under the given circumstances, an economy cannot afford to increase such inputs, as they would be detri- mental to sustainable agriculture. Moreover, the present use of resources should not deplete the resource-base to such an extent that the development process becomes dependent and is not sustainable in the future. There are some suggestions to improve the Indian agriculture:

- New agricultural strategies are almost confined to food grains. It must be extended to non food grains as well. It must be extended to other agricultural crops also.

Table 3
Progress of Major inputs used in Food Grain Production in India: 1950-51 to 1999-2000

Year	*Irrigation (a)*	*Index*	*Fertilizer (b)*	*Index*	*HYV (c)*	*Index*	*Rainfall (d)*
1950-51	17.56	100	0.48	100	NA	-	-
1960-61	18.51	105	1.91	398	NA	-	-
1967-68	19.44	111	9.40	1,958	NA	-	-
1983-84	29.37	167	42.9	8,937	41.0	100	113
1989-90	32.81	187	63.5	13,229	48.3	118	101
1990-91	33.58	191	67.5	14,062	50.9	124	106
1991-92	35.21	200	69.8	14,542	53.1	129	91
1999-2000	39.21	223	88.85	18,510	63.5	155	96
% Growth rate in 1999-2000 over 1950-51	123.29		18,410.00		54.88		
Annual compound growth rate	1.62		11.00		2.61		

Note:
(a). Irrigation: NIA as a % of NSA;
(b). Fertilizer: Per hectare consumption of chemical fertilizer;
(c). HYV: HYV area as % of area under food crops, and
(d). Rainfall: Actual rainfall as percentage of normal rainfall.
Source: Indian Economic Survey.

- Irrigation facilities must be increased.
- There must be revolutionary changes in the methods of cultivation of small farmers.
- Extension of new agricultural strategies to dry farming areas must be taken up.

Nearly 70 per cent of cultivated land in India is still under dry farming because they do not have irrigational facilities. Construction of minor-irrigation projects, scientific and optimum use of available water resource in these areas, development of new methods of water utilization etc., are some of the steps to extend Green Revolution to dry areas. In other worlds, effective programme has to be launched for "green new areas".

References

Government of India (2001), "National Agricultural Policy", *Yojana,* Vol. 45, No.1, 4-11.

Handbook of Statistics on Indian Economy (2001), Reserve Bank of India, Ministry of Agriculture, Government of India, New Delhi.

Iqbal, C. (1979), "High Yielding Varieties of Seeds and their Impact on Agricultural Development", in A. Mohammad (ed.) book *Dynamics of Agricultural Development in India,* Concept Publications, New Delhi, India, 71-80.

Mohammad, A. (1979), *Dynamics of Agricultural Development in India,* Concept Publications, New Delhi, India.

Rao. C.H.H. (2001), "Technological Change in Indian Agriculture: Emerging Trends and Perspectives", in K.S. Dhindsa and A.Sharma, (ed.), *Dynamics of Agricultural Development,* Concept Publications, New Delhi. Vol. 2, 31-49.

Singh, K.K., Khan, M. and Shekhawat, M.S. (2000), "Green Revolution - How Green it is?" , *Yojana,* Vol. 44, No. 6, 26-28.

Tilak, J.B.G. (1993), "Education and Agricultural Productivity in Asia: A Review", *Indian Journal of Agricultural Economics,* Vol.48, No. 2, 187-200.

24

Political Economy Through Education

V. Krishna Murthy, R. V.L.N. Ratnakar Rao

Introduction:

According to Karl-Marx "Behind every political action, there is an economic intention". Political economy should include Education For All (E.F.A), so that the political action as well as its economic intention result in national development. Trained and Educated on sound lines, the population wrongly considered so far as a burden of the nation truly becomes an asset in accelerating economic growth and in ensuring social change in desired directions as education develops basic skills and abilities and fosters a value system conducive to national development goals.

Education is the Key

Since mankind development started, education -- incidental and informal in the beginning and formal and functional later has served as the main instrument for disseminating various accomplishment of human civilization. Now there are special government efforts like closing the gap between urban and rural educational spending, especially in building new facilities as well as upgrading and refurbishing education infrastructure in rural schools. Despite these noble efforts, the divide between rural and urban education still persists. A rational policy on rural education may help. Part time education, mobile school, compensatory education, inclusive education are some of the suggested ways to help children residing in rural and urban slum areas. At the place where school is not possible, the mobile schools or itinerant teachers (visiting teachers for visually handicapped children etc). can be run by education department bringing "education to the door steps" of the rural learner.

Functional Education–Features

Functional education consists of activities like training, education, development, performance, appraisal and so on. All this activities are interconnected, interrelated and interdependent

1. Functional education is a system having several interdependent subsystems. Therefore change in any one subsystem leads to changes in other parts
2. Functional education is a planned process of systematic way of developing people. It is undertaken on a continues basis as learning is a lifelong process and goes on and on.
3. Functional education involves development of competencies at different levels i.e., at the individual level (eg. literacy), at interpersonal level (eg. relationship), at group level (eg. Team work) and at organization level (eg. Goals).
4. Functional education is interdisciplinary in nature and so it is an amalgamation of various concepts, principals, laws and practices drawn from soft sciences like sociology, psychology etc.,

Empowerment through Education

As Mahatma Gandhi said," India will not progress economically, educationally and socially unless rural people are empowered through education". India lives in villages as the major portion i.e., 74.28% is living in 5,76,126 villages.

For empowerment to take place, education is a primary requirement. Perhaps the major aspects of empowerment are a corollary to education.

One With education comes employment

Two With employment comes economic freedom

Three Economic freedom is the basis upon which the edifice of empowerment is built

Education is the key to make people self - reliant and gives them the confidence to pursue their goals and achieve success in what ever field they desire. It is therefore acknowledged that education leads to empowerment and life long sustained education or continuing education improves the quality of human life. For example : 1. Education in general helps women : a) to overcome social prejudices b) take control of their lives and c) assume the status and identity beyond child-bearing and child-rearing 2. Now women mix up freely in public life. The interaction with people develop women as an individual and made her economically independent

Total Literacy Campaign (TLC)

Total literacy campaign is basically a mass based campaign with the district as a unit. Organizations like Akshara Mahila followed a group based selective approach. The same self - help spirit of the self - help groups which organized as groups in economic activity is extended to literacy to satisfy their functional leads. The programme is planned in such a way that the group identifies the learners from other groups, selects the volunteers from the group members and decides the timings and place.

1. The expenditure for training the volunteers and teaching material is met by the group itself.
2. Zilla Saksharatha Samithi – ZSS (District Literacy Unit) provides only learning material
3. The teaching learning process in TLC is for 6 months and it does take into account the variations in agricultural seasons.

The National Literacy Mission (NLM), through the TLC has played a key role in raising awareness on issues of gender equity like the women development programme, "Mahila Samakhya" (Women Forum) and several other programmes. The National Perspective Plan for women (1988-2000) was drawn up in 1988 as an important strategy to change social attitudes.

Educational for All: (E.F.A)

Educational For All is a concept which insists universalizing education in the country. Primary education is the basic foundation on which the future depends as it helps to promote national integration and therefore great need for an integrated and value oriented education with a national perspective is required. Eradication of adult illiteracy, that too in rural sectors becomes the major thoughts in our plans. The illiterates in the age group of 15-35 in rural areas must be linked effectively with various development programmes. The strategies of EFA include:

1. The very programme should be taken to collect information about the drop outs and non-school going children, the teacher should remain incharge of undertaking the survey in consultation with the members of the community.
2. Taking into consideration the need and aspirations of the people, a programme of development should be pursued by the help of different agencies. Eg. The Home Science Departments of the Universities and Government Food and Nutrition Unit should help the village girls and women the art of preparing and preserving fruit juice, jams, jellies and pickles and also stitching.
3. In E.F.A emphasis must be given to Health Education, Nutrition Education, Games and Arts etc., in order to make education functional and develop total personality.

4. To implement the programme of E.F.A, the Minimum Levels of Learning (MLL) and women's education must be improved.

Jan Shikshan Samsthan (JSS) – Institute of People's Education (IPE)

Removal of illiteracy and imparting the knowledge of 3 Rs (reading, writing and arithmetic) to all the illiterate people in the age group of 15-35 in India is the main target of National Literacy Mission established in 1988. because it is regarded that basic literacy can be meaningful for an individual only when he is able to use it in his daily life and only when it enable to him to earn his livelihood i.e., when it becomes functional. To make this happen the scheme of Shramik Vidya Peeths are in operation for the last 34 years but due to intensive coverage of almost the whole country under the literacy programme and the advent of continuing education programme, Government felt it necessary to make some changes in this scheme. Consequently, name of Shramik Vidya Peeth has been changed to Jan Sikhshan Samsthan (JSS) and it has been decided by the government of India that it will cover not only the labourers but also the neo-literates, people belonging to the weaker sections of the society, scheduled caste, scheduled tribes, women etc. It has also been decided that these JSSs will operate not only in the urban areas but also in the rural areas.

Jan Sikshan Samsthan is the Institute of People Education. It is conceived for non-formal, adult and continuing education. It would also provide academic and technical resource support to Zilla Saksharatha Samithis (District Literacy Units) in both urban and rural areas. Their activities include:

1. Vocational and skill development programmes for neo-literates in both industrial / urban and rural areas
2. Training programmes for key resource persons, master trainers and trainees in vocational courses and also for neo-literates.

3. Programmes based on the polyvalent or multi dimensional approach to adult education.

Polyvalent or Multi Dimensional Approach:

The polyvalent approach attempts to provide knowledge and skills in an integrated manner and rests on the following principles

- A worker / neo-literate must have continuous access to education and training through out his life – principle of life long education
- Each programme should be need based: a satisfied individual is an important determinant in increasing his individual or group effectiveness
- Since needs vary widely, programmes have to be diversified, flexible, adoptable to varying situation
- The polyvalent approach takes into account learning needs, convenience of place and time both for learners and instructors
- There should be variety in content, duration, methods and instructional arrangements
- The methodology includes theory (eg. Guest lectures), practical (eg. Demonstration) and field work experience (eg. Visits and observations) .Thus JSSs seeks to improve the quality of life of the beneficiaries

Rural Education

Education is much more important for the rural people of the country for the following reasons. 1) backwardness of the village life and agriculture, lack of education is responsible for agricultural backwardness 2) village life is guided and controlled by various superstitions and they take loans on account of social customs and traditions eg. Money for marriages. 3) education is the only solution to help the villages to overcome these problems and financial burdens 4) the present system of educations in rural areas does not teach the students the ways through which they can earn their livelihood in rural areas, preserving and developing the rural rich environment and resources 5) craft centered education should be introduced for the rural people as suggested by Gandhi 6) adult literacy should be increased in rural areas.

Conclusion

Therefore education provides employment, economic freedom and there by empowerment along with fulfilling the national objectives and goals.

25

Political Economy—Workers Education Programme

R.V.L.N. Ratnakar Rao, V. Krishna Murthy

Introduction

Man power or human resource may be thought of as the total knowledge, skills, creative abilities, talents, aptitudes etc., of an organizations work force as well as the values, attitudes and benefits of the individual involved. According to Habison, Human Resource are the energies, skills, talents and knowledge of people which are applied to the production of goods or rendering of useful services.

Education is the understanding and intervention of knowledge. It does not provide definitive answers but rather a develops the logical and rational mind that can determine relationships among pertinent variables and thereby character and understanding of basic principles and develop the capacities of analysis, synthesis and objectivity. Usually workers education is outside the scope of an organization's functions. Hence workers education is organized by the Central Board for Workers Education (CBWE) set up in 1958

Political economy is the name given to an important division of the science of the government. The object of Government ought to be the happiness of men, united in society. It seeks the means of securing to them the highest degree of felicity compatible with their nature, and at the same time of allowing the greatest possible number of individuals to partake in that felicity for example, Workers of an Organization.

What the Literacy or HRD Can Do?

HRD or literacy helps to achieve :

- Higher income
- Higher standard of living
- Higher productivity
- Better awareness
- Better social or human relationship
- Improves labour relations
- Improves employee - employer relations
- Awareness of social problems
- Awareness of poverty
- Awareness of inequalities
- Enhances human dignity
- Achievement of individual goals
- Achievement of social justice
- Achievement of national goals

Change and Upgradation of Skills and Knowledge

The beginning of 2000 has already seen sweeping changes both at macro and micro levels. To adopt the changes, skills and knowledge up gradation is necessary. Today we are in the world of change and therefore changing knowledge, skill and technology alone will determine the political economy.

The world's 3W's i.e., the world of wealth (economic development), the world of work (production) and the world of word (information) should be brought together as they are the means as well as the ends of real progress. The level of development of a country is expressed in terms of parameters like economy, education and enlightened man power because of their role in moulding the citizens of the nation and lead them towards progress and development. Education in its broad sense includes not only formal schooling but also non - formal, informal, incidental and distant modes of importing knowledge, skills, attitudes and habits through appropriate information, messages and instructions through programs like workers education.

Workers Education

One of the important factors which led to the introduction of workers education of scheme in India was the alarming rate of illiteracy among the masses. According to the 1971 census, 71 of percent of the total population was illiterate. As far back as 1930, Royal Commission on labour remarked in its report that the illiteracy rate of Indian industrial labour was unduly high and that with introduction of technologically advanced products in industries it is perilous to have illiterate workers handling the new or advanced machines because of the risk involved. The Government of India in cooperation with the Ford Foundation appointed an international committee of experts for advise on the scheme. The committee submitted its report in March 1957. On the basis of the committee's recommendations, a semi - autonomous agency, the Central Board of Workers Education (CBWE) was set up in 1958 to administer and implement the scheme. The CBWE was constituted by having representatives from the Central Organizations of both workers and employers, Central and State Governments and educational institutions. In 1959-60 an ILO experts visited India to study the working of the workers education scheme of the CBWE and made a few recommendations to the Government of India related to the improvement of methods and techniques of instructions, productions of audio - visual aids and the need to give a high priority for preparing booklets in regional languages.

Focus and Stages of Workers Education

The focus of workers educations program is to create awareness among all sections of the working class about their

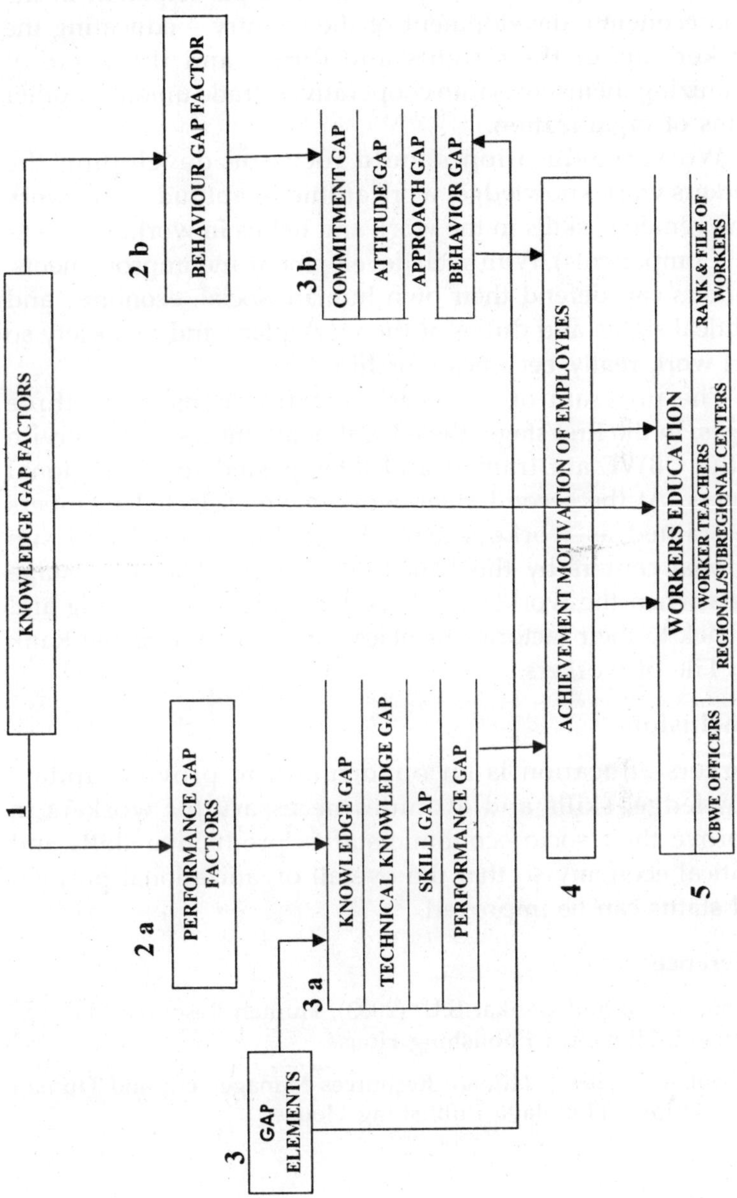

Gap Factors in Workers' Education : Conceptual Frame

rights and obligations for their effective participation in the socio economic development of the country - educating the workers about their rights and duties and the value of organizing themselves into cooperatives, trade unions or other forms of organization.

Workers education should focus on developing the workers work knowledge, work attitudes, aptitudes and work achievements, skills in the work and habits in working (K-A-S-H Components). With such development and improvements, workers can defend their own human, social, economic and political rights and duties at the work place and in society so that work really becomes worship.

The program of workers education consists of three stages: In the first stage, the educational officers in the service of the CBWE are trained and later posted to the regional centers. At the second stage workers i.e., selected members are trained as workers teachers at the regional and sub regional centers by the education officers. The third stage starts when the worker teachers complete their training and go back to their factories or places of work to train the Rank and File of workers.

Conclusion

Workers education is an opportunity to provide update knowledge, skills and attitudes necessary for workers to improve their socio economic status, productive skills and political economy so that the overall organizational position and status can be improved.

References

Memoria, C.B and Gankar S.U. (2003), Human Resource Management, Himalaya Publishing House.

Michael, V.P. (2002), Human Resources Management and Human Relations, Himalaya Publishing House.

26

Impact of Social Capital on Poverty in India

Kavitha Venkatachari

Introduction

It is important for policy makers to understand the mechanisms through which poverty can be reduced. In the post war period, the development paradigm has been evolving from an almost exclusive focus on physical capital towards a people centered approach to sustainable development, emphasizing the social dimensions of development, in particular the role of human and social capital. This paper picks up on some of the themes of contemporary interest; concentrating on the role of social capital in development and examining whether there are economic payoffs to enhancing social capital.

The literature on social capital has focused on problems of conceptualizing and measuring social capital and studies of the economic payoffs to social capital have relied on large, detailed survey data to capture the effects of social capital. As a consequence these studies have tended to focus on industrialized countries and small scale studies in developing countries. This paper looks at the problems of analyzing the economic payoffs to social capital, in particular their impact on poverty reduction, in developing countries. Whereas other empirical studies on social capital in developing countries have focused on micro level analysis, this paper analyses social capital at the macro level; at the state level in India.

India is a country of enormous ethnic, linguistic, and cultural diversity; consisting of a federation of 25 states; 13 states have populations in excess of 20 million people, six have more than 60 million three have 80 million, and one has a population of 140 million. There is a great deal of variation in the ethnic composition, religious orientation,languages,natural resources, composition, religious orientation, languages, natural resources, and economic and social performance of the states.

According to the 2001 census the total urban population was 285.35 million, 27.8 percent of the total population. The level of urbanization in the country has been steadily increasing since 1951.Though the overall level of urbanization in the country is presently estimated as 29.3 percent, the corresponding absolute number of estimated urban population is a massive 332 million and expected to continue to increase at an average growth rate of 2.46 percent per annum for the next 25 years (United Nations 2005).

Poverty in India has been falling, on average, at a rate of 0.9 percent per annum over the last thirty years. However it can be seen that some states have been more successful than others at reducing poverty. This paper attempts to explain the reasons for differences among India states in reducing poverty. In particular this paper tests the hypothesis that those states which have been relatively well endowed with social capital have had greater success at reducing poverty. Panel data, at the state level is used and an econometric model is constructed which integrates social capital into a broader model of poverty.

Highlights of this Paper

Section One: Reviews the literature on social capital and looks at problem of conceptualizing and measuring social capital. Section Two: Looks at poverty in India at the state level

Section Three: Outlines a model of poverty and social capital Section Four: Considers the data used in this study, focusing on the availability and quality of data on social capital. Section Five: Applies the data to the econometric model and the results are reported.

Conceptualisaton of Social Capital

The definition and measurement of social capital remain two issues which are yet to be resolved in the literature; there is a problem of mapping the concept of social capital into an operational measure which can be used to carry out systematic studies. This section reviews some of the literature where attempts have been made to measure social capital. It will be seen that the difficulties in conceptualizing social capital are mapped onto operationalising problems. There is a problem of discussing social capital in highly abstract terms, of building castles in the clouds, which leads to ambiguity surrounding what is meant by social capital.

Several studies have been carried out on the link between social capital and economic development [Helliwell and Putnam (1995), Putterman (1995), Knack and Keefer (1996)]. This focus on the link between culture and economy; the extent to which social factors determine economic success. They use a variety of approaches, conceptions and measures of social capital to address this issue. It can been seen that in most of these cases the analysis appears to be constrained by the availability of data. It is interesting to look at the way in which these studies have overcome the data limitations in analyzing social capital. In his paper, 'Social capital and development capacity: the example of rural Tanzania' (1995), Putterman asks these questions:

- how and when do cultural conditions facilitate or retard economic development? And
- are there any cultural preconditions for development? He argues that changes in attitudes, practices and knowledge, though not necessarily correlated with indicators of economic development, may contribute to the potential of such development. Putterman sees

> social capital as an expanded form of human capital; broadened to consider its social and cultural dimensions and the importance of informal learning. The dichotomous concept of modern and traditional is discarded in favour of a notion of varieties of social organization and it is within this conceptual framework that Putterman analyses the case of rural Tanzania. Putterman concludes that human capital needs to be understood as a socially embedded and multidimensional phenomenon that takes time to be reshaped and to be accumulated. It is argued that social capital augments human capital and facilitates economic development through increasing a country's capacity to absorb modern technologies and forms of organization.

Helliwell and Putnam, Knack and Keefer and Rose, and have attempted to measure social capital. Knack and Keefer, following Solow (1995), argue that if social capital is to become more than just a "buzzword" then some form of measurement needs to be identified. Similarly Rose argues that argues that the "the measurement challenge is to turn anecdotes about social networks into quantified data".

Rose, in his paper "Social capital: definition, measure and implications" (1996), criticizes using the "number of formal institutions in a society" as a measure of social capital, because it ignores important informal social networks. It is stressed that far more people rely on informal social capital than on formal institutions of state and market resources to deal with there problems. Rose suggests using sample survey techniques to collect data about behavior, including interaction with national institutions of civil society and the state. The form of measure varies with the level of development of the society and Rose warns that in less developed societies there is likely to greater problems associated with aggregating up to the national (state) level.

Rose uses survey data, from Russia, to illustrate his paper. Types of social capital are identified by asking the question: "on whose help do you rely in the first instance when having problems?". The significance of social capital for coping in transition economies was measured by considering the "percentage able to get by in a year without spending savings or borrowing". Social capital for social protection was measured by asking "whether a friend would loan as much as a week's wages if your household was very short of money". Rose gives two measures of trust: i) the percentage of workers who trusted/distrusted union officials, and ii) asking households who they would trust with their savings.

In their paper, 'Does Social Capital Have an Economic Payoff? a cross country investigation' (1996), Knack and Keefer, use data from the World Values Surveys and other sources to look at the relationship between interpersonal trust, norms of civic co-operation , and economic performance. In their study survey indicators are used which are "no doubt inexact - due to translation difficulties, sampling error, and response bias - but which produce values that are consistent with data from independent sources and with anecdotal evidence regarding differences among countries." [Knack and Keefer (1996)].

Using the World Values Surveys, Knack and Keefer identify indicators for: i) trust, and ii) the strength of norms of civic co-operation. The measure of trust was the percentage of respondents who replied that "most people can be trusted". The strength of norms of civic co-operation was measured by people's attitudes, measured on a scale of 1 (always justifiable) to 10 (never justifiable), as recorded in the survey, to the following: i) "claiming benefits when you are not entitled to ", ii) "avoiding a fare on public transport", iii) "cheating on taxes if you have the chance", iv) "keeping money that you have found", and v) "failing to report damage you have done accidentally to parked vehicle".

They outline three variables of principal interest; i) an index of civic community - made up of a measure of political behavior of citizens (newspaper readership and the availability of sports and cultural associations) and a measure of breadth and depth of civic community (turnout in referenda and the incidence of preference voting); ii) an index of institutional performance - a composite measure on the comparative performance of regional governments. It covers 12 separate elements from timeliness of budgets to legislative innovation; and iii) an index of citizen satisfaction - the share of respondents who were "very" or "rather" satisfied with their regional government - based on large sample survey between 1977 and 1988. For more detail on the choice of indicators the reader should refer to Putnam (1993).

Table 1
Total and Urban Population (in Millions) in India

Year	*Total*	*Urban*	*Percent*
1951	361.09	62.44	17.3
1961	439.23	78.94	18
1971	548.16	109.11	19.9
1981	683.33	159.46	23.3
1991	846.39	217.55	25.7
2001	1027.02	285.35	27.8
2007*	1134.25	332.01	29.3

Source: * Estimated using United Nations (2005) projections of growth rates

In their paper, 'Cents and Sociability: Household Income and Social Capital in Rural Tanzania' [Narayan and Pritchett (1997)], Narayan and Pritchett measure village level "social

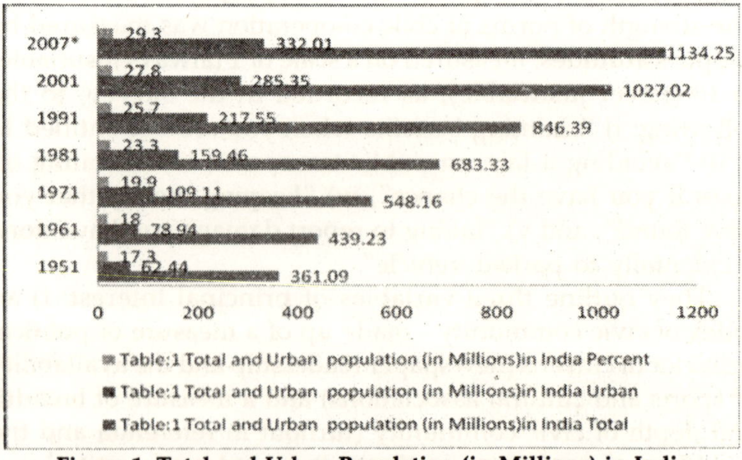

Figure 1: Total and Urban Population (in Millions) in India

capital" in rural Tanzania using data from a household survey designed to measure trust and the extent and characteristics of associational activity. Their study shows that higher village social capital is associated with higher levels of individual's incomes, even after controlling for household education, physical assets, and village characteristics. They argue that the quantitative effect of social capital is surprisingly large: a one standard deviation increase in village social capital predicts expenditures per person (their proxy for income) increase by 20 to 30 percent for each household in the village.

This impact is as large as tripling either the level of education or stock of non-farming physical assets. Three strands of evidence are suggested for a link between social capital and income: i) only the social capital of the household's village, not of the household itself is related to incomes, ii) instrumental variables estimates are used to purge the potential joint endogeneity of incomes and social capital: iii) proximate mechanisms are identified through which social capital affects incomes. These include better publicly provided services, greater use of modern agricultural inputs, more community activity on roads, and greater use of credit in agriculture.

It can be seen that there are considerable problems in conceptualizing and measuring social capital. Here a parallel can be drawn between poverty and social capital. The debate on poverty has focused on narrow versus broad ("vulnerability", "dignity" and "assets") conceptions of poverty [Baulch (1996), HDR (1997)].

The former focuses on income/consumption poverty, whilst the latter incorporate "vulnerability", "dignity", "assets" and "autonomy". Similarly social capital, the extent of social networks, can be conceptualized at various levels. A narrow approach would be to view social capital as the extent of civil society. A broader approach would include aspects of trust, informal networks of relations and ideas of kinship.

In conceptualizing social capital a distinction can be made between formal and informal social capital. Formal social capital refers to formally defined patterns of behavior, norms of exchange, networks and institutions. Informal social capital refers to those networks which operate outside of this formal system; it refers to things such and kinship, informal networks between individuals, families and groups. It is useful to make this distinction, because it illustrates the difficulties in operationalising the concept of social capital. Whilst measures of the first kind of social capital can be found: e.g. the extent of civil society (measured by the number/membership of NGOs in economy). The second kind is more problematic, requiring surveys of household to be carried out. The collection of such data is expensive, and in the absence of this data, presents problems for the study in hand. A distinction can be drawn between the extent of social networks and the quality of social networks. It is into the latter that the concept of trust is important.

It should also be noted that with regard to poverty, social capital might be considered a component of a broader conception of poverty; with lack of social capital itself being a facet of poverty. In the context of poverty, social capital can be seen as either a means to an end, or as an end in itself, depending on the definition of poverty. For the purposes of this paper narrow conceptions poverty and social capital are used; poverty is defined in terms of income and social capital in terms of the extent of civil society. The rationale for this is that whilst recognizing the broader conceptual issues, the modeling of poverty and social capital at the macro level is constrained by the availability of good, reliable data. Broader issues related to social capital and poverty are more effectively captured in specific case studies.

Heller's paper 'Social capital as a product of class mobilization and state intervention: industrial workers in Kerala, India' provides a good example of the way in which qualitative data on social capital can be used to augment quantitative studies in order to gain a greater understanding of social capital in a specific area. In his paper, Heller argues that state intervention and class mobilization in the state of Kerala have produced two forms of social capital. Kerala's high level of social development and successful redistributive reforms can be interpreted as a direct result of mutually reinforcing interactions between a programmatic labor movement and a democratic state. This synergy between state and labor has also created the institutional forms and political processes required for negotiating the class compromises through which redistribution and growth can be reconciled. These dynamics are explored through a close examination of both the organized factory sector and the unorganized (informal) sector.

In concluding this section on conceptualizing social capital, it can be seen that a positivistic parallel can be drawn between social capital and chemistry. Any student of basic thermodynamics will be able to tell you that the effect of applying heat to a reacting solution is that it speeds up the rate of the reaction.

There are two reasons for this: i) the particles become more excited and therefore move around more, increasing the probability of collision with other particles; and ii) by having more energy, once particles are brought into contact, there is a greater probability that they will react. Similarly social capital affects the economic system in two principal ways: i) through increased social networks, there is greater probability of contact between agents, making transactions more likely (this can be thought of as a kind of multiplier effect); and

ii) through the enhanced quality of the relationships between agents, which makes transactions between agents more efficient and more probable (this part acts to reduce the transactions cost of exchanges). Like heat in the chemistry experiment, social capital speeds up the rate of reaction, making the system run faster and more smoothly.

The studies reviewed here illustrate some of the main problems associated with measuring social capital, and the divergent approaches to overcoming these. Within the context of the study of social capital in the states of India, these problems are exacerbated for two reasons: i) comparable data is required at the state level, and ii) the less developed nature of India vis-à-vis the countries in the studies reviewed above, creates problems of generalizing up to the state level.

Poverty Reduction in the States of India

This paper uses the dataset prepared by Dev and Ravi, which they allowed us to use and from which they produced their papers on poverty in India [Dev and Ravi (2007, Government of India2002b). What are the patterns in poverty reduction in the states of India? Following Dev and Ravi, the poverty line used is based on a nutritional norm of 2400 calories per person per day, and is defined as the level of average per capita expenditure at which this norm is typically attained [Planning Commission (1997, 2000)]. The poverty line was thus determined at a per capital monthly expenditure of Rs. 49 at October 1973-June 1974 all-India prices.

State -Specific Poverty Lines in 2004-05

(Rs. Per Capita Per Month)

State/UT	*poverty line*
Andhra Pradesh	542.89
Assam	378.84
Bihar	435
Chhattisgarh	560
Delhi	612.91
Goa	665.9
Gujarat	541.16
Haryana	504.49
Himachal Pradesh	504.49
Jammu Kashmir	553.77
Jharkhand	451.24
Karnataka	599.66
Kerala	559.39
Madhya Pradesh	570.15
Maharashtra	665.9
Orissa	528.49
Punjab	466.16
Rajasthan	559.63
Tamil Nadu	547.42
Uttar Pradesh	483.26
Uttarkhand	637.67
West Bengal	449.32
Dadra &NagarHaveli	665.9
All -India	538.6

Source: Govt of India (2007)

Country: India (Rural)								
Svy Year	*Mean$*	*PL*	*H(%)*	*PG(%)*	*SPG(%)*	*Watts*	*Gini(%)*	*MLD*
1977.5	37.51	38.0	69.02	24.52	11.26	0.3453	34.20	0.2077
1983	41.03	38.0	57.78	18.06	7.57	0.2456	30.06	0.1499
1987.5	42.85	38.0	55.60	16.27	6.43	0.2112	30.13	0.1548
1993.5	43.76	38.0	52.46	14.33	5.36	0.1828	28.59	0.1393
2004.5	49.93	38.0	43.83	10.66	3.65	0.1325	30.46	0.1595

Income/Consumption Distribution (Rural) Calculated by Author

		*Income/Consumption share by deciles(%)**			
I/C	*Year*	*1*	*2*	*3*	*4*
C	1977.5	3.57	4.70	5.69	6.58
C	1983	3.83	5.05	6.06	7.01
C	1987.5	3.95	5.24	6.12	6.94
C	1993.5	4.14	5.45	6.30	7.13
C	2004.5	4.09	5.30	6.11	6.90

Contd.

*Income/Consumption share by deciles(%)**					
5	*6*	*7*	*8*	*9*	*10*
7.48	8.46	9.61	11.12	13.65	29.14
7.96	8.96	10.15	11.73	14.33	24.92
7.83	8.81	10.00	11.56	14.06	25.49
7.99	8.94	10.09	11.60	13.96	24.40
7.71	8.65	9.78	11.30	13.80	26.36

Country: India (Urban)								
Svy Year	*Mean$*	*PL*	*H(%)*	*PG(%)*	*SPG(%)*	*Watts*	*Gini(%)*	*MLD*
1977.5	45.07	38.0	54.79	18.61	8.42	0.2554	35.74	0.2153
1983	48.28	38.0	48.25	14.62	5.99	0.1923	33.33	0.1873
1987.5	50.89	38.0	47.50	14.43	5.78	0.1916	35.57	0.2090
1993.5	54.91	38.0	40.77	11.39	4.24	0.1491	34.34	0.1929
2004.5	62.43	38.0	36.16	10.16	3.80	0.1336	37.59	0.2333

Income/Consumption Distribution (Urban)

		*Income/Consumption share by deciles(%)**			
I/C	*Year*	*1*	*2*	*3*	*4*
C	1977.5	3.13	4.44	5.38	6.33
C	1983	3.46	4.70	5.63	6.54

C	1987.5	3.44	4.40	5.31	6.24
C	1993.5	3.52	4.50	5.42	6.36
C	2004.5	3.14	4.10	5.02	5.98

Contd.

*Income/Consumption share by deciles(%)**					
5	*6*	*7*	*8*	*9*	*10*
7.32	8.47	9.85	11.69	14.68	28.71
7.53	8.65	10.00	11.77	14.61	27.11
7.21	8.32	9.67	11.54	14.71	29.16
7.36	8.48	9.85	11.73	14.91	27.87
7.00	8.18	9.62	11.63	15.07	30.26

The income/consumption shares by decile are based on estimated Lorenz curves. Households are ranked by income or consumption per person. Distributions are population (household-size and sampling expansion factor) weighted.

Modelling Poverty and Social Capital

This paper builds upon the model of poverty reduction used by Dev and Ravi (2007). In this section the model is explained, its limitations discussed and modified to include the effects of different endowments of social capital. The model contains three main components: i) the dependent variables-which consist of various measures of poverty, ii) the time-dependent explanatory variables, and iii) the initial conditions. The model therefore captures the way in which the evolution of poverty over time is a function of certain time specific factors (income, inflation, the real wage etc.) and also the states' initial endowments of physical, human capital. It is the object of this paper to extend this model to examine the effect of social capital as a determinant of poverty reduction. The diagram below shows an expanded model structure, where social capital is included.

The following econometric model is estimated for measured poverty in region i at date t (P_{it}).

$$\ln P_{it} = \square \ln Y_{it} + \square' X_i t + \square_i + \square_{it} \quad (1)$$

where Y_{it} is a matrix of time dependent variables, X_i is a matrix of the initial conditions, $\square_i$ are the time invariant state-specific fixed effects and $\square_{it}$ is an error term which is assumed to follow an AR(1) process. The model is estimated using a Least Squares Dummy Variable (LSDV) approach [Greene (1993), Maddala (1992)]. This, fixed effects approach, assumes that differences across units can be captured in the intercept term. In the formulation above, each $\square_i$ is an unknown parameter to be estimated.

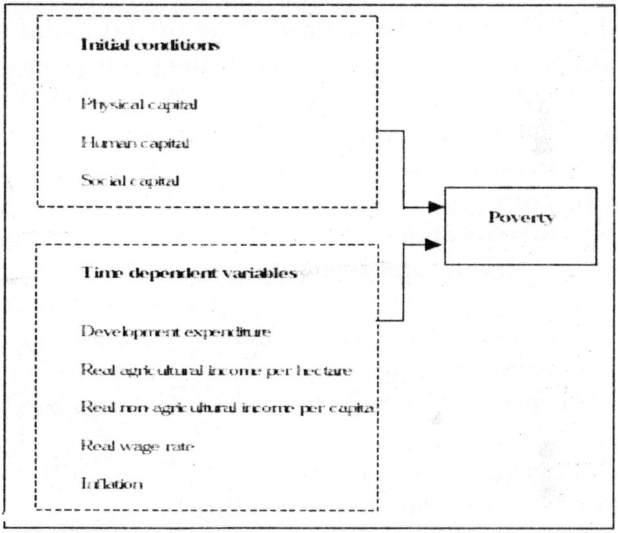

Description of the Data

This section outlines indicators of social capital and reviews the data used by Dev and Ravi (2007). The data come from various rounds of the Indian NSS. Annex One (A1) shows the variables used in the model; the first section of the table show the variables used by Dev and Ravi and the third shows variables indicating social capital.

Variables which affect the consumption/income of a person on or near the poverty line will also affect the evolution of the poverty measure. Dev and Ravi (2007) suggest important roles for agricultural yield, non-farm income, inflation and the real wage rate. In addition to this, development expenditure is included to examine the impact on poverty of government spending. The data on time dependent variables comes from NSS rounds. Dev and Ravi (2007) make the following points about the time-dependent explanatory variables: i) the data on some of the time dependent variables contains gaps, ii) the data is spaced $(0.9<t<5)$ and the NSS rounds do not cover a full 12 month period. To overcome the first problem rounds 13, 14, 15 and 46 are excluded from the dataset. The second problem is overcome by log-linearly interpolating the annual data to the midpoint of each NSS round The initial conditions, summarized in Annex One (A1), reflect initial stocks of physical and human capital, adopted by Dev and Ravi. These variables come from a range of data sources and correspond to values around the year 1960. The variables cover: i) infrastructure-ELCT, ROAD and IRR, ii) landlessness-NOLAND, iii) education-LITM, LITF, iv) health/demography -GFR, and v) urban-rural disparity-MCR.

Dev and Ravi do not include these physical and human capital indicators at time dependent explanatory variables for two reasons: i) times series data is unavailable, and ii) including these indicators as time dependent variables would raise problems of endogeneity due to the development expenditure variable-refer to Annex Two (A2) for the composition of development expenditure.

This ability of this model to overcome the lack of data on physical and human is attractive in that it allows us to overcome some of the problems of deficient social capital data. The social capital data comes from a variety of sources and corresponds to values around the year 1960. Data on social capital is at best scarce, so in order to the measure the stock of social capital indirect measures have been used; measures of the extent of the press, local organizations, social demographics, rural-rural linkages and voting patterns. These indicators are summarized in Annex One (A1) and the values reported in Annex Three (A3). The following variables (all in log form) were chosen for describing the initial conditions of social capital:

- *Extent of the Press:* Here, the number of newspaper per state (NOPAP), the circulation of newspapers in hundreds of thousands (CIRC) and the average circulation of papers (AVCIRC) were used [Nair (1995)].
- *Local Organizations:* The indicators here correspond to the numbers of youth clubs and women's groups for each state. Specifically the indicators were: i) the average number of youth clubs functioning per block (YC), ii) membership of youth clubs functioning per block (MYC), iii) average number of membership in youth clubs functioning per 100 youths (MYC100), iv) the average number of Mahila Samitas (women's groups) functioning per block (MS), v) average membership of Mahila Samitas per block (MMS), vi) average number of Balwadis/nurseries functioning per block (NURS), and vii) average membership of Balwadis/nurseries per block (MNURS) [Government of India (1966)].
- *Social Demographics:* Here the indicators used were: i) the endogamy rate-the percentage of births in rural areas occurring at the child's mother's village (ENDOG), ii) the marriage distance (MARDIST), and the percentage of the rural population widowed, divorced or separated (FEM) [Sopher et al.(1980)].
- *Rural-Rural Linkages:* Where member of the family (village) migrate from one rural location to another, migration may act as a proxy for linkages between villages in rural areas. The variables used are: i) net female rural to rural migration (MIGF), and ii) net male rural to rural migration (MIGM) [Sopher et al. (1980)].
- *Voting Patterns:* voting patterns indicate the extent to which people are included within and linked into networks of the democratic process. The variables used are: i) the turnout at the 1962 general election as a percentage of the electorate (TURN), ii) the

number of spoilt papers as a percentage of the total electorate (SPOILT), and iii) the number of candidates per seat (CAND) [Butler et al. (1991)]

These measures are far from ideal and do not convey fully the multidimensional nature social capital. In particular they capture some aspects of the strength of civic community; however they fail to capture any of the effects of trust.

The ability to disentangle the effects of the various initial conditions is related to there degree of correlation with one another; high levels of correlation indicate multicollinearlity within the model and lead to inefficient estimators. Annex Four (A4) shows the correlation matrix for the initial endowments of social capital. The table shows that in most cases there is only weak correlation. There are a few cases of strong correlation but these present no serious problems; for example strong correlation between male and female literacy rates, between the number of papers and circulation, between number of organisations and membership etc. The implication of this is that where there is strong correlation between similar variables (e.g. number and circulation of newspapers) a decision has to me made to drop one or the other.

Estimation of the Econometric Model and Results

Does social capital have an economic payoff in terms of reduced poverty and do differences in social capital help to explain the differing performances amongst states at raising rural living standards? This question is dealt with in two ways: i) by comparing social capital and poverty reduction performance for each state, and running an econometric model to assess the poverty reducing impact of social capital, whilst holding other factors constant. These crude results indicate that there is a relationship between social capital and poverty, however to confirm this result the econometric model identified in equation (1) is estimated.

The initial specification of the model consisted of the time dependent variables (Y_{it}) which comprise current and lagged values of the lnYPH, lnNSA, lnYNA, lnCPIAL and lnDEVEX. This is further refined so that the matrix of time dependent variables is made up of: i) the sum of current and lagged lnYPH, the sum of current and lagged lnYNA, Inflation [given by (lnCPIALit - $lnCPIAL_{it-t}$)/ t_t], and lagged lnDEVEX. In addition to these time dependent variables, the log of the real wage rate (lnRWAGE) is also included

This equation was used as the starting point

$$lnP_{it} = p_1 lnY_{it} + p_2 Y_{it-1} + g^* X_i t + h_i + e_{it} \quad (2)$$

Hypothesis tests were carried out and it was found that many of the social capital variables were not significant; many of them were highly correlated with one another.

Refining the regression, the following two models were developed. The first considers the effect of social capital in the form of civil society on poverty reduction. The sector considers social capital in the form of political participation.

Regression 1

$$\ln P_{it} = \alpha_1 *(lnYPH_{it} + lnYPH_{it-1}) + \alpha_2 *(lnYNA_{it} + lnYNA_{it-1}) + \alpha_3 *lnDEVEX_{it-1} + \alpha_4 *INFLN_{it} + \alpha_5 *RWAGE_{it} + \beta_1 *(lnIRR_i *T) + \beta_2 *(lnIMR_i *T) + \beta_3 *(lnCIRC_i *T) + \beta_4 *(lnMEMMS_i *T) + \beta_5 *(ENDOG_i *T) + \beta_{it} \quad (3)$$

	Mean Consu-mption (Mean)	*Head-count (H)*	*Poverty Gap (PG)*	*Squared Poverty Gap (SPG)*
Current plus lagged real agricultural income per hectare	(-4.62)	(-3.87)	(-4.41)	(-4.72))
Current plus lagged real non-agricultural income per capita	(-7.92)	(-7.33)	(-8.62)	(-8.40)
Lagged read development expenditure per capita	(2.99)	(-1.85)	(-2.48)	(-2.58)
Inflation	(-4.45)	(-2.94)	(-2.93)	(-2.69)
Real wage	(-2.55)	(-3.87)	(-3.88)	(-3.67)
Infant mortality rate	(-5.66)	(-4.58)	(-5.43)	(-4.99)
Newspaper circulation	(-4.98)	(-5.62)	(-5.53)	(-4.79)
Percentage of spoilt papers	(-4.75)	(-4.43)	(-4.98)	(-4.62)
Election turnout	(-2.43)	(-2.51)	(-2.74)	(-2.55)
AR1	(-4.91)	(-3.99)	(-3.43)	(-3,45)

Figures in parantheses are t-ratios

Regression 2

$$\ln P_{it} = \alpha_1*(\ln YPH_{it} + \ln YPH_{it-1}) + \alpha_2*(\ln YNA_{it} + \ln YNA_{it-1}) + \alpha_3*\ln DEVEX_{it-1} + \alpha_4*INFLN_{it} + \alpha_5*RWAGE_{it} + \beta_1*(\ln IMR_i*T) + \beta_2*(\ln CIRC_i*T) + \beta_3*(\ln SPOILT_i*T) + \beta_4*(TURN_i*T) + \varepsilon_{it} \quad (4)$$

	Mean Consu-mption (Mean)	*Head-count (H)*	*Poverty Gap (PG)*	*Squared Poverty Gap (SPG)*
Current plus lagged real agricultural income per hectare	(4.45)	(-3.76)	(-4.98)	(-4.56))
Current plus lagged real non-agricultural income per capita	(7.34)	(-7.87)	(-7.78)	(-7.38)
Lagged read development expenditure per capita	(2.76)	(-1.67)	(-1.89)	(-1.87)
Inflation	(-4.56)	(2.88)	(2.64)	(2.45)
Real wage	(2.56)	(-3.98)	(-3.67)	(-3.45)
Infant mortality rate	(-6.34)	(6.77)	(6.67)	(5.99)
Newspaper circulation	(1.67)	(-2.78)	(-1.77)	(-1.12)
Members of Mahila Samatis	(2.83)	(-2.87)	(-2.58)	(-2.78)
Endogamy rate	(-.88)	(1.89)	(1.67)	(1.12)
AR1	(5.45)	(4.45)	(3.98)	(4,12)

Figures in parantheses are t-ratios

By looking at the elasticities for the social capital variables, the impact of social capital on poverty reduction can be assessed. The signs on the coefficients suggest those states which have been relatively well endowed with social capital have been more successful at reducing poverty.

Looking at the two social capital regressions which were run, the first included variables on: i) newspaper circulation, ii) members of mahila samatis and iii) the endogamy rate, and the second included: i) spoilt papers and ii) election turnout. The first regression shows that higher newspaper circulation and membership of women's groups lead to higher mean consumption and lower poverty being observed. Similarly, lower endogamy rates are associated with higher mean consumption and lower levels of poverty.

The second regression shows that social capital in the form of higher levels of participation (in elections), measured by the proportion if spoilt paper and election turnout, is associated with higher levels of mean consumption and lower levels of poverty.

Whilst this study does provide evidence for a relationship between social capital and poverty reduction, it is limited in the extent of its analysis for the two main reasons: i) the lack of detailed data on social capital, ii) the modeling complexities involved in modeling broad conceptions of social capital and poverty. It therefore follows that for an effective understanding social capital; this approach needs to be augmented by more detailed state specific case studies.

Conclusion

There are many problems associated with conceptualizing and measuring social capital. The idea of considering narrow versus broad conceptions of social capital is useful because it allows us to examine the limitations of various approaches to analyzing the economic impact of social capital. Here I have drawn a parallel with poverty, where the kinds of research questions which can be addressed depend crucially on the way in which the concept is conceived. The studies reviewed in this paper show that there are two main types of study on the economic payoffs to social capital: i) micro level studies based on sample data, and ii) macro level studies based on national and sample data. It can be seen that within the developing country context, the former has been the exclusive vehicle for analysis; allowing detailed study of the effects for broadly conceived social capital. However these approaches suffer from a limitation, in that they provide no means for aggregating up and looking at social capital from the macro level. The studies which have focused on social capital at the macro level have tended to focus on industrialized countries, where there is available data. In the developing country context this kind of data is scarce making analysis more problematic. In this paper a model has been constructed that makes efficient use of limited data. It can be seen clearly from the analysis that those states which were initially well endowed with social capital were also more successful at reducing poverty.

Appendix

A1: Explanatory variables Time dependent (Y)
Denotion
log of real agricultural SDP per hectare of net sown area*
YPH
log of net sown area per person in state
NSA
log of real non-agricultural state domestic product per person in state*
YNA
log of rate of inflation in rural sector**
INFLN
log of real wage rate
RWAGE
log of per capita real state development expenditure***
DEVEX

Initial Conditions I (X) - physical and human capital
log of % of villages with electricity
ELCT
log of km. of rural roads per 100 sq. km. of area
ROAD
log of % of operated area irrigated
IRR
log of % of households landless
NOLAND
log of female literacy rate (per '000 popn.)
LITF
log of male literacy rate (per '000 popn.)
LITM
log of infant mortality rate (per '000 live births)
IMR
log of ratio of urban-to-rural mean consumption (%)
GFR
log of general fertility rate (per '000 females aged 15-44)
MCR

Initial conditions II (X) - social capital
log of number of newspapers
PAP
log of circulation of papers (,000)
CIRC
log of average circulation of papers
AVCIRC
log of average of youth clubs functioning per block
YC

log of average membership of youth clubs functioning per block
MYC
log of average number of membership in youth clubs per 100 youths
MYC
100
log of average number of Mahila Samitis (women's groups) functioning per block
MS
log of average membership of Mahila Samitis per block
MMS
log of average number of Balwadis/nurseries functioning per block
NURS
log of average membership of Balwadis/nurseries per block
MNURS
log of endogamy rate (% of births in rural areas occurring at child's mother's natal
ENDOG

village)
log of marriage distance
MARDIST
log of net female rural-to-rural migration
MIGF
log of net male rural-to-rural migration
MIGM

* Real values of agricultural and non-agricultural SDP are calculated using adjusted CPIAL for each state as the deflator.

** The rate of inflation in the state is measured by the change per year in the natural log of (adjusted) CPIAL; $INFLN_t = (CPIAL_t - CPIAL_{t-?})/?_t$

*** Development expenditure consist of spending on both economic and social services - summarised in A2.

A2: Composition of development expenditure

Economic services	*Social services*
Agriculture and allied activities Rural development	Education
Special area programs	Medical and public health
Irrigation and flood control	Family welfare
Energy	Water supply and sanitation
Industry and minerals	Housing
Transport and communications Science	Urban development
Technology	Labour and labour welfare
Environment	Social security and welfare
	Nutrition
	Relief (on account of natural calamities)

A3: *Initial Conditions II (X) - Social Capital*

	pap	*circ*	*avcirc*	*yc*	*myc*	*myc100*	*ms*	*mms*	*Bn*	*mbn*	*endog*	*fem*	*migf*	*migm*	*mardist*	*spoilt*	*turn*	*cand*
Andhra Pradesh	567	848	1447	22	336	5	17	264	3	29	16.11	14.8	-17194	-45139	13.9	0.718	4.169	1.23
Assam	110	186	1691	16	343	5.2	13	359	2	65	2.2	6.1	94472	205481	10.6	0.8	3.966	1.23
Bihar	225	578	2569	23	355	5.3	4	96	2	43	9.02	11.2	-164238	-346479	10.1	0.687	3.85	1.48
Gujarat	527	1544	2930	23	547	7.5	10	199	5	151	6.18	9.3	23936	24960	13.2	0.923	4.06	1.13
Karnataka	398	1235	3103	15	378	5.7	4	118	4	1.4	15.17	13.3	64537	106037	15.1	1.004	4.082	1.22
Kerala	569	2536	4457	18	720	7.9	11	1206	6	170	17.68	12.3	21994	-3525	8.7	0.405	4.257	1.02
Madhya Pradesh	467	605	1295	26	372	5.5	8	135	5	76	9.71	11.8	97018	137373	16	0.579	3.637	1.21
Maharashtra	1706	6145	3602	34	660	11	18	400	6	166	18.05	12.7	9129	33939	15.6	1.077	4.1	1.34
Orissa	119	208	1748	34	788	13	8	234	10	237	4.66	12.5	-18450	-42824	9.6	0.408	3.161	0.9
Punjab	427	595	1393	13	178	2.4	11	200	4	89	12.97	12.2	-37949	-99265	19.4	0.803	4.18	1.58
Rajasthan	572	634	1108	20	298	3.8	8	139	2	46	6.23	9.6	-32815	-25598	20.8	0.755	3.958	1.62
Tamil Nadu	870	4942	5680	6	129	1.9	9	202	4	95	14.23	14.1	-127664	-128442	10	0.786	4.231	1.31
Uttar Pradesh	1473	2273	1543	8	129	1.8	6	47	9	89	4.09	9.9	-34224	-164964	14	0.756	3.931	1.64
West Bengal	1204	2729	2267	20	578	7.9	5	148	2	81	5.88	13.5	83450	286301	8.2	0.543	4.022	1.13
Jammu & Kashmir				4	49	0.8	0.5	6	0	60	2.66	11.3	-1588	-5020	5	0.3955	4.01	0.916

A4: Correlation Matrix of Initial Conditions - Social Capital

	Pap	*circ*	*avcirc*	*yc*	*myc*	*myc100*	*ms*	*mms*	*Bn*	*mbn*	*endog*	*fem*	*mardist*	*spolit*	*turn*	*cand*
pap	1															
circ	0.892	1														
avcirc	0.254	0.662	1													
yc	-0.269	-0.311	-0.222	1												
myc	-0.218	-0.093	0.162	0.912	1											
myc100	-0.259	-0.133	0.144	0.925	0.989	1										
ms	0.08	0.058	-0.015	0.614	0.616	0.588	1									
mms	-0.139	0.081	0.402	0.632	0.772	0.724	0.878	1								
bn	0.109	0.133	0.108	0.471	0.523	0.511	0.7	0.605	1							
mbn	0.089	0.085	0.037	0.14	0.144	0.132	0.258	0.23	0.261	1						
endog	0.415	0.538	0.459	0.292	0.325	0.29	0.459	0.522	0.358	-0.19	1					
fem	0.421	0.472	0.308	0.029	0.057	0.066	-0.038	0.028	0.076	-0.14	0.702	1				
mardist	0.192	-0.091	-0.515	0.426	0.241	0.217	0.628	0.359	0.526	-0.2	0.408	-0.044	1			
spoilt	0.4	0.392	0.176	0.02	-0.03	-0.035	0.336	0.134	0.095	-0.39	0.337	-0.145	0.584	1		
turn	0.522	0.599	0.413	-0.388	-0.256	-0.33	0.1051	0.1371	-0.263	-0.22	0.416	0.1075	0.068	0.595	1	
cand	0.328	0.092	-0.344	-0.045	-0.221	0.26	0.285	0	0.191	-0.14	0.164	-0.161	0.695	0.575	0.27	1

27

Learning New Computer Skills in the Workplace: A Stress or Pleasure?

Kavitha Venkatachari

Introduction

Information and communication technologies (ICTs), especially computers, have dramatically changed the way we work and live. According to the survey, nearly six out of ten Indian workers used a computer (personal computer, mainframe or word processor) at work, with the majority (78%) using it to perform various tasks on a daily basis. The adoption of ICTs and its far-reaching effects have attracted considerable interest. The majority of earlier literature centers around the effects on productivity and job quality, which Rubery and Grimshaw (2001) sub-divide into three main dimensions: 1) employment relations and protection (e.g., employment opportunities, employment relations, career opportunities, job protection and collective bargaining, pay); 2) time and work autonomy (e.g., work intensity, power and autonomy, work/life balance, work relations); and 3) skills and careers (e.g., skills, job prospects).

Polarized views on the effects of ICTs can be found in the literature in terms of each of these dimensions. For example, the pessimistic argues that ICTs destroy employment opportunities through automation and rationalization, reduce pay by downgrading skills and weakening workers' collective bargaining power. To the exact opposite, the optimistic hypothesizes that ICTs create jobs through developing new markets and human capital, increase pay by augmenting skills. Entorf and Kramarz (1996)) has argued that workers who use computers earn more than other employees (those who do not) not because of their computing skills per se, but rather because they are endowed with more other unobservable or immeasurable skills. Other work (e.g., Baldwin, Diverty and Sabourin (1995)) has shown that the adoption of computers and other new technologies is a key element to firms' success because these technologies are correlated with market share increases, productivity gains, product and delivery quality improvements, increased flexibility, production costs reduction, and so on (e.g., Baldwin and Lin (2002)).

There are many other aspects on which ICTs may have significant impacts too. For example, using a special supplement to the December 1998 Current Population Survey (CPS), Kuhn and Skuterud (2000) show that 15% of unemployed job seekers in the United States used the internet to search for jobs in 1998, so did half of all job seekers with online access from home. They further demonstrate that internet job search rates exceeded those of traditional job search methods such as services provided by private employment agencies, contacting friends and relatives, using trades unions or professional associations.

With employers fiercely competing for technological advantages by widely adopting and frequently upgrading ICTs, workers constantly find themselves being surrounded by these technologies. What impacts does the adoption of ICTs have on workers? Specifically, what psychological impacts do ICTs and the constant need to learn new computer skills may have on workers? Do they cause extra stress or worry? Are some workers affected more than others? Answers to questions such as these are important if we are going to better understand the profound impacts the ICTs revolution has caused.

"The computer revolution has given the modern workplace an array of new options and improved efficiency. But far from having a calming effect on overworked employees, computerization has itself become a source of increasing psychological stress."(August14, 1992:703)

Further, although actual overall job stability and security changed very modestly in both Canada and the United States up to the mid-1990s, this small change in the aggregate masks rather sharp declines or rises for certain groups of workers (e.g., Neumark, Polsky and Hansen (1999), Picot, Lin and Pyper (1998), Schmidt and Svorny (1998), Picot and Lin (1997)). Does the adoption of ICTs contribute in any way to changes in job security and stability? If so, are the impacts felt uniformly across the board or diversely across different groups of workers?

In addition, ICTs have increasingly replaced humans to perform a great number of complex and challenging tasks. As a result, many processes and tasks have been automated or routinized. Has this made work more or less interesting/ boring? If yes, are the impacts invariant across all workers or some workers are affected more than others? While effects of ICTs on such areas as productivity, wages, firm performance are well researched and documented, there has been far less effort and work on job quality as measured in psychological stress, job security and work interest.

Objectives of the Study

- To learn new computer skills cause extra stress or pleasure.
- To learn new computer technologies affect work at what extent.
- To learn computers make work more or less interesting.
- To what extent that work is affected, do computers make job more or less secure.

Methodology

A questionnaire was designed, pilot study was conducted, and then it was modified to capture the data across sectors in

Mumbai. A Structured modified questionnaire was used to collect the data in various companies in Mumbai. In this study we have taken the variables like, gender, age, education, employment type, industry, and occupation. A total of 150 questionnaires were sent out, 110 were received and used for the analysis. The overall response rate was 73 %.

Some of the factors that commonly cause work-related stress include:

- Job insecurity
- change to duties
- Heavy workload
- tight deadlines
- Harassment
- Changes within the organization
- insufficient skills for the job
- Poor relationships with bosses or colleagues
- Discrimination
- Long hours

Stress as a Source of Workplace Model

Karasek model is based on three variables:

1. Demands(psychological demands)the pressure put on the individual by the work environment including

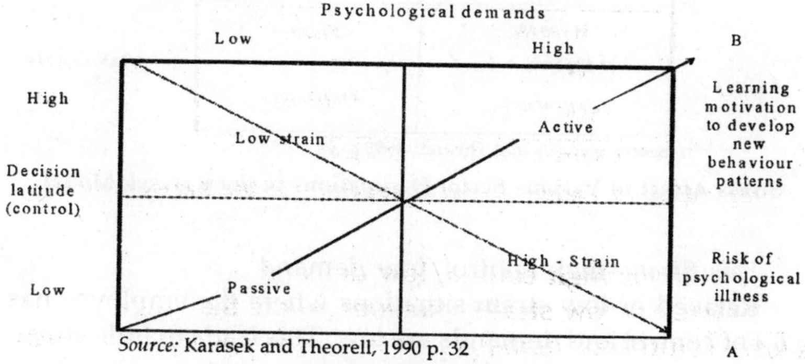

Source: Karasek and Theorell, 1990 p. 32

The Karasek Model

workload, pace of work, length of working hours, time schedules, tight deadlines etc

2. Control (decision latitude) the individual's capacity to respond to work demands and pressures, including autonomy, responsibility, skill, training, experience etc.
3. Support (social support)the characteristics of the social environment in which working activities are performed including organizational culture, working climate, management style, help from co-workers, involvement, participation, team working etc.

By combining control and demand four situations can be identified, they are represented in four quadrants in the fig:

Passive:-low control/low demand

Passive situations where the employee has little control but where demands are also low. This leads to stress in the form of monotony and boredom.

High Strain:-low control/high demand

Situations where the employee has little control but demands are high. This leads to high stress.

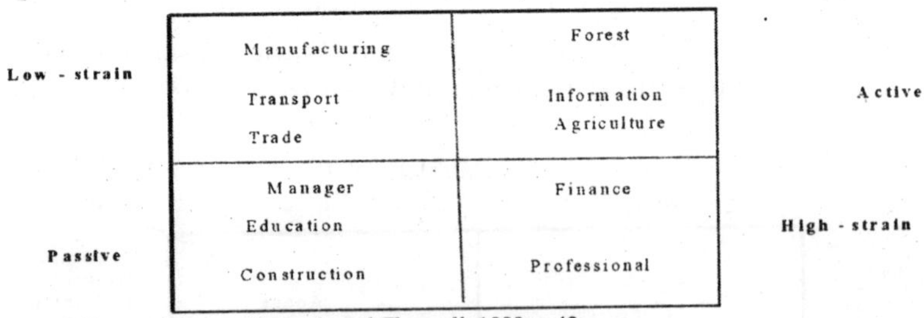

Source: Karasek and Theorell, 1990 p. 43

Stress Affect in Various Sector Occupations in the Karasek Model

Low Strain:-high control/low demand

Relaxed or low strain situations where the employee has a lot of control and demands are low. This leads to little stress.

Active:-high control/high demand

Situations where the employee has to respond to high demands, but at the same time can exercise high control. This leads to an active situation were most people feel they can somehow manage stress.

According to the model, the low strain, high strain and active and passive people are differentiated and put in the table. In this diagram, people who are working in Finance department and Professional are having High strain, because their working culture and time schedules are making them high stress. People who are working in manufacture, transport department and trading they are having less strain because the work pressure and management style are vary from one industry to another.

Estimation: Work place stress: Effects of computers

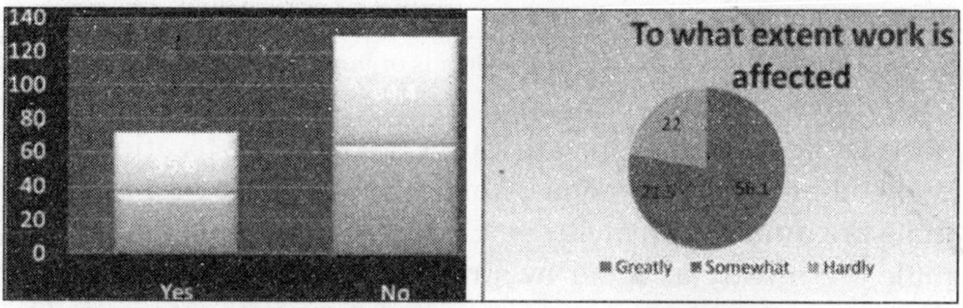

Source: Primary data collected from various organizations in Mumbai(Fig1)

Does the need to learn new computer skills by computers?

To what extent work is affected cause workplace stress?

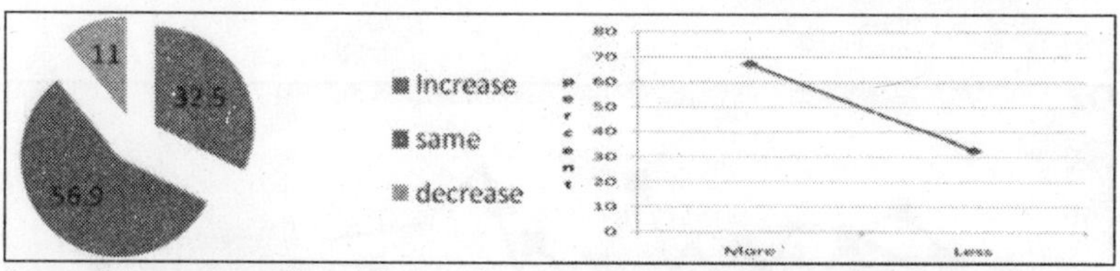

Source: Primary data collected from various organizations in Mumbai (Fig 2)

How do computers change job security?

Do computers make job more or less interesting?

The first question we try to address is whether having to learn new computer skills causes' excess worry or stress in the workplace and if so, whether the stress varies with

Table:1
Stress Caused and Work Affected by Computers

	Stress%	*Hardly%*	*Somewhat%*	*Greatly%*
Male	19.7	30.1	20.6	29.6
Female	16.1	31.4	20.4	32.1
Age15-24	13.1	40.8	15.1	31
Age25-34	13.1	34.5	15.2	37.2
Age35-44	17	23.1	22.4	37.5
Age45-54	21.4	33.7	24.5	20.4
Age55-64	20.5	19.6	25.1	34.8
EduSSC	18.7	45.7	20.5	15.1
EduHSC	18.1	24.5	25.1	32.3
EduUG	18.1	34.5	27.6	19.8
EduPG	13.5	13.8	24.3	48.4
Rural	16.7	20.1	25	38.2
Urban	16.1	28.2	19.5	36.2
Fulltime	16.7	22.5	25.7	35.1
Part time	16.7	40.7	21.5	21.1

Source: Primary data collected from various organizations in Mumbai

observable demographic attributes, geographic locations, and work characteristics. The Table 1 shows that 32.1% of the male are affected great stress. Compare with male and female male are mostly affected by stress. If we are comparing with the age group 35-44 age group people are affected more. The people who are living in rural they are affected because their education level is less and they cannot cope with the envronment. It affects a lot.

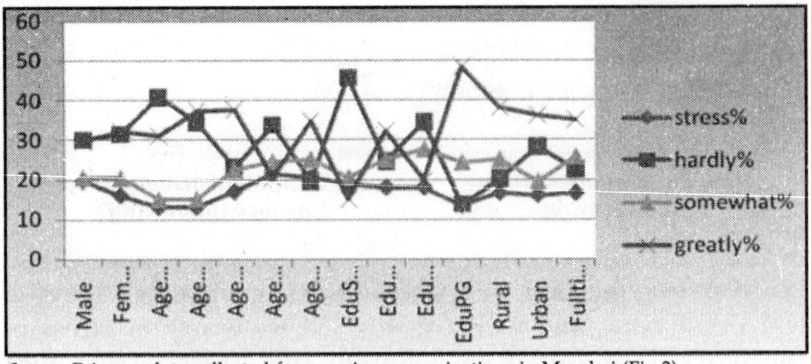

Source: Primary data collected from various organizations in Mumbai (Fig 3)

The second question we attempt to answer is whether work is affected by computers and if so, the extent to which work is affected. The survey provides four mutually exclusive answers. We combine the "hardly" and "not at all" cases into one category and thus, the dependent variable takes on three values: one for "work being greatly affected"; another for "work being somewhat affected"; and the remaining for "work being hardly or not at all affected".

Table:2
Stress Affected by Various Sectors in Mumbai

	Stress%	*Hardly%*	*Somewhat%*	*Greatly%*
Manufacture	14.2	26.5	20.2	39.1
Agriculture	10.2	20.5	25.2	44.1
Forest	10.1	32.1	17.7	40.1
Construction	15.2	55.7	22.5	21.8
Trade	15.2	37.6	25.7	36.8
Transport	15.2	37.8	25.7	36.5
Finance	18.9	23.9	23.4	52.7
Professionals	15.2	25.7	24	50.3
Managers	20.7	39.9	25.6	34.5
Education	22.2	41.5	25.5	33.1
Health	15.2	53.5	23.2	23.3
Information	15.2	30.7	25.2	44.1

Source: Primary data collected from various organizations in Mumbai

The Table 2 shows that 39.1% of the people are affected more stress in manufacturing field and 44.1% of the people are affected by the agriculture department and finance

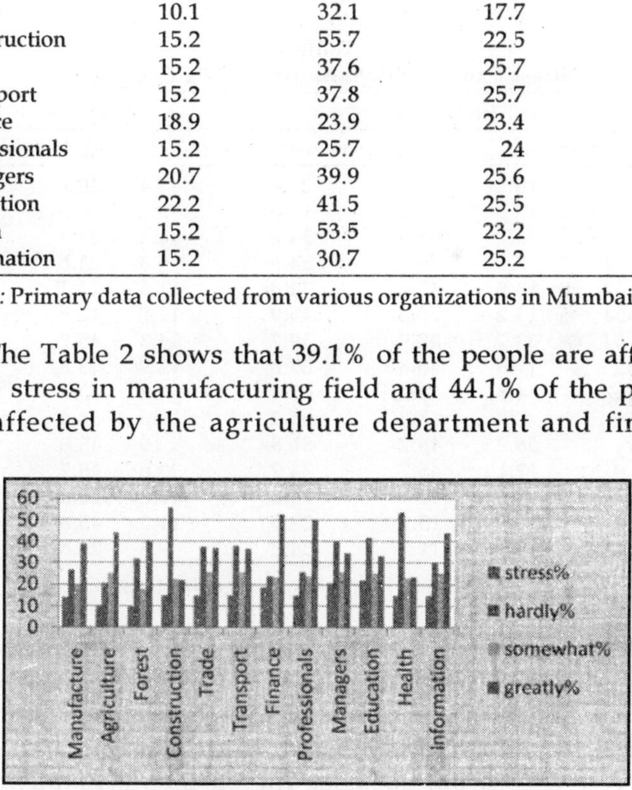

Source: Primary data collected from various organizations in Mumbai (Fig 4

department people 52.7%. Because their age and education is also affecting to maintain their job. They can not learn new computer skills because most of the people are living in the rural areas. In construction field 55.7% of the people are affected stress in a low level

The sample of those who state that their work is greatly or somewhat affected by computers is further asked if computers have changed their job security and work interest. Our third research question is thus how computers have changed job security. In the context of the survey, the dependent variable has three discrete and ordinal values: one for "job security has increased"; another for "job security has stayed the same"; and the rest for "job security has decreased".

Table 3
Stress Caused and Work Affected by Computers

	Job Security			*Work Interest*		
	Decreased%	*Same%*	*Increased%*	*Decreased%*	*Same%*	*Increased%*
Male	10.2	69.8	23.7	4	38.7	57.9
Female	12.5	67.9	17.6	9.7	56.5	67.8
Age15-24	6.2	55.8	34.6	34.2	23.4	45.7
Age25-34	7.5	56.5	54.6	6.8	23.6	34.7
Age35-44	13.8	45.7	34.8	11.5	23.7	34.8
Age45-54	14.2	70.6	45.9	12.7	12.9	34.8
Age55-64	23.7	37.9	59.7	34.3	45.7	23.8
EduSSC	11.6	45.8	67.8	12.9	23.8	34.8
EduHSC	34.8	78.2	67.4	4.8	43.7	52.6
EduUG	23	68.9	65.2	19.3	36.6	57.9
EduPG	56.2	45.2	56.8	19	45.6	13.8
Rural	12.1	45.7	34.2	23.6	45.7	67.2
Urban	34.6	12.1	15.8	12.8	34.6	45.9
Fulltime	34.9	15.9	23.5	11.2	45.8	56.8
Part time	45.9	11.7	34.7	9.5	23.8	34.9

Source: Primary data collected from various organizations in Mumbai

The table shows that job security and work interested are affected by the introduction of computers. Male workers benefit more from computers in terms of job security than their female counterparts. It is estimated that 24% of men are observed with a job security increase as a result of the introduction of computers compared to 18% among women. On the other hand 10% of men are detected with a job security decrease relative to 12.5% of women.

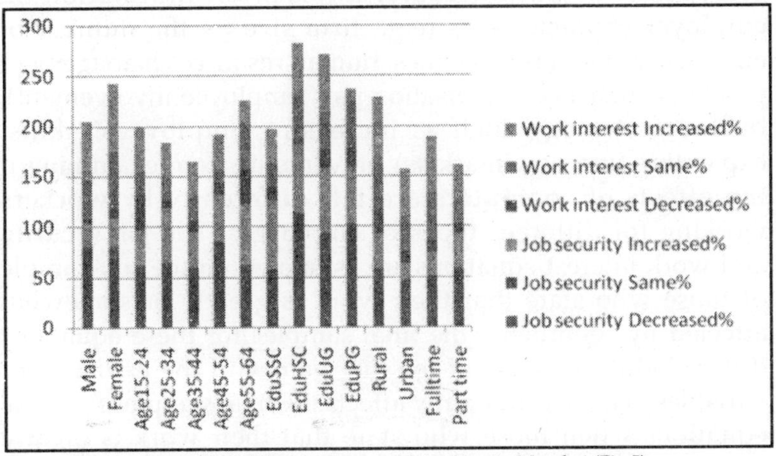

Source: Primary data collected from various organizations in Mumbai (Fig 5)

Finally, the fourth question addressed in the paper is how computers have changed work interest. The survey provides three mutually exclusive answers: "work has become more interesting"; "no change in work interest"; and "work has become less interesting". Explanatory variables for all four models are workers' demographic attributes, geographic areas, and work characteristics. Within the context of our data, demographic attributes include gender, age, education attainment.

Mumbai is a metropolitan city composed of economically diverse regions. As computer use varies somewhat from one area to another effects of computers are also expected to vary. Further, as computer usage differs substantially across a set of work characteristics, effects of computers are also expected to vary along these dimensions. Within the context of our data, these work characteristics include full-time or part-time work schedule, employee or self-employed (with or without paid help) employment type, industry, and occupation.

Along with the wealth of information on respondents' personal characteristics, the data permit an in-depth analysis for the first time on use of and particularly, the effects of computers. Most noticeably, the lack of information on employer characteristics (e.g., firm size by the number of employees or assets/revenues; human resources management practices such as compensation pay, employee involvement); business strategy such as increasing employees' skills, expanding into new markets) prevents us from examining if the effects of computers are felt differently by workers working for different types of employers. The job security and work interest equations are estimated on the sub-sample of those who state that their work is greatly or somewhat affected by computers, the final samples for these equations differ slightly because of missing values in the explanatory variables, which also slightly affects the final samples for these equations when those who state that their work is greatly affected by computers are split from those who state that their work is somewhat affected. Non-respondents ("Don't know" or "Refused") to this variable amount to about one-third of the sample.

Conclusion

Computers have reached nearly every corner of our lives, whose impacts are inevitably wide spread and profound. The result demonstrates that variables are significantly associated with workplace stress caused by the need to learn new computer skills include age, education, industry and occupation. Specifically, having to learn new computer skills is more likely to cause stress for middle age employees in the age group 35-44. Because of the recession and job cut, people who are having higher level of education they are greatly affected by stress. There is also an issue of equity - all workers are affected in different ways in different sectors. Their indeed exist substantial variations in these effects over demographic and job specific characteristics. Some industries are affected more and some industries are affected more favorably.

References

Autor, D., L. Katz and A. Krueger (1998), "Computing Inequality: Have Computers Changed the Labor Market?" Quarterly Journal of Economics, 113 (4), 1169 - 1213.

Bakker, C. (2000), Information and Communications Technologies and Electronic Commerce in Canadian Industry, Ottawa: Statistics Canada Catalogue 88F0006XIB-00004.

Baldwin, J. and Z.L in (2002), "Impediments to Advanced Technology Adoption for Canadian Manufacturers," Research Policy, 31, 1-18.

Carayon-Sainfort, P. (1992), "The Use of Computers in Offices: Impact on Task Characteristics and Worker Stress," International Journal of Human-Computer Interaction, (4(3), 245-61.

Cohen, R. (1995), "The Economic Impact of Information Technology," Business Economics, 30 (4), 21-25.

CQ Researcher (1992), "Workplace Stress: Is the Computer a Friend or Foe?" Work, Family and Stress: Can Overworked Americans Cope with Today's Time Crunch? 2 (30), 703, Washington: Congressional Quarterly Inc.

Dinardo, J. and J. Pischke (1997), "The Returns to Computer Use Revisited: Have Pencils Changed the Wage Structure too?" Quarterly Journal of Economics, 112 (1), 291-303.

Gera, S., G. Wulong and F. Lee (1999), "Information Technology and Labour Productivity Growth: An Empirical Analyis for Canada and the United States," Canadian Journal of Economics, 32 (2), 384-407.

Greenan, N. and J. Mairesse (2000), "Computers and Productivity in France: Some Evidence," Economics of Innovation and New Technology, 9 (3), 275-315.

ILO (2001), "Life at Work in the Information Economy," World Employment Report 2001, Geneva: International Labour Organization.

Kling, R. and C. Dunlop (1993), "Controversies about Computerization and the Character of White Collar Worklife,"The Information Society, 9, 1-29.

Kuhn, P. and M. Skuterud (2000), "Job Search Methods: Internet versus Traditional," Monthly Labor Review, 123 (10), 3–11.

Lehr, B. and F. Lichtenberg (1999), "Information Technology and Its Impact on productivity: Firm-Level Evidence from Government and Private Data Sources, 1977–1993," Canadian Journal of Economics, 32 (2), 335–62.

28

INTELLECTUAL PROPERTY RIGHTS IN INDIA — A CASE FOR THEIR PROTECTION

G. Durga Prasad

The Intellectual Property is the foundation of knowledge based economy. It pervades all sectors of economy and is increasingly becoming important for ensuring competitiveness of the enterprises. The Intellectual Property Rights (IPRs) have become important in the changing trade environment which is characterized by global competition, high innovation risks, short product cycle, need for rapid changes in technology, high investments in R & D, production and marketing and the need for highly skilled resources. With the opening up of trade in goods and services, the IPRs have become susceptible to infringement leading to inadequate return to the creators of knowledge. Hence, the interests of the innovators are protected under the TRIPS agreement. The term Intellectual Property (IP) reflects the idea that its subject matter is the product of the mind or the intellect.

New ideas and inventions which keep on emerging in every conceivable field of science and technology are the outcome of manipulation of human mental faculty. The resulting outcome of human intelligence is known as 'intellectual property'. It is, therefore, essential to protect such intellectual property so that nobody else can enjoy the fruits of other's efforts. The IP is intangible unlike inanimate objects, since it is the creation of the human intellect. The distinctive feature of IP is that it "relates to information which can be incorporated in tangible objectd6s and reproduced in different locations and can be used by several persons at the same, unlike immovable or movable tangible property"[1]. There are variations as to the set of rights forming the basket of IPRs. Under the WTO Agreement, the IPRs include a. literary, artistic and scientific works, b. performances of performing artists, phonograms, and broadcasts, c. inventions in all fields of human endeavour, d. scientific discoveries, e. industrial designs, f. trademarks, service marks, and commercial names and designations, and g. protection against unfair competition and all other rights resulting from intellectual activity in industrial, scientific, literary or artistic fields[2].

One expects a large number of IPRs would be generated and protected all over the world including India in all areas of science and technology, software and business methods. It is essential not only in the interest of the individual but country and society at large that scientific inventions, new technologies and creative achievements are protected. Hence, all publicly funded institutions and agencies will have to come to terms with the new ground realities and take positive steps to direct research suitably to generate more IPRs, protect and manage them efficiently[3].

Objectives of the Paper

The emergence of globalization and information technology has had a profound impact on the economic development of India. This has made the IPRs highly significant in the process of economic development. India's decision to join the Paris Convention may finally lend the much-needed direction to the rather haphazard approach the country has taken towards preparing itself for the patent regime. The present paper is an attempt to study how IPRs are protected in the country. In this endeavour, the paper is divided into two Sections. Section I deals with various dimensions of IPRs in the country taking into account the legislative enactments. In Section II, an evaluation of IPRs is provided. In this Section, a discussion is made with respect to how TRIPS Regime is implemented in the country; impact of globalization on higher education, patent applications by the universities; R&D expenditure; and policy initiatives.

The TRIPS Agreement

The Agreement on Trade Related Aspects of Intellectual Property Rights is resolved in final Uruguay Round text. The text is divided into 7 different parts containing a total of 73 Articles. Part I is on general provisions and basic principles. The standards for specific intellectual property rights, copyrights, copyright and related rights, trade marks, geographical indications, industrial designs, patents, layout designs of integrated circuits and protection of undisclosed information have been contained in Par II. There is also a section on the control of anti-competitive property rights. While Part IV talks about the acquisition and maintenance of intellectual property rights, Part V is on dispute, prevention and settlement. Part VI covers the transitional arrangement. Lastly, Part VII deals with institutional arrangements.

Thus, IPRs under the TRIPS Agreement cover

- Copyright and Related Rights
- Trade Marks
- Geographical Indications
- Registered (Industrial)Designs
- Patents
- Layout-Designs (Topographies) of Integrated Circuits.
- Protection of Undisclosed Information
- Control of Anti-Competitive Practices in Contractual Licenses.

What is Intellectual Property?

Because IP is the creation of human mind and intellect, this kind of property is called "intellectual" property is created by incorporating information in tangible objects capable of multiplying in unlimited number of times at different locations anywhere in the world. The property is basically in the concept, idea, thought and thereafter is the actual product, work or process, etc. According to the World Intellectual Property Organization (WIPO), the intellectual property includes rights relating to inventions in all fields of human endeavour, scientific discoveries and industrial designs. It also contains trade marks, service marks and commercial names and designations, literary, artistic and scientific works and performance of artists, phonograms and alike. Further, the protection against unfair competition and all other rights resulting from intellectual activity in the industrial scientific, literary or artistic fields have been aptly given space in the domain of intellectual property.

IPRs are largely territorial rights except copyright, which is global in nature in the sense that it is immediately available in all the members of the Berne Convention. These rights are awarded by the State and are monopoly rights implying that no one can use these rights without the consent of the right holder. It is important to know that these rights have to be renewed from time to time for keeping them in force except in case of copyright and trade secrets. These IPRs have fixed time except trade marks and geographical indications which have indefinite life. Unlike other moveable and immovable properties, these rights can be simultaneously held in many countries at the same time. IPRs can be held by the legal entities, which have the right to sell and purchase property. The other important feature is that what is known in public domain cannot be protected. Hence, these rights are associated with something new or original.

Dimensions of IPRs in India

India has specific legislations on the first 6 of the above IPRs listed[4]. The IPRs can be broadly classified into copyright and related rights and industrial property rights. Copyrights and related rights relate to the cultural field and cover all literary and artistic expressions as well as artistic performances and broadcasts. Industrial Property Rights are so called because they are of great relevance to production and distribution of industrial goods.

1. Copyright and Related Rights

Copyright means all the rights conferred by the Act upon its owner in respect of his literary, dramatic, musical or artistic work or in respect of cinematographic film or record. The creators and producers are called 'authors' and their products 'works'. Literary work includes computer programmes and software. It is not necessary that a high quality literary work is needed before a tangible creation is protected. A simple arithmetic book is considered as a literary work and can be given the copyright. These are protected under Indian Copyrights Act. In a work, copyright means the exclusive right to do things specified in the right. It also includes the right to exclude others from committing those acts which are protected under the copyright act. The rights consist of rights of reproduction, distribution, communication to the public, translation, adaptation and so on[5]. Copyrights generally last during the3 life term and till the end of 60 years after the3 de3ath of the authour[6]. For cinematographic films, records, photographs, posthumous publications, works of government and international agencies, the term of license is 60 years. Also, for broadcasting the term is 25 years. Thus, copyright offer4s protection to original works of authorship in any tangible medium of expression[7].

On the other hand "Related Rights" include rights of performers and broadcasting organizations who communicate works of authors to the public through performance or broadcasting. In this, performer's rights last for a period of 50 years[8]. Nevertheless, once a performer has consented to the incorporation of his performance in a cinematographic film he ceases to have performer's right in that performance[9].

Regarding the transfer of the copyright, the owner of the copyright in an existing work or prospective owner of the copying in a future work may assign to any person the copyright either wholly or partially.

2. *Trade Marks*

Trademarks are distinctive signs which identify a particular product as the product of a particular company or manufacturer. Trademarks may one or combination of words, letters, and numerals. They may also consist of drawings, symbols, three dimensional signs, or colours used to distinguishing feature. It could be an artistic label, design or mark. However, capability of the mark for being graphically represented is a condition for registration in India[10]. A certification Trademark can be obtained to mark the goods or services, quality, accuracy or other characteristics. The right to trademark lasts for a period of 10 years and can be renewed from time to time for an unlimited period with a payment of renewal fee[11]. A trademark gives exclusive rights o the owner to use it to identify his goods or services and any use by unauthorized persons is punishable.

The Indian Trademark Act, 1999 is a big leap forward from the Trade and Merchandize Marks Act, 1958 and Trademark Act, 1940. This is to bring the law completely in line with India obligation in the TRIPS Agreement.

3. *Geographical Indications (GI)*

A geographical indication is a sign used on goods which posses certain qualities or reputation because of their geographical origin. Indications which identify a good as originating in the territory of a member or a region or a locality in that territory, where a given quality reputation or other characteristics of the good is attributable to its geographical origin. The concept of identifying GI and protecting them is a new concept in India perhaps in most developing countries. Typical examples of GI are Basmati (India & Pakistan), Scotch whisky (Scotland) and Champagne (France). These are the products identified as typical to a geographical region. This gives the right to producers only from these regions to name the produce by these names. Produce from any other region cannot be named similarly.

According to TRIPS, GI which is not or cease to be protected in its country origin or which has fallen into disuse in that country cannot be protected. The GI identifies such goods as agricultural goods, natural goods or manufactured goods as originating, or manufactured in the territory, where a given quality, reputation or other characteristic or such goods is essentially attributable to its geographical origin land in case where such goods are manufactured goods one of the activities of either the production of processing or preparation of the goods concerned takes place in such territory, region or locality, as the case may be[12].

A registered geographical indication can be used only by the authorized person and if any other person uses the same by any means "that indicates or suggests that such goods originate in a geographical area other than the true place or origin of such goods in a manner which misleads the persons as to the geographical origin of such goods" that will be an infringement[13]. The registration of a geographical indication lasts for 10 years and can be renewed from time to time for an unlimite3d period with a payment of renewal free[14]. This is the same as in the case of Trademarks.

4. Industrial Design (ID)

There are many varieties and brands of the same product in the market, which look quite different from each other. If the products have similar functional features or have com parable price tags, the eye appeal or visual design of a product determines the choice.

"Design" as defined in the Designs Act, 1911 relates to the features of shape, configuration, patterns or ornamental decoration applied to an article by any industrial process or means. The features of the designs in the finished article should appeal to and are judged solely by the eye.

As industrial design is an outcome of inventive activity, initially, mentally conceived and then put on a drawing board, followed by the mechanics of giving a concrete shape to the basic new idea in the design and then finally contriving a method for mass manufacturing lthe4 same to put forth a product in the market for the benefit of the consumer. A new design thus conceived or invented is, therefore, an intellectual property. Industrial Designs are the external features of a product. They are the ornamental or aesthetic aspects of a product or article which make the ar4ticle attractive and appealing. The design may consist of three dimensional fealtur4es, such as the shape or surface of an article, or of two-dimensional features such as patterns, lines or colour or a combination of the two[15]. The owner of the registered design gets a copyright in the same for 10 years which can be extended for 5 years more by making an application and by paying a fee of Rs.2000/- be3fore the expiry of the initial 10 year period[16]. Therefore, the total term of a registered design is 15 years. While sanctioning the copyright, "first to file rule" is applied for registrability of design.

5. Layout Designs of Integrated Circuits

Layout Design is an obligation agrees upon initially under the Washington Treaty for which India is a signatory. Later this agreement was incorporated in the TRIPS Agreement in the Uruguay Round.

This prote4cts the semiconductor IC layout designs, India has enacted Semiconductor Integrated Circuits Layout Design Act, 2000 to give protection to IC layout design. Layout design is la layout of transistors and other circuitry elements and includes lead wires connected such elements and expressed in any manner in a semiconductor integrated circuit[17]. Semiconductor IC means a product having transistors and other circuitry elements which are inseparably formed on a semiconductor material and designed to perform an electronic circuitry function. The term or registration is 10 years from the date of filing[18].

6. Protection of Trade Secrets (Undisclosed Information)

Undisclosed information is generally known as trade secret/ confidential information includes formula, pattern, compilation, programme, device, method, technique or process. Protection of undisclosed information is least known to player4s of IPR and least talked about, although it is perhaps the most important form of protection for industries, R&D institutions and other agencies dealing with IPRs. Nevertheless, in India the Contract Act of 1872 covers many aspects of trade secrets.

It is very difficult to define the term, undisclosed information in concrete terms. However, broadly speaking the term may be defined as "a formula, pattern, device or compilation of information used in one's business and given an opportunity an advantage over competitors who do not know the use of it". A trade secret is a valuable piece of information with the essential requirement that the information be treated as such, i.e. as a secret. The value of a trade secret resides in the fact that competitors or other interested parties do not have access to it. The owner has the exclusive right to use/exploit as long as it remains a secret. A chemical composition of a product falling in, say, a soft-drink category needs to be protected through a trade secret rather than patent which is a publicly known document. In respect of a machine tool, so long as the company keeps its internal secret as trade secret, it refers to a trade secret. The moment the product is in the market, many people will know how to copy the product and the moment the product is copied the trade secret associated with the copied aspects will no longer remain valid and secret hence the protection will be lose and the term of the protection will be over. This would be true in the case of design features, but trade secret can be maintained about, say, composition of materials used and the process conditions adopted for manufacturing a product.

The IPRs Agreement requires the members to protect the undisclosed information and data submitted to governments or governmental agencies. In India, there is no separate and exclusive law for protecting undisclosed information/trade secret or confidential information.

7. Patents

A patent is an exclusive right granted by a country to the owner of an invention to make, use, manufacture and market the invention, provided the invention satisfied certain conditions stipulated in the law. Patents are exclusive rights in inventions. Exclusive right implies that no one else can make, use, manufacture or market the invention without the consent of the patent holder. A patent can be granted to a product or a process providing a new way of doing or a technical solution to a problem. Patents are the protection accorded by a government to an inventor for a fixed number of years during which period he will hold full rights to exclude others from exploiting. In return for this right, the inventor discloses details of his innovation to the people. Therefore, a patent will come into the public domain unlike a trade secret. A patent is a property right that can be gifted, inherited, assigned, sold or licensed. The right can be revoked by the country even if it is sold, licensed, manufactured or marketed.

In 1856, the first Indian Patent Law was promulgated. Later, after independence, the Indian Patent Act, 1970 was passed. The Act was amended radically to become fully compliant with the provisions of TRIPS Agreement. The recent, amendment was made in 2005 which was preceded by the Amendments in 2000 and 2003. In addition, India was a member of the Paris Convention, Patent Cooperation Treat and Budapest Treaty.

The Patents Act, 1970 defines "invention" as a "new product or process involving an inventive step capable of industrial application"[19]. New invention means any invention or technology which has not been anticipated by publication in any document or used in the country or elsewhere in the world before the date of filing of patent application with comp0lete specification, i.e. the subject matter has not fallen in public domain or sit does not form part of the state of the art. An inventive step means a feature of an invention that involves technical advance as compare3d to existing knowledge or having economic significance or both and that makes the invention not obvious to a person skilled in the art[20]. Such invention must be capable of being made or used in an industry. Generally, novelty, non-obviousness and commercial/industrial application are the principles on which patents are granted. The Indian Patent Act, 1970 gives a long list of inventions or discoveries which are3 not patentable in India[21].

Moreover, no patent is granted in India for an invention relating to atomic energy[22]. As of now, the method or process of manufacture and not the product perse is patentable. But under the TRIPS regime, product patenting must be introduced by 2005 in all the member countri3es. This process patenting in India gives monopoly to the patentee to produce the patented invention[23]. The term of patent will be 20 years from the date of filing for all types of inventions.

The Indian Patent Act has now a specific provision in regard to patenting of micro organisms and microbiological processes. It is now possible to get a patent for a microbiological process and also products emanating from such process. With effect from December 17, 2001 India became la member of the Budapest Treaty.

Further, there are mail-box provisions for pharmaceutical industry and EMR provision in respect of drugs and agro chemicals for those countries which do not have product patents.

In India, new plant varieties can also be protected providing rights to the farmers to use the seeds from their own crops for planting the next crop. This comes under the New Plant Variety and Farmers Rights Protection Act, 2001. The total period of protection is 10 years from the date of registration.

8. Other Protective Measures

India enacted the Biodiversity Act, 2002 to ensure maintenance, sustenance and development of its biodiversity. The Act has specific provisions about ownership of IPRs associated with exploitation of biodiversity. The other Act having its influence over other Acts related to IPRs is the Information Technology Act, 2000 which looks at the security aspect of material being transacted on internet.

SECTION II: EVALUATION OF IPRS

Implementation of TRIPS Regime in India

In India, the administration of IPRs is done through the Department of Industrial Policy and Promotion (DIPP) which is the nodal Department for all matters concerned World Intellectual Property Organization (WIPO). The World Body administers treaties in the field of IP for which India is a Member. India is also a member of 2 major treaties, viz., Paris Convention, 1883 for the Protection of Industrial Property relating patents, trademarks, designs, etc. The other treaty is Berne Convention, 1886 for the Protection of Literary and Artistic Works relating to copyright. In addition, India is also a member of the Patent Cooperation Treaty (PCT) which facilitates obtaining of patents in several countries by filing a single application.

The DIPP mentioned in the preceding paragraph is concerned with legislations relating to Patents, Trade Marks, Designs and Geographical Indications in India. These are administered through the Office of the Controller General of Patents, Designs and Trade Marks (CGPDTM). The CGPDTM is also in charge of the Office of the Patent Information System, Nagpur and the Intellectual Property Training Institute, Nagpur. Also, an Intellectual Property Appellate Board (IPAB) has been set up at Chennai to hear appeals against the decisions of Registrar of Trademarks, Geographical Indications and the Controller of Patents.

India has entered into Bilateral Cooperation Agreements, i.e. MOUs with UK, France, USA, European Patent Office and Japan. These focus on human resources development, capacity building and awareness and outreach activities. Moreover, India has entered into Multilateral Cooperation arrangements. India has an active cooperation programme in IP matters with WIPO which include, inter alia, organization of job seminars and workshops and study programmes, besides technical assistance by WIPO experts.

Regarding enforcement of IPRs in the country, civil and criminal provisions exist in various laws for dealing with counterfeiting and piracy. DIPP has set up an Inter-Ministerial Committee to coordinate IP enforcement issues.

The following Table shows data on patent approvals. The table shows that only a minor proportion of applications field for the grant of Patent Rights are granted patents during the period under study. For instance, during the 8 year period, the proportion of patent applications granted patent rights constitute 18.72% only. In absolute terms, of the total applications filed 118761, 22228 applications are granted patents during the period under study. In 2003-04, the percentage of approvals forms only 10.94 of the total applications filed.

Table I: Extent of Patent Approvals, 1999-00 to 2006-07

Years	*Applications Filed*	*ApplicationsExamined*	*PatentsGranted*
1999-00	4824	2824	1881
2000-01	8503	4264	1318
2001-02	10592	5104	1591
2002-03	11466	9538	1379
2003-04	12613	10709	1911
2004-05	17466	14813	4320
2005-06	24415	11569	4320
2006-07	28882	14119	7359

Regarding Trademarks, Table 2 provides the extent registrations during the 8 year period under study. For instance, the backlog of unexamined applications of approximately 5 lakh cases brought down to zero. Renewal of Trademarks certificates being done instantaneously in clear cases and new applications are examined within one week. As against only 8010 registrations in 1999-2000, 13 times more Trademarks were registered in 2006-07, that is 109361. During the last 3 years under study, 3.38 lakh trademark certificates were issued, whereas only 1.65 lakh trademarks were registere3d in 64 years since 1940 to 2004.

Regarding geographical indications, since September 2003, 39 geographical indications have been registered. These include Chanderi Saree, Pochampalli prints, Sholapur Chaddar, Mysore Silk, Kullu Shawl, Bidriware, etc.

The applications concerning Designs have increased from 2874 in 1999-00 to 5372 in 2006-07. The number of applications examined has also gone up to 5179 in 2006-07 as against 2067 in 1999-00. The number of registrations has also gone up from 1382 in 1999-00 to 4431 in 2006-07.

Table 2: Extent of Trade Mark Registrations Approved during 1999-00 to 2006-07

Year	*Filed*	*Examined*	*Registered*
1999-00	63378	42500	8010
2000-01	84275	70115	14202
2001-02	90236	159735	6204
2002-03	94120	249003	11190
2003-04	92251	89958	39762
2004-05	78996	72091	45015
2005-06	85699	79200	184325
2006-07	103419	85185	109361

In the context of latest policy changes, the government has approved a proposal for establishment of a National Institute for Intellectual Property Management (NIIPM) at Nagpur. The Institute will perform training, education, research and think tank functions.

Impact of Globalization on Higher Education

Globalization means different things to different people. What is more, the word globalization is used in two ways[24]. It is used in a 'positive' sense to describe a process of integration into the world economy. It is used in a 'normative' sense to prescribe a strategy of development based on a rapid integration with the world economy. Therefore, economic integration straddles national boundaries as liberalization has diluted the significance of borders in economic transactions[25].

India has started opened its economy since July 1991 and became a founder member of WTO. January 1, 1995 came and brought with it the full impact of WTO along with the Agreement on TRIPS. The Indian system rose to the new occasion and through its efforts has taken successful steps towards transition to a new culture by updating its existing laws, enacting new legislations, instituting new mechanisms for enabling creation of IP and its protection. The spread of markets and the momentum of globalization during the past two decades have transformed the world of higher education almost beyond recognition. Market forces, driven by the threat of competition or the lure of profit, have led to the emergence of higher education as business. In India, aims of publicly funded institutions such as universities, colleges, autonomous bodies and PSUs are multifaceted and are not purely driven by economic considerations, but they are primarily driven by social obligations. This approach has helped us in creating a pool of highly educated population land also building an inherent strength in research and development and core competency.

On the negative side, this system has bred complacency which blunted the spirit of innovation and fire for being ahead of others. Globalization has taught us many new lessons by opening our eyes to the existing and forthcoming ground realities. These realities are going to stay. Since the beginning of 1990s new approaches started taking roots in respect of such institutions, especially related to their management and source of funding. It is observed that educational and R&D institutions are being asked to generate their own funds and depend less and less on block grants by central or state governments. For this, a new paradigm shift has been taking place in educational sphere to make inventions a reality.

Moreover, in India, not even 8 percent of the people are reaching to the higher education level. In the advanced West, the percentage is 40 percent. India is now contemplating to increase this to 15% at least by increasing the number of universities in the state on its own and by inviting the private entrepreneurs to form universities. Also, needed curriculum changes with practical approach are urgently taken care of to improve the inventive aptitude among the younger generations.

Filing of Patent Applications by the Academic Institutions

In India, the Universities and Academic Institutions have no habit of filing applications for patents until 1995 for protecting their inventive works. For instance, only 4 applications w3ere filed by the Academic Institutions other than IITs and IISc in

1995. On the other hand, the later category of institutions filed 31 applications during the same year. By 2002, the number of applications filed by the academic institutions other than IITs and IISc rose to 33. On the other hand, the number in respect of IITs and IISc increased to 46 by the same year. As against this, the total applications for patents increased from 35 in 1995 to 96 in 2001 and fallen to 79 in 2002.

R&D Expenditure

The R & D expenditure, though increasing over a period, is staggering at a very low level. For instance, it is around 0.81 percent of GNP in 1998-99. Of this, the Centre contributed 67.5 percent, private sector 21.6 percent, state governments 8 percent and the higher education sector 2.9 percent. It may be noted that in the coming years, the R&D expenses by the education sector is likely to go up as the academic institutions interact more and more with the industry and are thereby motivated to spend their own resources in R&D. In this context, the UGC, the Central Government, and other public and private funding agencies have determined to extend liberal assistance to the Universities, Colleges, and Research Institutions for the emergence of innovative activity in the country. Therefore, the role of the government in capacity building in management of IPR is fundamental and of utmost importance in the country.

In order to create an inventive-India, the task of spreading literacy is an uphill task, in view of the size of population and country. Hence, spread of knowledge takes sufficiently longer time. In addition, creation of awareness among scientists, technicians, etc., has remained an unsatisfied goal for the protection of their inventive ideas. Hence, the print and electronic media, internet, videos, etc are to be used to make them unde4rstand the novelty of their invention. In this context, the universities, therefore, are provided with necessary technical, financial and legal help to create awareness regarding inventions made.

Policy Initiatives

In order to enhance motivation of scientists, research institutions and universities in the projects funded by various Departments at the Centre like Department of Science and Technology, Department of Biotechnology, Department of Scientific and Industrial Research and Department of Ocean Development, the Ministry of Science and Technology issued guidelines in 2000 for Technology Transfer and IPRs. Moreover, by means of tax-waivers, government of India is encouraging innovative activity on the part of industries. For example, the advantage of a 3 year excise duty exemption or exemption from Drugs Price Control Order may generate income which may offset the cost towards R&D. Besides, weighted tax deduction at 150% on R&D expenditure is available to companies engaged in the business of biotechnology, or the business of manufacture or production of drugs, pharmaceuticals, electronic eq2uipment, computers, telecommunication equipment, chemicals and manufacture of aircraft and helicopters. Other measures include tax holiday to R&D companies, accelerated depreciation allowance, income tax relief on R&D expenditure, and income tax deduction for sponsoring research, etc.

Conclusion

The agreement of TRIPS is expected to protect intellectual talents of the member countries and by doing so it is hoped to reap gains from the commercial exploitation of the idea or product. Being a part to the Agreement, India has made rapid strides in implementing the TRIPS regime in the country by enacting several laws. But the patenting abilities of Indian institutions, scientists, technicians, etc are conspicuous by their absence. This is due lack of awareness to get patents on the one hand, and on the other Indian scientific talent has failed to withstand the competition from the foreign companies. Since most of the inventions have been made and are taking place in the developed world, developing countries are at a disadvantageous position in reaping gains from the TRIPS

Agreement. Also, the government is in fact failing to disseminate information through various media to improve the awareness. In this context, our Indian Universities are not an exception. But patenting of inventive ideas is the need of the hour in the light of the fast picking up globalization trends in the country particularly in view of the globalization of higher education. Though the government had provided several fiscal incentives for encouraging innovative ideas by the industries, academic institutions, the R&D expenditure is at a lower level. Therefore, encouraging research activity by an intensive funding mechanism on the part of the Universities, IITs, IISc, research institutions is urgently called for. They must be encouraged to go for patents. Also, academic curriculum has to be changed by introducing practical orientation and by taking into account the requirements of the country for encouraging innovative abilities in the younger minds.

References

T.C.James, "Intellectual Property Rights and Rural Development", **Kurukshetra,** April, 2004, pp.12.

Annex 1C, "**TRIPS Agreement**" agreed upon April, 15, 1994 and came into force on Jan.1, 1995.

R.Saha, **Management of IPRs in India**, p.1

The Copyright Act, 1957; the Trade Marks Act, 1999; the Geographical Indications of Goods (Registration and Protection) Act, 1999; the Designs Act, 2000; the Patents Act, 1970; and the Semiconductor Integrated Circuits Layout Design Act, 2000.

Sec.14 of the Copyright Act, 1957.

Sec.22 of the Copyright Act, 1957.

Atul Chandra and Shantanu Kumar, "IPRs: Issues, Status, and Strategies", **Yojana,** Octo.1999, p.17.

Sec.38, of the Copyright Act, 1957.

Sec.38 (4) of the Copyright Act, 1957.

Sec.2 (1) (zb) of the Trade Marks Act, 1999.

Sec.25, ibid.,

Sec.2 (1) (e) of the GI of Goods (Registration and Protection) Act, 1999.

Sec.22. ibid.,

Sec.18 (1), ibid.,

Sec.2d of the Designs Act, 2000.

Sec.11, ibid.

Sec.2 (h) of the Semiconductor Integrated Circuits Layout-Design Act, 2000.

Sec.16, ibid.

Sec 1 (j) of the Patent Act, 1970.

Sec.1 (ja) ibid.

Sec. 3 ibid.,

Sec.4, ibid.,

Sec.48, ibid.

Deepak Nayyar, "Globalization: What does it mean for Higher Education?" **EPW**, Dec.15, 2007, pp.30-35.

Ibid. p.30.

Index

F

G